THE PSYCHOLOGY OF
GROUP AGGRESSION

WILEY SERIES IN
FORENSIC CLINICAL PSYCHOLOGY

Edited by

Clive R. Hollin
Centre for Applied Psychology, The University of Leicester, UK

and

Mary McMurran
School of Psychology, Cardiff University, UK

COGNITIVE BEHAVIOURAL TREATMENT OF SEXUAL OFFENDERS
William L. Marshall, Dana Anderson and Yolanda Fernandez

VIOLENCE, CRIME AND MENTALLY DISORDERED OFFENDERS:
Concepts and Methods for Effective Treatment and Prevention
Sheilagh Hodgins and Rüdiger Müller-Isberner (*Editors*)

OFFENDER REHABILITATION IN PRACTICE:
Implementing and Evaluating Effective Programs
Gary A. Bernfeld, David P. Farrington and Alan W. Leschied (*Editors*)

MOTIVATING OFFENDERS TO CHANGE:
A Guide to Enhancing Engagement in Therapy
Mary McMurran (*Editor*)

THE PSYCHOLOGY OF GROUP AGGRESSION
Arnold P. Goldstein

THE PSYCHOLOGY OF GROUP AGGRESSION

Arnold P. Goldstein

School of Education, Center for Research on Aggression
Syracuse University, USA

JOHN WILEY & SONS, LTD

Other Wiley Editorial Offices

John Wiley & Sons, Inc., 605 Third Avenue, New York, NY 10158-0012, USA

Jossey-Bass, 989 Market Street, San Francisco, CA 94103-1741, USA

Wiley-VCH Verlag GmbH, Pappelallee 3, D-69469 Weinheim, Germany

John Wiley & Sons Australia, Ltd, 33 Park Road, Milton, Queensland 4064, Australia

John Wiley & Sons (Asia) Pte Ltd, 2 Clementi Loop #02-01, Jin Xing Distripark, Singapore 129809

John Wiley & Sons Canada Ltd, 22 Worcester Road, Etobicoke, Ontario, Canada M9W 1L1

Library of Congress Cataloging-in-Publication Data

British Library Cataloguing in Publication Data

A catalogue record for this book is available from the British Library

ISBN 0-470-84515-5 (cased)
ISBN 0-470-84516-3 (paper)

Typeset in 10/12 pt Palatino by TechBooks, New Delhi, India
Printed and bound in Great Britain by Antony Rowe Ltd, Chippenham Wiltshire
This book is printed on acid-free paper responsibly manufactured from sustainable forestry
in which at least two trees are planted for each one used for paper production.

Publishers' note

As this book is being prepared for publication, the Publishers have learned the sad news of Arnold P. Goldstein's death. We hope this book will be seen as a worthy part of Professor Goldstein's substantial contribution and legacy to research on aggression, to his colleagues, and to students of psychology and education.

All of us at John Wiley & Sons, Ltd., extend our deepest sympathies to his family and friends

CONTENTS

ABOUT THE AUTHOR

Arnold P. Goldstein, PhD, was the Director of the Center for Research on Aggression at Syracuse University, Director of the New York State Task Force on Juvenile Gangs, and co-founder of the International Center for Aggression Replacement Training. He served on the American Psychological Association Commission on Youth Violence and on the Council of Representatives for the International Society for Research on Aggression. He was the author of 55 books and 100 articles on violence, aggression, delinquency, abuse, and related issues. His work was honored with numerous awards, including the Career Achievement Award from the American Psychological Association's Committee on Children, Youth, and Families (1996), the Senior Scientist Award from the APA Psychology Division (1996), and most recently, the 2002 Devereux Massachusetts Legacy of Caring Award.

SERIES EDITORS' PREFACE

ABOUT THE SERIES

At the time of writing it is clear that we live in a time, certainly in the UK and other parts of Europe, if perhaps less so in other parts of the world, when there is renewed enthusiasm for constructive approaches to working with offenders to prevent crime. What do we mean by this statement and what basis do we have for making it?

First, by "constructive approaches to working with offenders" we mean bringing the use of effective methods and techniques of behaviour change into work with offenders. Indeed, this might pass as a definition of forensic clinical psychology. Thus, our focus is application of theory and research in order to develop practice aimed at bringing about a change in the offender's functioning. The word *constructive* is important and can be set against approaches to behaviour change that seek to operate by destructive means. Such destructive approaches are typically based on the principles of deterrence and punishment, seeking to suppress the offender's actions through fear and intimidation. A constructive approach, on the other hand, seeks to bring about changes in an offender's functioning that will produce, say, enhanced possibilities of employment, greater levels of self-control, better family functioning, or increased awareness of the pain of victims.

A constructive approach faces the criticism of being a "soft" response to damage caused by offenders, neither inflicting pain and punishment nor delivering retribution. This point raises a serious question for those involved in working with offenders. Should advocates of constructive approaches oppose retribution as a goal of the criminal justice system as incompatible with treatment and rehabilitation? Alternatively, should constructive work with offenders take place within a system given to retribution? We believe that this issue merits serious debate.

However, to return to our starting point, history shows that criminal justice systems are littered with many attempts at constructive work with offenders, not all of which have been successful. In raising the spectre of success, the second part of our opening sentence now merits attention: that is, "constructive approaches to working with offenders *to prevent crime*". In order to achieve the goal of preventing crime, interventions must focus on the right targets for behaviour change. In addressing this crucial point, Andrews and Bonta (1994) have formulated the *need principle*:

> Many offenders, especially high-risk offenders, have a variety of needs. They need places to live and work and/or they need to stop taking drugs. Some have poor self-esteem, chronic headaches or cavities in their teeth. These are all "needs". The need principle draws our attention to the distinction between *criminogenic* and *noncriminogenic* needs. Criminogenic needs are a subset of an offender's risk level. They are dynamic attributes of an offender that, when changed, are associated with changes in the probability of recidivism. Non-criminogenic needs are also dynamic and changeable, but these changes are not necessarily associated with the probability of recidivism. (p. 176)

Thus, successful work with offenders can be judged in terms of bringing about change in noncriminogenic need *or* in terms of bringing about change in criminogenic need. While the former is important and, indeed, may be a necessary precursor to offence-focused work, it is changing criminogenic need that, we argue, should be the touchstone of working with offenders.

While, as noted above, the history of work with offenders is not replete with success, the research base developed since the early 1990s, particularly the meta-analyses (e.g. Lösel, 1995), now strongly supports the position that effective work with offenders to prevent further offending is possible. The parameters of such evidence-based practice have become well established and widely disseminated under the banner of "What Works" (McGuire, 1995).

It is important to state that we are not advocating that there is only one approach to preventing crime. Clearly there are many approaches, with different theoretical underpinnings, that can be applied. Nonetheless, a tangible momentum has grown in the wake of the "What Works" movement as academics, practitioners, and policy makers seek to capitalise on the possibilities that this research raises for preventing crime. The task now facing many service agencies lies in turning the research into effective practice.

Our aim in developing this Series in Forensic Clinical Psychology is to produce texts that review research and draw on clinical expertise to advance effective work with offenders. We are both committed to the ideal of evidence-based practice and we will encourage contributors to the Series to follow this approach. Thus, the books published in the Series will not be practice manuals or "cook books": they will offer readers authoritative and critical information through which forensic clinical practice can develop. We are both enthusiastic about the contribution to effective practice that this Series can make and look forward to it developing in the years to come.

ABOUT THIS BOOK

It is with mixed emotions that we write about this book. On one hand, we were delighted to have attracted Professor Goldstein to write a book for our Series. Professor Goldstein's research and writing on the topic of aggression and violence has had a significant impact among the academic community of teachers and researchers. More importantly, his work on changing violent behaviour, particularly his programme Aggression Replacement Training (ART; Goldstein, Glick, & Gibbs, 1998), has influenced the efforts of practitioners all over the world. The worldwide influence of ART was seen in 2001 with formation of the International Center for

Aggression Replacement Training (ICART). The formation of ICART was marked with a conference in Malmö, Sweden, which attracted over 750 delegates from 20 countries. That the first day of the conference was 12 September 2001 added a certain sombre emphasis to the proceedings. It is a remarkable testimony to Professor Goldstein's work that his research and publications are so relevant to today's issues, and that his contribution should be recognised on such a global stage.

The book Professor Goldstein has written for our Series looks at the phenomenon of aggression that takes place in groups. While there are, of course, singularly aggressive individuals who habitually behave in a violent manner, there are also occasions when the group takes over and the pack rules. On such occasions even the seemingly mildest of people can act in ways they would not have thought possible. The psychology of the group and, indeed, the crowd is well documented in the mainstream social psychology literature.

Like all good applied psychologists, Professor Goldstein knows his theory and he marshals what we know about group dynamics as a platform for understanding real-life aggressive behaviour. It is tempting to think of aggression and violence in its most extreme forms, such as robbery, rape, and murder, but aggression is much more pervasive than as seen in its most extreme forms. Anyone who has been the target for gossip, rumour, innuendo, harassment or bullying will testify that such forms of "low-level" aggression can be extremely damaging, in terms of both psychological and physical well-being. Professor Goldstein begins this book by considering various manifestations of low-level aggression, adding significantly to our understanding of how aggression is an implicit part of our culture. Moving through the more obvious groups – delinquent gangs and the mob – Professor Goldstein arrives at intervention. The overview he gives of types and styles on intervention begins to show just what is possible, the depth of effort and expertise needed to be effective, and the size of the task. As with all Professor Goldstein's books, his easy writing style makes it a pleasure to read and learn.

Our delight at having Professor Goldstein's book in our Series pales at the news of his recent death. The loss of Professor Goldstein is a major blow to the communities of academics and practitioners committed to reducing aggression in society. There is no doubt that Professor Goldstein had a great deal still to give and now that has been taken away.

If I (Clive) might be permitted at individual note, the loss of Arnie is deeply felt for me personally. I first corresponded with Arnie at the very beginning of my career and took great encouragement from the fact that so venerable a figure from the literature should write to me, concerned about my fledging efforts at research and practice. Of course, when you knew the man, you understood that that was exactly what he would do: he cared deeply about the prevention of aggression and, and as I'm sure others will also testify, encouraged the efforts of all those with similar concerns. Over the years, through continued correspondence, contributions to each other's edited books, and meeting at conferences, I came to count Arnie as one the closest of my academic friends. I last saw him in Malmö at the ART conference. I was honoured to be asked by Arnie give the opening paper at that conference and can honestly say that I have never been so nervous in my life! It's no easy task to present a theoretical paper on aggression in front of the master. Anyway, he said I did okay and that's good enough for me. I'll miss him dreadfully.

Clive Hollin and Mary McMurran

REFERENCES

Andrews, D. A., & Bonta, J. (1994). *The Psychology of Criminal Conduct*. Cincinnati, OH: Anderson Publishing.

Goldstein, A. P., Glick, B., & Gibbs, J. C. (1998). *Aggression Replacement Training: A Comprehensive Intervention for Aggressive Youth* (Rev. Ed.). Champaign, IL: Research Press.

Lösel, F. (1995). Increasing consensus in the evaluation of offender rehabilitation? *Psychology, Crime, & Law, 2*, 19–39.

McGuire, J. (Ed.). (1995). *What works: Reducing reoffending*. Chichester: John Wiley & Sons.

PREFACE

Human history, written with a gloomy but accurate pen, is a litany of groups of persons seeking to hurt other such groups. Such efforts at, often successful, bodily and psychological injury go by many terms—rumor-mongering, group bullying, gang rape, mob aggression, feuds, riots, rebellions, insurrections, mass murder, war, genocide. Perhaps no human quality has been more evident, more damaging, and more enduring.

A wide array of professions center their efforts and energies on seeking better understanding of group aggression in its many incarnations, and in attempting to devise and implement means for its prevention, moderation, or control. Psychology is among these professions, and the present book seeks to present and examine its contribution in this context. I claim no primacy for what psychology has to offer. Instead, I seek to place its efforts alongside those of sociology, political science, criminology, and other relevant disciplines. The problem is uniquely immense. All contributions are welcome.

I begin by reflecting the fact that group aggression is typically a *group* phenomenon, not merely a behavior emanating from a random collective of separate individuals. As such, this book's journey begins with a detailed presentation of theory and research on those dimensions of group life that bear apparent or even probable relevance to the domain of aggression. How and why groups form, their goals, leadership, cohesiveness, conflict, norms, power structure, communication patterns, and, especially, relations with other groups, are among the topics considered. These and other arenas of group organization and functioning are offered in Chapter 1 as a template for informed consideration, in the chapters that follow, of the various major forms group aggression has taken.

Using this group dynamics template, I invite readers to join me in seeking to understand more fully the causes, nature, and modification of low-level group aggression (Chapter 2), bullying and harassment (Chapter 3), gang violence (Chapter 4), mob aggression (Chapter 5), and both established and emerging means for intervening effectively in this domain (Chapter 6).

Psychology's contribution to understanding and moderating group aggression is both modest (given the enormity of the problem), and yet significant as but one large piece in a multicomponent intervention effort. I explore this contribution here toward the dual goals of the continued expansion of its substance and continued application of its fruits.

October, 2001   Arnold P. Goldstein

Part I

INTRODUCTION

Chapter 1

AGGRESSION-RELEVANT GROUP DYNAMICS

Over the past 75 years, a substantial wealth of literature has grown dealing with the structure and functioning of human groups. Theory, research findings, and creative speculation are its diverse formats. Its specific contents are numerous and varied, and include both an array of intragroup concerns (e.g., cohesiveness, leadership, performance), and topics focused upon between-group phenomena (e.g., conflict, cooperation, aggression). The generators of this knowledge base are largely social psychologists, but also include sociologists, criminologists, mediators, group therapists, group trainers, and professionals from yet other disciplines. The present chapter seeks to summarize those segments of this literature that are of apparent or even possible relevance to group aggression, and to offer it as a pool of information, many of whose particulars we hypothesize to be potentially relevant to the main concerns of this book. It is our contention, and already some of our experience, that viewing the chief topics constituting the group aggression theme—e.g., bullying, gang violence, riots—through the lenses of the group dynamics literature can aid greatly both in understanding their source and substance, and in reducing their frequency and intensity.

As noted, I describe and examine this literature in the present chapter. Where and when possible, in subsequent chapters I seek to draw upon it as a template clarifying better our understanding of the structure and processes involved when groups either perpetrate or are the targets of aggression by multiple others. Our template applying effort is, however, but a mere beginning. We hope that by thusly providing and utilizing the accumulated group dynamics literature, others will similarly be encouraged to do so.

THEORIES OF GROUP DEVELOPMENT AND BEHAVIOR

Realistic Conflict Theory

Competition between groups in the real world—nations, tribes, athletic teams, gangs, ethnic groups, and others—is a pervasive and enduring phenomenon, a phenomenon of major social and political salience and significance. As Forsyth (1983) observes:

The simple hypothesis that conflict is caused by competition over valued but scarce resources has been used to explain the origin of class struggles (Marx & Engels, 1947), rebellions (Gurr, 1970), international warfare (Streufert & Streufert, 1979), and the development of culture and social structures (Simmel, 1950; Sumner, 1906). (p. 377)

The resources competed for may be power, prestige, territory, status, or wealth. As Sidanius and Pratto (1999) observe, the Realistic Conflict Theory seeking to explain the nature and consequences of such competition describes it as a zero-sum conflict over real material or symbolic values. It is competitive (zero-sum) because, as Campbell (1965) noted earlier, one group's gain is perceived as another's loss. Such a sense of relative loss, Sidanius and Pratto (1999) note:

... translates into perceptions of group threat, which in turn causes prejudice against the outgroup, negative stereotyping of the outgroup, ingroup solidarity, [heightened] awareness of ingroup identity, and internal cohesion including intolerance of ingroup deviants, ethnocentrism, use of group boundary markers ... (p. 17).

To better understand the sources of such conflict-encouraging consequences and the conditions under which they may be promoted or ameliorated, a number of social scientists have sought to recreate and examine such intergroup competition under more controlled circumstances. Chief among these investigations of realistic group conflict are the seminal studies conducted by Muzafer Sherif and his research group (Sherif et al., 1961).

In each of these geographically dispersed field experiments, which have come to be known as the *summer camp studies*, approximately 24 white, middle-class 11- to 12-year-old boys participated. From the boys' perspective, their participation involved simply attending a summer camp for a three-week period. The camp was staffed by the researchers, whose study design planned three stages of camp programming: group formation, intergroup conflict, and conflict reduction. In the first stage of the experiments, the boys were transported to the camp in two separate groups. These groups were matched on an array of psychological and physical qualities and were constituted in such a manner that most pairs of boys who were friends before the two groups were formed were assigned to different groups, thus minimizing the preexperimental level of within-group attraction. Upon arrival at the camp, the two groups were situated in widely separated locations, out of possible contact with one another. During the week that this first phase of the experiment lasted, each group of boys engaged in athletics, hiked, camped, swam, and, as a concomitant of such interaction, developed a group structure with its associated norms and roles. Within each of the two groups, now self-named and self-decorated the Rattlers and the Eagles, high levels of cohesiveness and positive in-group attitudes were well evidenced. Toward the end of this first week, boys in each group began to realize that they were sharing the camp facilities with another group and began referring to "those guys" in increasingly comparative, competitive, and rivalrous ways. This minor aspect of the Sherif et al. (1961) studies—i.e., initiation by the group of comparative in-group favoritism in the absence of not only overt competition with the other group but without even having met them—will loom large later in this chapter as we examine the potent influence of mere categorization into groups on diverse in-group and out-group biases.

The researchers welcomed the boys' requests for competitive, between-group opportunities, for this is precisely what the research plan called for at stage two. A tournament was announced, to last four days, of baseball, tug-of-war, tent-pitching competition, cabin inspections, and other contests:

> At first, the tension between the two groups was limited to verbal insults, name calling, and teasing. Soon, however, the intergroup conflict escalated into full-fledged hostilities. After losing a bitterly contested tug-of-war battle, the Eagles sought revenge by taking down a Rattler flag and burning it...A fist fight [followed]. Next, raiding began, as the Rattlers sought revenge by attacking the Eagles' cabin during the night. The raiders...swept through the Eagles' cabin tearing out mosquito netting, overturning beds, and carrying off personal belongings. During this period, the attitudes of each group toward the other became more and more negative, but the cohesiveness of each became increasingly stronger. (Forsyth, 1983, pp. 375–376)

Indeed, each group's rapid march from friendly rivalry to overt hostility was accompanied by widely evidenced increases in within-group favoritism. Such heightened cohesiveness, attraction, and solidarity for example, emerged in a series of miniexperiments (within the larger camp experiment) disguised as games. One such game was a bean toss in which a large quantity of beans was scattered in the grass. Each group had a fixed amount of time to pick up as many beans as possible. Later, the experimenters projected a picture of what was purported to be each boy's pickings, and all boys had to estimate the number of beans displayed. In reality, the amount was the same in every instance, arranged in diverse configurations. Boys' estimates showed a highly consistent bias favoring their own group members. Such favoritism, as a second example, was also fully reflected in the youths' sociometric choices. When asked to indicate their best friends, over 90 % of the boys in both groups chose someone in their own group even though, it will be recalled, less than two weeks earlier their (then) best friends had been placed in the other group.

In quite a different experimental context, Blake and Mouton (1961, 1986) sought to replicate and extend the Sherif et al. (1961) findings, in this instance with adults. Participants were management-level employees of various industrial organizations, constituted into groups of 20 to 30 each, purportedly to discuss and examine an array of relevant interpersonal and organizational topics and problems. Over the course of their research effort, Blake and Mouton established 150 such groups, but at any given time at least two and often more groups were functioning—and their members were aware of this. As each group entered into its problem discussions, a degree of in-group cohesiveness began to develop. Along with this rise in attraction and solidarity within each group, the awareness of other, similar groups appeared to elicit rumblings of a desire for competition. The investigators, in the study's next phase, posed an identical problem to pairs of groups, instructing each group to find the best solution. Although explicit competitiveness had still not been instituted at this point by the researchers, group member comments repeatedly revealed it to be alive and running in their own minds. When, in fact, problem solution reports were duplicated and exchanged for study and analysis on a cross-group basis, both in-group favoritism in the form of overvaluation of their own group's solution and out-group discrimination in the form of pejorative evaluation of out-group solutions regularly emerged. In company with such biases, the competitiveness flowered and with it came frequent displays of out-group hostility. In fact, Blake and Mouton (1986) reported that "Sometimes intergroup antagonism grew so intense that the experiments had to be discontinued" (p. 72). Various strategies were implemented and evaluated as possible moderators of intergroup hostility—isolating groups, forcing combinations, adjudicating differences, mediation, and conciliation—but each appeared to have little positive impact. What did seem to function to reduce antagonisms was, again, positive interdependency in the form of intergroup collaboration and cooperation vis-à-vis superordinate goals. Other investigators, working in diverse settings, with diverse types of groups, and in diverse cultures, have similarly reported perceived or actual intergroup competition, as well as the ameliorative impact on such biases of the imposition of superordinate goals (Bass & Dunteman, 1963; Diab, 1970; Ryen & Kahn, 1975; Turner, 1981; Worchel, 1979; Worchel, Andreoli, & Folger, 1977). In this last regard, it is useful to note that Brewer and Miller (1996) subsequently distinguished between superordinate *goals* and superordinate group *identity*, asserting that it is the latter that causes the coming together, ameliorative effect, not the share goals per se.

Turner (1981) succinctly summarizes the combined results of these several investigations:

> Where two groups come into contact under conditions that embody a series of incompatible goals—where both groups urgently desire some objective that can be attained only at the expense of the other—competitive activity towards the goal changes over time into hostility between the groups; also: (a) unfavorable attitudes and images (stereotypes) of the out-group come into use and become standardized, placing the out-group at a definite social distance from the in-group; (b) intergroup conflict produces an increase in solidarity within the groups; and (c) increased solidarity and pride in one's own group lead to in-group biases which overevaluate the characteristics and performances of in-group members and underevaluate those of out-group members. Where conflicting groups come into contact under conditions that embody a series of superordinate goals, cooperative activity towards the goal has a cumulative impact in improving intergroup relations; in reducing social distance, dissipating hostile outgroup attitudes and stereotypes, and making future intergroup conflicts less likely. (p. 68)

Though the perspective on in-group–out-group conflict emerging from this body of work was termed *Realistic* Conflict Theory, and spoke in name to conflict over both real material and symbolic resources, most consideration of it has emphasized the former, i.e., real, tangible, touchable resources. So very often, it appears that it is the symbolism inherent in the struggle over realistic resources that lies at the heart of conflict generation and maintenance. As frequently happens in the realm of interpersonal aggression, small and even trivial differences, competition or insults, via what they are perceived to symbolize in the minds, hearts, and—eventually—fists of the protagonists may grow by means of what has been described as a "spiraling character contest" into full blown aggression.

And indeed, the matter or matters in realistic or symbolic contention can be, and often are, decidedly trivial. As Rothbart (1993) observed, Jonathan Swift in *Gulliver's Travels*

> ...implied that the conflict between the Protestants and the Catholics in Europe was equivalent to a war between nations that differed in their preference for breaking an egg on its large or its small side. Freud (1926/1959) later described the phenomenon in which we exaggerate the importance of negligible differences as 'the narcissism of small differences.' (p. 95)

Whether the differences in contention are large or small, real or symbolic, the consequences of the resultant in-group–out-group competition seem both well established and substantial. Some investigators, however, reacted to this series of findings by wondering whether, for the in-group–out-group biases and their several consequences to occur, competition might be sufficient but not necessary. Recall that in the Sherif et al. (1961) and Blake and Mouton (1961) series, as well as in some of the subsequent research, in-group favoritism, out-group discrimination, and even the gathering of the clouds of intergroup conflict began *before* formal intergroup competition or even its announcement. Further, both Ferguson and Kelly (1964) and Rabbie and Wilkins (1971) found evidence for intergroup favoritism in clearly noncompetitive conditions. Doise et al. (1972), in an early contribution to what became known as *social categorization theory* and, later, as *social identity theory*, reported that simply being divided into groups, without social interaction, face-to-face contact, or anticipated intergroup behavior, can create in-group bias. Billig (1973), responding to these early findings and impressions, proposed that

> the social categorization involved in group formation, and the development of in-group consciousness and identity in relation to other groups initiates the process of intergroup attitude development: overt intergroup competition is not a necessary condition for intergroup attitudes. (p. 320)

Thus, the groundwork was prepared for the next phase of experimentation on in-group—out-group relations, the era of social identity theory.

Social Identity Theory

To test the proposition that the mere division of individuals into what they believe to be two or more groups is by itself sufficient to elicit both in-group favoritism and out-group bias, Tajfel and his research team conducted what appropriately came to be known as the *minimal group studies* (Tajfel, 1970; Tajfel et al., 1971). In part, their research hypotheses and design grew from investigations in what appears to be quite another field, object perception. Bruner (1957) had earlier explored the role of categorization in human perception. Campbell (1958) broadly proposed that the diverse principles guiding such object perception might well apply with equal relevance in the domain of person perception. Similarly, Doise and Weinberger (1973) and Doise, Deschamps, and Meyer (1978), with direct applicability to the evolution of social identity theory, found that perceptual categorization accentuated the perceived similarity of items within a category and the perceived differences between items differentially categorized, a finding which, they suggested, might also hold at the social level for the perception of persons categorized into different groups.

In the minimal group research, participating subjects were divided into two "groups" ostensibly on the basis of some trivial criteria, for example, their preference for the works of one or another of two painters they had never heard of before. In reality, assignment to a "group" was made randomly. The subjects did not interact during the experiment, either within or between the "groups." Each subject was told to which "group" he belonged, but the membership of all other participants, whether in his own "group" or the other, remained anonymous to him. Each subject, working alone, was asked to make a series of decisions regarding the allocation of money to two other subjects, designated only their "group" membership and individual code number. Three types of designated recipient–subject pairs were used: (1) one from each "group," (2) both from own "group," and (3) both from the "out-group." Across a series of such investigations, including one (Billig & Tajfel, 1973) in which subjects were assigned to "groups" not on the basis of purported aesthetic preferences, but on a random toss of a coin conducted in front of the subject, most subjects consistently allocated monies in the direction of favoring, in their decisions, anonymous members of their own "groups" at the expense of anonymous members of the "out-groups." Thus, in the absence of social interaction between or within groups, contact, conflict of interest, previous hostility, any links between self-interest and group membership, or any other form of functional interdependence within or between groups, the mere perception or cognition that one belonged to a particular group appeared to be sufficient to elicit discrimination in favor of purported in-group members, and against those perceived to belong to the out-group. The discriminatory potency of this minimal group effect is highlighted by the fact that in a number of the relevant investigations, not only did subjects give more money to in-group than to out-group members when this was unrelated to their personal gain, but they also gave less in an absolute sense to in-group members in order to give them relatively more than out-group members.

The original minimal group studies, given their explicit challenge to the earlier realistic-group-conflict theory, generated a considerable amount of subsequent research. Time and again these follow-up minimal group investigations replicated the basic findings of in-group favoritism and out-group discrimination, even though such research often varied the purported basis for categorization, or measured discrimination differently, or was conducted in a different culture (Brewer, 1979; Doise, 1971; Turner, 1975, 1980; Vaughan, 1978; Wetherell, 1982; Wetherell & Vaughan, 1979). To underscore further the potency of the social categorization process beyond its central discrimination consequences, it also produces more positive attitudes toward, and more reported liking of, in-group than out-group members; ethnocentric biases in perception, evaluation, and memory; an altruistic bias toward in-group members, and a strong tendency to view one's in-group co-members in a heterogeneous, individuated, differentiated manner, whereas the outgroup is regarded as an undifferentiated, homogeneous mass (Brewer & Miller, 1996; Deaux, 2000; Forsyth, 1999; Howard & Rothbart, 1978; Turner, 1978). Further, the in-group is perceived as possessing greater entativity (Hamilton, Sherman & Lickel, 1998) or a sense of "groupness" by its members, more distinct syntality or "personality" (Shaw, 1981), and is more likely to be given the benefit of the doubt in ambiguous circumstances, i.e., a "leniency bias" (Brewer & Miller, 1996). Given the breadth and depth of the perceptual, affective, and cognitive consequences of categorization, it is understandable that Tajfel (1978) paradoxically wondered whether they ought to be called maximal groups instead!

Tajfel's (1970) early explanation for these findings, generic norm theory, proposed that the regularity across cultures of discrimination against out-groups implied the broad existence of discriminatory norms which were taught, internalized, and regularly applied in "us" versus "them" contexts. However, both the circularity of such reasoning, as well as the existence of individuals and groups that are not highly ethnocentric, led to the generic norm explanation being short lived. Why else might social categorization reliably produce such a broad array of substantial, psychosocial effects? Gerard and Hoyt (1974) invoked an experimenter-bias explanation. Experimental instructions and tasks, they held, led subjects to believe that biased behavior was expected of them, and they conformed to such expectations.

A third explanation raised the possibility that the core explanatory mechanism was perceived similarity, that is, perhaps the discriminatory behavior was a result of the subject's perception—due to the purported basis on which the categories were constructed (e.g., shared aesthetic preference)—that he or she was, on this criterion, similar to in-group members and different from out-group subjects. Yet factorial studies in which the separate and combined effects of similarity and "pure" (random) categorization, devoid of any basis in similarity, were examined clearly demonstrated that categorization and not similarity was the potent condition (Billig & Tajfel, 1973; Billig, 1973; Rabbie & Huygen, 1974; Wilder & Allen, 1978).

Following these early explanatory efforts, social identity theory began to emerge as a comprehensive basis for categorization effect phenomena. The theory rests on the sequential unfolding of three processes—social categorization, social identity, and social comparison—employed by the individual or group in an effort to create positive group distinctiveness.

> The knowledge of our membership in various social categories, or groups of people, and the value attached to it is defined as our "social identity." Social identity, however, only acquires meaning by comparison with other groups. We interpret the social environment and act in a manner enabling us to make our own group favorably distinctive from other groups with which we may compare it. Such positive distinctiveness from relevant outgroups affords a satisfactory or adequate social identity. (Williams, J. & Giles, 1978, p. 434)

To return to the minimal group studies that provided the initial impetus for the social identity perspective, it is argued (Turner, 1975) that it is not the division into groups per se that causes the reliable discrimination effects, but rather a more basic motivation to seek and find positive self-evaluation. Thus, to restate the core of this perspective, it is held that social categorizations are internalized to define the self in social situations, and such identity-shaping categorizations engender a self-evaluative social comparisons process. One's self-esteem as a group member, it is held, depends on the evaluative outcomes of such social comparisons between in-group and out-group. Since individuals desire positive self-esteem, the social comparisons search is for positive distinctiveness for the in-group as compared to the out-group. Hence the reliable in-group favoritism and out-group discrimination biases.

The manner in which this sequence unfolds, and its yield of positive distinctiveness self-esteem, is held by the theory to be a function of a number of factors, some of which are absolute or relative qualities of the groups being compared, and others of which concern the availability and perceived desirability of alternative routes to positive distinctiveness. One important moderating consideration is described in the theory by the concept of *insecurity*. Social relationships between groups, as Brown and Ross (1982) observe, are seldom static, and since any significant changes in intergroup power or status relations will influence the outcome of intergroup comparisons, the nature of the social identity dependent on such comparisons will also change. It is such changes which the theory describes as *manifestations of insecurity*. Insecurity is more likely to occur, the theory posits, when the power or status of one of the groups is seen as being illegitimately acquired. Further, the consequences of insecure social identity are a renewed search for positive distinctiveness—perhaps through direct competition, but also possibly by other means. The group member may engage in individual mobility: he or she may leave the group and even attempt to assume the positively valued qualities of the out-group, i.e., engage in a process of assimilation. Alternatively, the person may seek positive distinctiveness by engaging in what the theory describes as *social creativity*, essentially an attempt to alter or redefine the elements of the intergroup comparative situation. One can seek to compare one's in-group with the out-group on a new dimension, a comparison more likely to yield positive distinctiveness. Otherwise, one may seek a different (lower status, less powerful) out-group against whom to compare one's in-group. Finally, group members may attempt to change their own values, transforming from negative to positive the valence of those qualities that define one's own identity, the oft-cited example of such a transformation being the "Black is beautiful" slogan.

The overview we have presented of social identity theory highlights the especially significant role of social categorization, as moderated by a number of intra- and intergroup characteristics, in the consequent search for identity-enhancing positive distinctiveness. Social categorization and the consequent promotion of in-group favoritism and out-group discrimination, it may further be noted, may be accentuated by external labeling, the use of intragroup symbols (name, flag, territory), and other sources of increased salience of group membership; by intergroup competition, as in the studies underpinning realistic-group-conflict theory; the more important is the attribute upon which the categorization is based to the social identity of ingroup members; and the more comparable the out-group is to the in-group. A number of factors have also been shown to reduce, at least under some circumstances, categorization-based in-group favoritism and out-group discrimination: common fate; value, attitude, or belief similarity; proximity; cooperative interdependence; anticipated and actual between-group interaction; and perception of a common enemy. Particularly useful for such discrimination-reducing purposes have been intergroup restructurings known, respectively, as decategorization, recategorization, and cross-categorization. Decategorization (or individuation) are procedures designed to reconfigure the manner in which outgroup members are perceived by those in the in-group, so that the former are viewed as individuals rather than "typical," undifferentiated "others." (Brewer & Brown, 1998). The challenge of this approach concerns minimizing the likelihood that the decategorized out-group member with whom an in-group member has, because of the decategorization, established positive content with, will be seen by the in-group member as an "exception to the (negative) rule," rather than as someone who might serve as a generalized springboard, as it were, to positive perception of the out-group as a whole. Recategorization, reflecting the superordinate group strategy utilized by Sherif et al. (1961), collapses the in-group and out-group into a single, larger group. Instead of emphasizing group member individuality, as in decategorization, here is stressed shared group membership (Dovidio et al., 1998). This strategy is also known as "the common ingroup identity model" (Dovidio et al., 1998). Finally, in cross-categorization, other group memberships held by in-group and out-group members, including especially other memberships they may share, are made salient. As Brewer and Miller (1996) note: "One possible effect of cross-category distinctions would be to dilute the meaningfulness of any in-group–out-group differentiation and eliminate category accentuation effects. In this case, in-group–out-group differences would be reduced or eliminated." (p. 9)

Information Processing

Once in-group favoritism and out-group discrimination are set in motion, whether as a result of categorization or on other bases, an array of information-processing sequences often combine to maintain their existence and potency. In an article aptly titled "On the Self-Perpetuating Nature of Social Stereotypes," Snyder (1981) sought to apply information-processing research on memory to the domain of stereotyping. In this now widely subscribed-to view, memory is construed to not be a replaying of some fixed memory traces but, instead, an active, reconstructive process (Bodenhausen, 1985; Hamilton & Sherman, 1996; Macrae & Bodenhausen, 2000). Exploring such notions as *retrospective reinterpretation, preferential remembering,* and *reconstructing the past by cognitive bolstering,* Snyder argues:

> Stereotypes influence and guide the remembering and interpretations of the past in ways that support and bolster current stereotyped interpretations of other people ... How might such reconstruction processes operate? First of all, the individual may search preferentially for stereotype-confirming factual evidence. Second, when the individual is in doubt about specific events in the target's past, these same stereotypes may provide convenient sources of clues for augmenting or filling in the gaps in his or her knowledge with evidence that further bolsters and supports current stereotyped beliefs. Third, stereotypes ... may provide guidelines for interpreting remembered events in ways that enhance their congruence with current stereotyped beliefs about the target. From this perspective, stereotypes function as "theories" that not only contain within them anticipation of what facts ought to be found in one's memory, but also initiate and guide the process of remembering and interpretation in ways that provide the individual with stereotype confirming evidence. (p. 191)

Such stereotype-driven cognitive bolstering may, in this view, be prospective, influencing the interpretation of later learned knowledge about the target person or group, and/or retrospective, acting upon the remembering and interpretation of previously learned information. A self-fulfilling prophecy may be the resultant of these processes, as they generate behaviors on the part of the target that confirm the stereotype.

Rothbart (1981) points to similar categorization-associated information-processing influences that may operate during the encoding, retrieval, and interpretation of information. For example, he suggests:

> ...activation of a category label... structures both encoding and retrieval... The widespread perception of in-group superiority may be attributable to the fact that in-group–out-group categorizations implicitly activate the expectancy that "we" are better than "they," and subjects selectively learn to remember in-group and out-group behaviors consistent with that expectancy. (p. 161)

Such differential processing of in-group-relevant and out-group-relevant information permits one to conclude, suggest Hamilton and Trollier (1986), that the social categories we each construct and employ are more than just means to simplify and comprehend a complex interpersonal environment: "They are also categories that can bias the way we process information, organize and store it in memory, and make judgments about members of those social categories" (p. 133). The power of social categorizations to shape what we seek, what we see, what we remember, and what we believe is by now well established—not only by earlier work on person perception and on social identity theory, and not only by the just-cited information-processing research on memory encoding, retrieval, and interpretation, but also by social cognition theory and investigation of what have been termed *social schemata*. A schema, according to Taylor and Fiske (1981), is a cognitive structure that guides how people take in, remember, and make inferences about raw data. Stereotypes are held to be a particular type of schema, one that organizes both one's knowledge and one's expectancies about people who fall into certain socially defined categories. Such schemata influence perceptions of variability, complexity, and valence. Specifically, out-groups are stereotypically seen to be less variable, simpler, and more negative than one's in-group. Schemata are often robust and perseverant. Taylor and Fiske note that people often not only ignore many exceptions to the schemata, but they may even interpret the exception as proving the schemata! Thus it is clear that just as categorization and the consequent search for positive distinctiveness can powerfully initiate in-group–out-group biases, information-processing sequences may both accentuate and perpetuate such biases and their consequences.

Social Dominance Theory

A third theoretical position of clear apparent relevance to our theme of group aggression is social dominance theory (Sidanius & Pratto, 1999). Central to this approach is the notion that inter-group relations derive in large measure from perceived social hierarchies consisting of what Sidanius and Pratto (1999) term "stratification systems." One, they assert, is an age-based system, in which (especially middle-aged) adults have disproportionate power over both younger adults and children. The second common social hierarchy derives from gender, a stratification system in which male dominance is typically reflected in their disproportionate social and political power compared to females. The third they label arbitrary-set systems, e.g., socially constructed hierarchies based on ethnicity, race, social class, caste, religion, region, nation, "or any other socially relevant group distinction that the human imagination is capable of constructing." (p. 33) Arbitrary-set social hierarchies, they remind us, are pervasive, enduring, strongly resistant to change, and in the view of social dominance theory, the major progenitor of intergroup aggression.

> Most forms of group conflict and oppression (e.g., racism, ethnocentrism, sexism, nationalism, classism, regionalism) can be regarded as different manifestations of the same basic human predisposition to form group-based social hierarchies. (Sidanius & Pratto, 1995, p. 38)

An array of both hierarchy-enhancing and hierarchy-attenuated forces exists, and exercise counterbalancing influences on human social systems. Hierarchy enhancement, that is, forces producing and maintaining ever-higher levels of group-based social inequality and strife, include aggregated individual discrimination, aggregated institutional discrimination, and the systematic use of aggression by supraordinates to subordinates. Hierarchy-attenuation influences, those that seek to produce greater levels of group-based social equality have, for example, been concretized over time by various religious teachings, political movements, and human and civil rights beliefs and actions.

The between-group dominance central to the resilience, robustness, and stability of social hierarchies rests in large part on what the theory terms legitimizing myths. These are the beliefs, values, ideologies, and stereotypes that provide the moral and intellectual justification for hierarchy construction and maintenance. Internal attributions for the misfortunes of the poor, notions of individual responsibility, and much of the thinking subsumed under the term "political conservatism" fit here.

> What all these ideas and doctrines have in common is the notion that each individual occupies that position along the social status continuum that he or she has earned and therefore deserves. From these perspectives then, particular configurations of the hierarchical social system are fair, legitimate, natural, and perhaps even inevitable. (Sidanius & Pratto, 1999, p. 46)

Legitimizing myths may also be hierarchy attenuating in their substance, and seek to promote greater levels of between-group egalitarianism. Such myths or belief systems may be found in many sources, from the Bible, to the US Declaration of Independence, to the doctrines of such diverse political and social movements as socialism, communism, feminism, and elsewhere.

The potency of legitimizing myths, both those hierarchy-enhancing and those hierarchy-attenuating, is held by social dominance theory to be a function of four factors: consensuality, embeddedness, certainty, and mediational strength. Consensuality is the degree to which the beliefs or assertions constituting the myth are broadly shared within the larger system of which the social hierarchy is a part.

Relevant to the potency of consensuality, and skirting uncomfortably close to a "blame the victim" stance, the theory notes that "group oppression is very much a cooperative game" (p. 43) and

> ... we suggest that it is subordinates' high level of both passive and active coop-
> eration with their own oppression that provides systems of group-based social
> hierarchy with their remarkable degrees of resiliency, robustness, and stability.
> Therefore, seen from this perspective, social hierarchy is not maintained pri-
> marily by the oppressive behavior of dominants, but by the deferential and
> obsequious behavior of subordinates. (p. 44)

Myth embeddedness is the degree to which it is well anchored to and strongly associated with other aspects of the culture's ideology. Its certainty concerns the apparency of the myth's degree of moral, religious, or scientific certainty or truth. Finally, the potency of a legitimizing myth is also determined by its mediational strength, defined as the degree to which it serves as a link between the desire to establish and maintain a group-based social hierarchy on the one hand, and the endorsement of hierarchy enhancing or attenuating social policies on the other.

Social dominance theory is both a sociological position, in its concern with social hierarchies, enhancing and attenuating forces, and societal legitimizing myths, and also a psychological theory. Its main concretization of the latter rests in the concept of social dominance orientation. This is a person quality, defined "as the degree to which individuals desire and support group-based hierarchy and domination of 'inferior' groups by 'superior' groups." It is a human dimension reminiscent of earlier writing about ethnocentrism, authoritarianism, and even fascism. The theory hypothesizes that one's degree of social dominance orientation will be positively associated with being male rather than female; with education, religion, and a host of earlier socialization experiences; with temperamental predispositions, such as low empathy, and with the degree of one's identification with and membership in hierarchically dominant arbitrary-set groups. Sidanius and Pratto (1999), it should be noted, have developed and begun psychometrically establishing a Social Dominance Orientation Scale as a means of reliably measuring this person-level contribution to social hierarchy construction and maintenance.

Other Relevant Theoretical Approaches

I have singled out Realistic Conflict Theory, Social Identity Theory, and Social Dominance Theory as the three positions potentially most relevant to the task of better understanding and reducing group aggression. None of realistic conflict, out-group discrimination, and social dominance are identical to the standard definition of aggression as being intentional physical or psychological injury to another person. However, they appear to be closely related concepts, each embedded in the-
oretical positions that appear to capture the complexity and dimensionality of the forces promoting and sustaining group aggression, thus encouraging their future consideration, application and evaluation in this context.

As noted, I have focused on these three theoretical views for their a priori apparent relevance to group aggression. There exist several additional such theoretical

viewpoints, which at minimum deserve mention in this context and for such purposes. Perhaps their clarifying potential vis a vis group aggression is more indeterminate, but that is a matter for future speculation and investigation to determine. Thus, through briefly, I wish in this theoretical section to also point the reader to Authoritarian Personality Theory (Adorno et al., 1950), Value Conflict Theory (Rokeach, 1973), Terror Management Theory (Wilson, 1973), Relative Deprivation Theory (Stouffer, 1949; Gurr, 1989), Prospect Theory (Kahneman & Tversky, 1979), Sociobiology and Evolutionary Psychology (Dawkins, 1989; W. D. Hamilton, 1964), and Group Position Theory (Blumer, 1960).

GROUP STRUCTURE AND PROCESSES

In order better to understand the nature and functioning of human groups, it is helpful to have a framework or schema that meaningfully organizes events and processes within them. Tuckman (Tuckman, 1965; Tuckman & Jensen, 1977) has offered just such a framework. His perspective on the stages of group development, summarized in Table 1.1, shows the developmental sequence of the the typical human group. In this sequence, groups organize and establish themselves, begin dealing with potential obstacles to meeting their group goals, solidify their structure, "groupness" or entativity and the roles and norms that will facilitate goal-relevant performance, perform their task, and adjourn. As Table 1.1 indicates,

Table 1.1   Five stages of group development

Stage	Major processes	Characteristics
Forming	Development of attraction bonds, exchange of information, orientation toward others and situation	Tentative interactions, polite discourse, concern over ambiguity, silences
Storming	Dissatisfaction with others, competition among members, disagreement over procedures, conflict	Ideas are criticized, speakers are interrupted, attendance is poor, hostility
Norming	Development of group structure, increased cohesiveness and harmony, establishment of roles and relationships	Agreement on rules, consensus-seeking, increased supportiveness, we-feeling
Performing	Focus on achievement, high task orientation, emphasis on performance and productivity	Decision making, problem solving, increased cooperation, decreased emotionality
Adjourning	Termination of duties, reduction of dependency, task completion	Regret, increased emotionality, disintegration

Sources: Tuckman (1965); Tuckman and Jensen (1977). Reprinted from *An Introduction to Group Dynamics* (p. 20) by D. R. Forsyth, 1983, Monterey, CA: Brooks/Cole.

Tuckman (1965) labels these stages forming, storming, norming, performing, and adjourning. Forsyth (1999), in parallel, terms these steps in group development and evaluation: orientation, conflict, structure, work, and dissolution. We will employ Tuckman's (1965) five-stage sequence as a means of organizing this section.

Forming

Why do groups form? Why do people need, seek, and appear to derive benefit from the company of others? Early observers (Edman, 1919; McDougall, 1908) spoke of the "herd instinct," an answer that subsequently reappeared in sociobiological writings about a "biologically rooted urge to affiliate" (E. O. Wilson, 1975). Like instinctual explanations of other behaviors, such speculations, however elaborate, are essentially circular and untestable. An explanation of group behavior based on need satisfaction is more tenable. This is especially so when the formulation is sufficiently complex to include both need similarity and need complementarity among group members, as well as particular needs and need patterns that are demonstrated empirically to relate to the quality of the group experience and the quantity of the group product. Schutz's (1967) perspective on interpersonal needs as a prime influence on group process fits this description well. His work points to group formation and process as being a result of members' needs to express or receive inclusion (associate, belong, join), control (power, dominance, authority), and affection (cohesiveness, love, friendship). A related position on group formation as a function of interpersonal need emphasizes the need for affiliation as the central determinant of member behavior (H. A. Murray, 1938; Smart, 1965). The social-comparisons theory of group formation takes a somewhat more cognitive direction. According to Festinger (1954) and Schachter (1959), people affiliate into dyads or groups when doing so provides useful information derived from comparing oneself, one's attitudes, or one's beliefs with those of others. This basis for group formation is especially attractive, it is held, when one's attitudes or beliefs are shaken and the act of communicating with and comparing oneself to others has potential for restoring equanimity or clarity, or at least for providing a sense of safety in numbers. Social identity theory, as noted earlier, goes yet further in this direction, beyond equanimity, clarity, or safety, to grouping and group identification as a route to a sense of positive distinctiveness.

The social exchange view of group formation is rather more "economic" in its specifics. According to its proponents (Kelley & Thibaut, 1978; Thibaut & Kelley, 1959), individuals make group affiliation decisions based on their estimate of the interpersonal value of such participation. Value is defined in terms of both estimated rewards and potential costs. What are the primary rewards and costs of belonging to groups? Rewards may include social support, the group's process, or the group's activities themselves; the benefits of experiencing certain group member characteristics suggestive of likely success at group goals (e.g., authenticity, competence, sociability), and, especially, the group goals themselves. Costs of affiliation may be discomfort with the ambiguous or unfamiliar; the investment that may have to be made in time, energy, self-disclosure, or other resources; possible social rejection; inefficiency or ineffectiveness in progress toward the group's goals;

reactance (i.e., the loss of a sense of freedom, autonomy, or "choicefulness" as the group brings pressure to bear upon its members to conform, reach consensus, or behave in a synchronous manner), and, in the case of groups organized to perpetrate aggression toward other groups, there often exists the high cost of becoming such a target oneself.

Starting early in its formation and continuing throughout its life, the group develops a sense of cohesiveness. This centrally important quality of groups has traditionally been defined in terms of (a) the attraction members feel toward other group members and the group as a unit, (b) member motivation to participate in the group's activities and contribute to the group's goals, and (c) the coordination of member effort. Cohesiveness has sometimes been measured by questionnaire (e.g., Schachter et al., 1951). Among the questions often included in such measures are the following:

1. Do you want to remain a member of this group?
2. How often do you think this group should meet?
3. If it seems this group might discontinue, would you like the chance to persuade members to stay?

More typically, intermember attraction (which emerged as the prime definition of cohesiveness) has been measured by sociometrics, a technique for estimating the social relationships among group members (Moreno, 1960). Members are asked to indicate whom they like most and least, with whom they would most like to work, and so forth. Responses are plotted on a sociogram, which not only reflects the level, spread, and content of intermember attraction, but also reveals such cohesiveness-related selections as the group's stars, isolates, pairs, chains, rejections, and integration. Hogg (1992), Lott and Lott (1965), and numerous other investigators note that group cohesiveness may be promoted by propinquity, acceptance by others, cooperative interaction, externally imposed threat, status homogeneity, apparent group goal related skills, effortful initiation into the group, and member similarity in attitudes, values, or backgrounds.

In recent years, the definitional base for cohesiveness has broadened. Beyond but still including attraction, added to its meanings are notions of resistance to disruption, unification, satisfaction, adhesiveness, and commitment. The meaning of attraction-to-group has itself also been altered. The original concept, determined and measured by questionnaire or sociometrically, pertained to "measuring the levels of attraction of individual members and averaging them." (Evans & Jarvis, 1980, p. 359), As these same authors then note, "This technique assumes, with little justification, that the whole process is no greater than the sum of its parts." (p. 359) Stated otherwise, it was asserted that the traditional definition (and measurement) of cohesiveness occurred at the interpersonal, rather than group level. Hogg's (1992) definitional reformulation sought to move its meaning precisely in this group direction. Hogg (1992) observes:

> . . . a clear distinction can be drawn between two forms of attraction . . . social attraction and personal attraction . . . The phenomenology of both is a positive feeling that one person has about another. However, the generative process underlying each is quite different. Social attraction . . . is depersonalized liking

based upon prototypicality and generated by self-categorization. It is actually attraction to the group as that group is embodied by specific group members, so that the object of positive attitude and feelings is not actually the unique individual person, but the prototype that he/she embodies. Targets are relatively interchangeable—they are depersonalized. John is not liked for being John, but for being a more or less exemplary embodiment of the prototypical properties of the group . . . In contrast, personal attraction [the traditional, averaged base for defining cohesiveness] is idiosyncratic and grounded in specific interpersonal relationships . . . Personal attraction is tied to specific non-interchangeable targets. (p. 100)

Hogg's (1992) redefinition grows quite directly from Social Identity Theory and its exclusive focus on group-level variables. Given the contemporary ascendancy of this theoretical perspective on group behavior, one may predict the cohesiveness defined in *social* attraction terms will gain prominence in future research on this, still central, dimension of group development and process.

We have singled out cohesiveness as primary among the characteristics of group development because cohesiveness has been shown to be an especially powerful influence upon the character and quality of group interaction, as well as being a major determinant of the group's longevity and success in reaching its goals. The more cohesive the group, the more likely its members will:

1. Be more open to influence by other group members
2. Conform to group norms and standards
3. Place greater value on the group's goals
4. Perceive other group members as similar to oneself
5. Be active participants in group discussion
6. Be more equal participants in group discussion
7. Be less susceptible to disruption as a group when a member terminates membership
8. Evaluate the group positively
9. Be absent less often
10. Become aggressive in response to external insult
11. Remain in the group longer

Cohesiveness is indeed a crucial foundation of group formation and development. It will tend to diminish the more there is disagreement within the group, the more the group makes unreasonable or excessive demands on its members, the more the leader or other members are overly dominating, the higher the degree of self-oriented behaviors, the more group membership limits the satisfactions members can receive outside the group, the more negatively membership is viewed by outsiders, and the more that conflict exists within the group.

Storming

Groups may experience conflict at any stage in their development. We wish here to focus on the growth and resolution of such conflict not only to understand better this significant group dynamic but also because the resolution of intermember difficulties will often be prerequisite to satisfactory progress toward the achievement of group goals. Forsyth (1983) proposes that group conflict characteristically moves through five phases. The first is *disagreement*, in which members discover that two or more group members are in conflict regarding a group task, an interpersonal matter, or other group-related concern. *Confrontation* is the second phase of a typical group conflict. Here the opposing factions openly debate the issues in contention. This phase is often characterized by attempts to convert or discredit one's opponent, increased or intensified commitment to one's own position, heightened tension among the disputants and within the group at large, and the formation of coalitions as previously neutral group members elect to, or are pressured to, choose sides. Flowing from such positional commitment, heightened tension, and polarization within the group, the third conflict phase, *escalation*, may ensue. Forsyth graphically describes this process:

> Many groups are caught up in a conflict spiral... The final remnants of group unity are shattered as the combatants' exchanges become increasingly hostile, persuasive influence is dropped in favor of coercion, promises are replaced by threats, and in extreme cases verbal attacks become physically violent assaults. (p. 84)

If the group holds together and weathers the storm of disagreement, confrontation, and escalation, then the fourth phase of group conflict, *deescalation*, may occur. Group members tire of fighting, feel their efforts and energy are being wasted, become increasingly more rational, begin to accept a bit of the other side's perspective, and decide to reinvest their efforts in movement toward the group's original purposes and goals. Such deescalation will often not occur without the aid and intervention of third parties. Finally, the last phase, *resolution*, occurs when the conflict is terminated. Conflict may end via integrative, win–win solutions, in which creative outcomes give both parties all they sought, by compromise in which both sides gain some and yield some until an agreement is reached, via withdrawal in which one side essentially yields for the sake of peace and unity, via imposition in which by sheer power of numbers or authority one viewpoint is made to prevail, or by conversion, in which the discussion, persuasion, and promises of one side cause the other side to be won over and change its position.

Conflict, of course, may never occur. Many groups organize, set their tasks, get down to business, perform competently, and reach their goals with no disagreement, minimal tension, and general absence of conflict. As noted, when conflict does occur and the group members themselves are not able to resolve it, aid from others outside the group may be necessary. As I will elaborate in Chapter 6, such help may take several forms. Mediation is one possibility. Here a third party (an outsider or a neutral group member) seeks to help the disputants come to agreement. (In many school settings, it has become popular to use fellow students as peer mediators.) The mediator avoids offering answers or solutions but serves instead as a facilitator, a go-between, an aid to helping those in disagreement to express their views, to listen openly to the other side, and to move toward compromise or other solutions. When mediation fails, either because the disputants can't really hear each other or are themselves unable to suggest compromise solutions, the third party may do so. In this negotiator role, the third party proposes possible solutions, compromises, or other effective outcomes for the disputants to consider and agree upon. When negotiation also fails, or is inappropriate, the third party's role may become more direct—not that of a mediating go-between or a negotiating proposer of solutions but one of an arbitrator. Arbitration is a process in which both sides agree on a third-party decision maker who listens fully to the competing positions and then imposes a binding decision upon the contending group members.

Although we believe that mediation, negotiation, and arbitration may each serve a valuable role in the reduction of group conflict, we recommend a fourth approach. The routes to group conflict resolution just described may work, but none of them contributes to the disputants' or the group's ability to ward off further conflicts or to resolve them when they do occur. Training the group members to be effective communicators in conflict situations does, however, have the potential to reduce conflict in the future. In such a training effort (Goldstein & Keller, 1987), group members are taught techniques for preparing for communication effectively, and avoiding obstacles to its success. An outline of this communications training program is given as Table 1.2. Communication training offered in accord with this schema has been shown to reduce within-group conflict substantially (Carkhuff, 1969; Goldstein & Keller, 1987; Guerney, 1964; Rose, 1977).

Intergroup conflict is a second broad class of group-related storming. Intergroup competition increases the level of cohesiveness within groups (Coser, 1956; Sherif & Sherif, 1953), an effect that is particularly pronounced within the group that wins the competition (Dion, 1973; Ryen & Kahn, 1970). Intergroup competition tends to increase rejection of the other group's members. Such rejection by each group of the other is heightened or moderated by how similar the two groups are, by whether they anticipate that they will have to interact in the future, and by features of the competitive task itself (Brewer, 1979). Intergroup competition serves to establish and maintain boundaries between groups, as reflected in member tendencies to emphasize between-group differences and minimize between-group similarities (Cooper & Fazio, 1979). Intergroup competition often leads to significant misperception of the other group's behavior and intentions. The other group may be stereotyped, dehumanized, or seen as immoral or malevolent; one's own group may be idealized as being moral, overly powerful, or totally right in its views (Linville & Jones, 1980; White, 1970, 1977). I will have a great deal more to say about intergroup conflict both later in the present chapter as well as in subsequent chapters.

Norming

As the group deals effectively with potential and emergent intermember conflict, and as intermember attraction and group cohesiveness build, the way becomes clearer for the group to establish explicit and implicit norms or guidelines, to solidify its choice of leaders and leadership styles, to carve out and begin enacting individual roles for its members, and to settle on particular patterns of communication that members feel to be comfortable and effective. These group dynamics (norms, leadership, roles, and communication patterns) are the primary concerns of the present section.

Table 1.2 A communication training program for conflict resolution

Preparing for communication
1. Plan on dealing with one problem at a time, sequencing problems in order of significance if more than one exists.
2. Choose the right time and place, emphasizing privacy and minimizing interruptions or distractions.
3. Review your own position and hoped-for outcomes, as well as those of the other disputant, placing particular emphasis on possible mutually satisfying solutions.

Conducting constructive communication
1. Acknowledge subjectivity not only in the other's position, but also in one's own as a means of establishing a non-defensive climate for discussion.
2. Be rational in stating your views, the reasons underlying them, and your hoped-for outcomes.
3. Be direct in putting forth what you need, feel, prefer, or expect, and minimize censoring or half-truths.
4. Make ongoing communication checks by asking questions, restating your understanding of the other's position, and asking for hard-to-understand content be repeated in order to be sure that you and the other party are communicating accurately.
5. Focus on behavior and on actual actions that you and the other disputant have taken or might take (what, where, when, how often, how much) and do not focus on more difficult-to-change disputant qualities, such as motivations, beliefs, character, personality, or other non-observable inner characteristics.
6. Reciprocate by showing willingness to acknowledge your own role in problem causation and by showing your own openness to change behavior toward the goal of problem solution.
7. Be empathic, try to perceive accurately and overtly communicate your awareness of the other disputant's feelings relevant to the conflict in progress.
8. Pay attention to non-verbal behavior—it is central to an accurate understanding of the nature and intensity of the other disputant's views, feelings, and perhaps even willingness to continue engaging in the communication process.

Avoiding communication blocks
Communication in conflict situations may falter for a variety of reasons. Group members should become sensitive to—and actively avoid—the following behaviors:

1. Threats	10. Overgeneralization
2. Commands	11. Unresponsiveness
3. Interruptions	12. Exaggeration
4. Sarcasm	13. Speaking for the other person
5. Put-downs	
6. Counterattacks	14. Lecturing
7. Insults	15. Kitchen-sinking
8. Teasing	16. Building straw men
9. Yelling	17. Use of guilt arousal

Norms

Norms are the overtly stated or covertly assumed rules of action specifying which behaviors are appropriate (prescriptive norms) or inappropriate (proscriptive norms) for group members. Thus, norms are evaluative standards implying or even directly stating that some member behaviors are better or more desirable than others. Norms often come into being not so much by means of prior discussion and overt choice as by gradual use and implicit adoption. They may come to be assumed and taken for granted by group members and may only become evident when they are violated. Normative behavior may be adopted initially because of positive feelings of group cohesion, because continuation of membership is desired, or in order to avoid pressure, rejection, or other group sanctions. Eventually, such behavior comes to be internalized or "owned" by group members. Forsyth (1999) observes that norms provide group members with both direction and motivation, they organize member interactions, and help make other members' behaviors meaningful and predictable. Norms are the organizers, shapers, and broad guidelines determining much of what does or does not occur in any given group, what the group expects and aspires to achieve, how it allocates its resources, how it will be led, and much more. Shaw (1981) suggests that member conformity to group norms will be influenced by several factors. One is qualities of the individual member, for example, intelligence appears to relate negatively to such conformity, whereas persons high on authoritarianism are more likely to conform than those low on this characteristic. A second category of conformity-influencing factors is situational. Here are included such group features as its structure, communication patterns, size, and the degree of unanimity among members in norm conformity. Third, the kinds of stimuli, behaviors, issues, or concerns reflected by and inherent in the particular normative standard will help determine its conformity level. Finally, intragroup relationships. Shaw (1981) points in particular here to past success or failure at goal attainment by the group, the kinds and intensities of the conformity pressure applied, and the degree to which the member identifies with the group involved.

Leadership

The topic of effective leaders and leadership has been a central concern of group dynamics researchers. For decades, through the 1940s, the "Great Man" theory of leadership prevailed. This view essentially held that effective leaders are persons who are born with or have come to possess certain personality traits and who, by dint of such characteristics, can and do lead in a variety of settings and situations. The research task thus became one of leadership-associated trait identification and, in fact, leaders have been shown to be somewhat more achievement oriented, adaptable, alert, ascendant, conscientious, emotionally controlled, energetic, friendly, responsible, self-confident, self-controlled, and sociable than other group members (Bass, 1981; Forsyth, 1983). Over time, however, the correlations between these traits and effective leadership behavior proved modest. Although such traits certainly contribute to the success of leadership attempts, their importance is eclipsed by the potency of the group situation itself. Carron (1980) comments with regard to this more modern, situational view of leader effectiveness that:

> it is now generally accepted that there are no inherent traits or dispositions within an individual which contribute to ascendancy and maintenance of leadership [across situations]. Instead, it is believed that the specific requirements of different situations dictate the particular leadership qualities which will be most effective. (pp. 126–127)

Table 1.3   Leadership behavior dimensions in sport

Dimension	Description
Training behavior	Behavior aimed at improving the performance level of the athletes by emphasizing and facilitating hard and strenuous training, clarifying the relationships among the members
Autocratic behavior	Tendency of the coach to set himself (herself), apart from the athletes, and to make all decisions by himself (herself)
Democratic behavior	Behavior of the coach that allows greater participation by the athletes in deciding on group goals, practice methods, and game tactics and strategies
Social support behavior	Behavior of the coach indicating his (her) concern for individual athletes and their welfare and for positive group atmosphere
Rewarding behavior	Behavior of the coach that provides reinforcement for an athlete by recognizing and rewarding good performance

Note: From "Preferred Leadership in Sport" by P. Chelladurai and S. D. Saleh, 1978, *Canadian Journal of Applied Sport Sciences, 3*, p. 91. Reprinted by permission.

Such situational thinking about leadership led to two research tasks. The first was the identification of specific behaviors, not traits, characteristic of acts of leadership. The second was the prescriptive determination of which leadership behaviors were optimal for which group members in which situations. Successful leadership, in this perspective, is a matter of matching leadership behaviors with appropriate situations (members, tasks, goals, settings) for their use. The early but still relevant Ohio State Leadership Studies (Hemphill & Coons, 1957) identified the following behaviors as constituting what leaders actually do: initiation, membership, representation, integration, organization, domination, communication, recognition, and production. Consistent with the situational view of effective leadership, Chelladurai and Saleh (1978) applied the Ohio State results to coaching behavior in athletic contexts. Table 1.3 indicates how leader behavior is held to vary optimally by task demand.

Though their categories of leadership behavior vary somewhat, both studies yield two broad classes of effective leadership behavior—namely, those that are task oriented and focus on performance and group goals, and those that are relationship oriented and hence more concerned with enhancing group cohesiveness and reducing group conflict (Hersey & Blanchard, 1977). The view of group leadership behavior as consisting of two broad dimensions—task orientation and relationship orientation—has become quite popular in group dynamics theory and research, taking the several expressions reflected in Table 1.4.

As the situational view of effective leadership proposes, research demonstrates that neither a task nor a relationship orientation is uniformly optimal. With some groups, under some circumstances and when working toward certain goals, a task focus on work, production, performance, and solutions is appropriate. For other situations, support, relationships, conflict reduction, and similar emphases are appropriate. Not surprisingly, there appear to be many group situations in which the most effective leadership behaviors reflect a balanced combination of task and relationship orientations.

Table 1.4 The two basic dimensions of leadership in behavior

Leadership dimensions	Alternative labels	Conceptual meaning	Sample behaviors
Consideration	Relationship orientation Socioemotional Supportive Employee centered Relations skilled Group maintenance	Degree to which the leader responds to group members in a warm and friendly fashion; involves mutual trust, openness, and willingness to explain decisions	Listens to group members Easy to understand Is friendly and approachable Treats group members as equals Is willing to make changes
Initiating structure	Task orientation Goal oriented Work facilitative Production centered Administratively skilled Goal achiever	Extent to which leader organizes, directs, and defines the group's structure and goals; regulates group behavior monitors communication, and reduces goal ambiguity	Assigns tasks to members Makes attitudes clear to the group Is critical of poor work Sees to it that the group is working to capacity Coordinates activity

Sources: Halpin and Winer (1952); Lord (1977). Reprinted from *An Introduction to Group Dynamics* (p. 215) by D. R. Forsyth, 1983, Monterey, CA: Brooks/Cole.

Other categorizations of leadership behavior exist. Lewin's research team (Lewin, Lippitt, & White, 1939; White & Lippitt, 1968) early on offered the dimensions of authoritarian, democratic, and laissez-faire leadership. Vroom and Yetton (1973) have suggested autocratic, consultative, and group leadership behavioral patterns. What is noteworthy about these, and other, leadership categories is the uniform agreement that, whatever the system, one must first take account of the "attributes of the group situation to consider in judging which type of leadership to use" (Forsyth, 1983, p. 235). Regardless of which typology one applies, it is also most useful to heed Forsyth's (1999) view that leadership is a reciprocal process, in which leader and led influence one another: at its best a cooperative, transactional process, involving social exchange rather than the exercise of sheer power, and at its most effective, also transformational as it motivates, persuades, augments the confidence of, and ultimately satisfies those to whom it is directed.

Roles

Leader is but one of many roles assumed by group members. As is the case for the leader, the way in which an individual in the group behaves at a given point in time is partly a matter of that individual's dispositions or traits, but it is even more so a result of the situational demands and opportunities operating within the group. Such situational determinants of members' roles include the leader's behavior, the behavior of other group members, the group cohesiveness level,

Table 1.5 Task roles and socioemotional roles in groups

Role	Function
Task roles	
1. Initiator contributor	Recommends novel ideas about the problem at hand, new ways to approach the problem, or possible solutions not yet considered.
2. Information seeker	Emphasizes "getting the facts" by calling for background information from others.
3. Opinion seeker	Asks for more qualitative types of data, such as attitudes, values, and feelings.
4. Information giver	Provides data for forming decisions, including facts that derive from expertise.
5. Opinion giver	Provides opinions, values, and feelings.
6. Elaborator	Gives additional information—examples, rephrasings, implications—about points made by others.
7. Coordinator	Shows the relevance of each idea and its relationship to the overall problem.
8. Orienter	Refocuses discussion on the topic whenever necessary.
9. Evaluator-critic	Appraises the quality of the group's efforts in terms of logic, practicality, or method.
10. Energizer	Stimulates the group efforts in terms of logic, practicality, or method.
11. Procedural	Cares for operational details, such as the materials, machinery, and so on.
12. Recorder	Provides a secretarial function.
Socioemotional roles	
1. Encourager	Rewards others through agreement, warmth, and praise.
2. Harmonizer	Mediates conflicts among group members.
3. Compromiser	Shifts his or her own position on an issue in order to reduce conflict in the group.
4. Gatekeeper and expediter	Smooths communication by setting up procedures and ensuring equal participation from members.
5. Standard setter	Expresses, or calls for discussion of, standards for evaluating the quality of the group process.
6. Group observer and commentator	Informally points out the positive and negative aspects of the group's dynamics and calls for change if necessary
7. Follower	Accepts the ideas offered by others and serves as an audience for the group.

Reproduced by permission of Blackwell Publishing from Beene & Sheats, 1948. *Journal of Social Issues*, **4**, 46.

group tasks, group communication patterns, group goals, and other salient group characteristics. As it has for the role of leader, group dynamics thinking has gravitated toward categorizing member behavior in terms of task-oriented roles and relationship-oriented (socioemotional) roles, as detailed in Table 1.5.

Communication patterns

A final aspect of the norm-setting process occurring in groups is the establishment and maintenance of viable communication patterns or networks by means

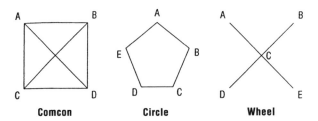

Figure 1.1   Communication networks relevant to group therapy leadership. (Reproduced with permission from *Psychotherapy and the psychology of behavior change* by A. P. Goldstein, K. Heller, & L. B. Sechrest, New York: Wiley)

of which the group will conduct its task- and relationship-oriented business. The communication network(s) established in any given group reflect many qualities of the group but most especially its preferred leadership style and the nature of its goals. Figure 1.1 depicts three of the more common communication patterns. Each letter in these networks represents a different group member, and each line represents a two-person communication linkage. Marked variability exists among these networks in the degree to which members are free to communicate with one another. Group member B, for example, is free to communicate with all other group members in the Comcon (or all-channel) network, with two other members (A and C) in the Circle network, and with only one other member (C) in the Wheel network. Differences also exist in member centrality—that is, in the number of linkages tied to members—and the number of linkages (distance) from them to each other member. In the Wheel network, member C is most central. Within the other two networks, all members are equally central or peripheral. Studies demonstrate that, in centralized networks like the wheel, central position members (leader, teacher, boss) are more satisfied than are peripheral members. Most people, in fact, tend to prefer one or another decentralized network since it permits, and may even encourage, independence of action, autonomy, and self-direction (M. E. Shaw, 1964). Centralized networks organize more rapidly, are more stable in performance, and are most efficient for the performance of simple tasks. However, as task complexity grows, the decentralized networks prove superior (M. E. Shaw, 1964). This finding is one more example of the need to vary a group characteristic depending on the situation—in this instance, the group's task.

Performing

As groups develop, deal with conflict, and establish participation norms and roles, they concomitantly seek to perform the tasks that motivated the group's formation in the first place. In this section, I will present the approaches that group dynamicists have taken to categorize group tasks, examine means that have been identified for improving group performance on such tasks, and consider the implications for member performance of the use of power to wield influence. Finally, we will turn to such collective behaviors as deindividuation and "groupthink." These latter two qualities of group performance appear to be particularly relevant to the emergence or promotion of aggressive behavior.

Group tasks

Forsyth (1983) points out that a group's specific tasks depend, in the first place, on the group's ultimate goals. Is the group organized to make decisions, solve problems, promote ideology, generate ideas, thwart other groups, learn facts, create products? Tasks to be performed, according to Shaw (1981), are also determined by (a) the difficulty of the group's overall problem, (b) the number of acceptable solutions, (c) the intrinsic interest level of the task, (d) the amount of cooperation required of group members for successful task performance, (e) the intellectual and related demands presented, and (f) member familiarity with task components. Steiner (1972, 1976) has proposed a system of classifying tasks based on task divisibility, the type of performance desired, and the manner in which group member inputs contribute to group goals (see Table 1.6). McGrath (1984; Arrow & McGrath, 1995) proposes that, at a general level of abstraction, group tasks are, sequentially, to generate, choose, negotiate, and execute. Generating is the group's planning task, its core is devising strategies to meet the group's goals. Choosing narrows its focus further including, for example, making decisions about which task-relevant issues are do-able or answerable, and which may not be. Negotiation is the group's effort to resolve task-associated conflicts or intermember differences. Task execution, the final step in the sequence, is its performance step.

How well will the group perform its designated tasks? In part, the answer depends on task characteristics. On additive tasks, for example, it has been shown that the larger the group, the lower the quantity or quality of each individual's contribution to task performance. This so-called *Ringelmann effect* (Forsyth, 1983) has been explained by Latane, Williams, and Harkins (1979) as being due to "coordination losses" (e.g., pulling on a tug-of-war rope at different times) and "social loafing" (i.e., working less hard when one's own contribution to task performance will remain unknown by other group members). Conjunctive group tasks, as a second example, pose a different performance problem. Here, because all group members must contribute to task performance, the group as a whole performs at the level of its weakest member. As Forsyth notes, the speed of a group of mountain climbers, a truck convoy, or a funeral procession is determined by its slowest member. However, conjunctive task performance can be improved if the task is divided and the weakest members are assigned to the least difficult subtasks.

Task performance is affected substantially by the group's task-relevant communication patterns. Deutsch and Krauss (1960), Harper and Askling (1980), Johnson and Johnson (1997), and numerous other investigators have shown that, in comparison to unsuccessful groups, successful groups have a significantly higher rate and accuracy of communication.

The techniques outlined earlier in this chapter for enhancing the quality of communication hold considerable potential for improving task performance. However, task performance may be impeded when the group's climate and associated communication patterns become defensive. Forsyth (1983) comments as follows:

Table 1.6 A summary of Steiner's typology of tasks

Question	Answer	Task type	Examples
Can the task be broken down into subcomponents or is division of the task inappropriate?	Subtasks can be identified	Divisible	Playing a football game, building a house, preparing a six-course meal
	No subtasks exist	Unitary	Pulling a rope, reading a book, solving a math problem
Which is more important: quantity produced or quality of performance?	Quantity	Maximizing	Generating many ideas, lifting the greatest weight, scoring the most runs
	Quality	Optimizing	Generating the best idea, getting the right answer, solving a math problem
How are individual inputs related to the group's product?	Individual inputs are added together	Additive	Pulling a rope, stuffing envelopes, shoveling snow
	Group produce is average of individual judgments	Compensatory	Averaging individuals' estimates of the number of beans in a jar, Weight of an object, room temperature
	Group selects the product from pool of individual members' judgments	Disjunctive	Questions involving "yes–no, either–or" answers such as math problems, puzzles, and choices between options
	All group members must contribute to the product	Conjunctive	Climbing a mountain, eating a meal, soldiers marching in file
	Group can decide how individual inputs relate to group	Discretionary	Deciding to shovel snow together, opting to vote on the best answers to a math problem, letting leader answer question

Source: Steiner (1972, 1976). Reprinted from *An Introduction to Group Dynamics* (p. 151) by D. R. Forsyth, 1983, Monterey, CA: Brooks/Cole.

> Whenever members of a group feel personally threatened, they begin to behave defensively. Effort is shifted from the group tasks to defensive tactics, and individual efficiency drops as concern over evaluations, worry about others' intentions, counterattack planning, and defensive listening escalate. (p. 163)

Gibb (1961, 1973) proposes a number of ways in which groups engender such defensive, task-impeding communication and also highlights the features of a more supportive, communication-encouraging group climate (see Table 1.7).

Table 1.7   Characteristics of defensive and supportive group climates

Characteristic	Defensive climate	Supportive climate
1. Evaluation versus description	1. People in the group seem to be judging your actions	1. People in the group are seen as trying to describe outcomes and information
2. Control versus problem oriented	2. Others are seen as manipulative, attempting influence	2. Others seem to be focused on the problem at hand
3. Strategy versus spontaneity	3. Members seem to plan out their "moves," interactions, and comments	3. Interaction seem to flow smoothly with little strategic control
4. Neutrality versus empathy	4. People in the group seem to react to you with aloofness and disinterest	4. People in the group seem to identify with your ideas and interests
5. Superiority versus equality	5. Others seem condescending, acting as if they are better than you are	5. Group members treat one another as equals
6. Certainty versus provisionalism	6. Some people in the group seem to feel that their own ideas are undoubtedly correct	6. People in the group are not committed to any one viewpoint, for they are keeping an open mind

Source: Gibb (1961, 1973). Reprinted from *An Introduction to Group Dynamics* (p. 164) by D. R. Forsyth, 1983, Monterey, CA: Brooks/Cole.

Power

Thus far, we have observed that performance in groups is significantly influenced by the nature of the group tasks, as well as by the rate and accuracy of members' task-relevant communication. However, task performance in group contexts is also a function of the relative power bases, levels, and tactics utilized by group leaders and group members. French and Raven (1959) have proposed that an individual's power in a group context may derive from one or more of several sources (see Table 1.8).

As is consistent with the situational view of group leadership, the effect and effectiveness of the six alternative bases for leader or member power or influence, as well as the effectiveness of whichever tactic(s) is/are employed to express them (see Table 1.9), are a function of characteristics of the particular group involved. Group cohesiveness, the manner in which the group leader has been selected, elected, or imposed, the group's size, and the group task and any deadlines associated with its completion are among the qualities determining the impact of expressed power.

Falbo (1977) has shown that the power tactics listed in Table 1.9 vary on two dimensions: rationality and directness. Bargaining, compromise, and persuasion are rational means for exerting influence on task performance, evasion, threat, and

Table 1.8 Six bases of power

Label	Definition
1. Reward power	The powerholder's control over the positive and negative reinforcements desired by the target person
2. Coercive power	The powerholder's ability to threaten and punish the target person
3. Legitimate power	Power that stems from the target person's belief that the powerholder has a justifiable right to require and demand the performance of certain behaviors
4. Referent power	Power that derives from the target person's identification with, attraction to, or respect for the powerholder
5. Expert power	Power that exists when the target person believes that the powerholder possesses superior skills and abilities
6. Informational power	Influence based on the potential use of informational resources, including rational argument, persuasion, or factual data

Source: J. R. P. French, Jr., & B. Raven (1959). (Reproduced with permission from French & Raven (1959) in Cartwright (Ed.), *Studies in social power*, Ann Arbor: Institute for Social Research)

deceit are non-rational means. Threats, persistence, and fait accompli are direct power tactics; hinting and thought manipulation are more indirect. Research has shown that group leaders and members who are especially concerned with being accepted and liked by their fellow group members make heaviest use of rational and indirect influence tactics, rather than non-rational and direct means. In contrast, non-rational and indirect tactics are the power methods of choice for manipulative group members.

The foregoing discussion provides a sense of how powerholders in groups seek to influence other group members. However, what are the effects of holding power over the powerholder? First, researchers have found in experimental groups that people with power clearly tend to use it (Deutsch, 1973; Kipnis & Consentino, 1969). If successful in its use, they often feel self-satisfaction, overestimate their interpersonal influence, and assign themselves unrealistically positive self-evaluations (Kipnis, 1974). They may assume that they themselves are the major determinant of other people's behavior (Kipnis et al., 1976), devalue those toward whom the influence was directed (Zander, Cohen, & Stotland, 1959), and in other ways distance from and derogate the targets of their power tactics (Sampson, 1965; Strickland, 1958). Powerful members of groups, in addition, will tend to protect the sources of their influence (Lawler & Thompson, 1979) and seek to expand upon it (McClelland, 1975).

Deindividuation

Deindividuation is the process of losing one's sense of individuality or separateness from others and becoming submerged in a group. A mob in a riot situation, an aroused audience at an athletic event or rock concert, a congregation at an emotional religious meeting, those listening to an impassioned speaker at a political rally, and

Table 1.9   Examples and definitions of sixteen power tactics

Strategy	Definition	Example
Reason	Any statement about using reason or rational argument to influence others	I argue logically. I tell all the reasons why my plan is best
Expertise	Claiming to have superior knowledge or skills	I tell them I have a lot of experience with such matters
Compromise	Both agent and target give up part of their goals in order to obtain some of them	More often than not we come to some sort of compromise, if there is a disagreement
Bargaining	Explicit statement about reciprocating favors and making other two-way exchanges	I tell her that I'll do something for her if she'll do something for me
Persuasion	Simple statements about using persuasion, convincing others, or coaxing	I get my way by convincing others that my way is best
Simple statement	Without supporting evidence or threats, a matter-of-fact statement of one's desires	I simply tell him what I want
Persistence	Continuing in one's influence attempts or repeating one's point	I reiterate my point. I keep going despite all obstacles
Assertion	Forcefully asserting one's way	I voice my wishes loudly
Manipulation	Making the target think that the agent's way is the targets own idea	I usually try to get my way by making the other person feel that it is his idea
Fait accompli	Openly doing what one wants without avoiding the target	I do what I want anyway
Hinting	Not openly stating what one wants; indirect attempts at influencing others	I drop hints. I subtly bring up a point
Emotion-target	Agent attempts to alter emotions of target	I try to put him in a good mood
Threat	Stating that negative consequences will occur if the agent's plan is not accepted	I'll tell him I will never speak to him again if he doesn't do what I want
Deceit	Attempts to fool the target into agreeing by the use of flattery or lies	I get my way by doing a good amount of fast talking and sometimes by some white lies
Emotion-agent	Agent alters own facial expression	I put on a sweet face. I try to look sincere
Evasion	Doing what one wants by avoiding the person who would disapprove	I got to read novels at work as long as the boss never saw me doing it

From "The Multidimensional Scaling of Power Strategies" by T. Falbo (1977), *Journal of Personality and Social Psychology*, 35, p. 540. Copyright © 1977 by the American Psychological Association. Reprinted with permission.

the crowd assembled at a potential public suicide are all examples of large groups in which one can psychologically lose one's sense of self in the collective experience. Some have tried to explain this phenomenon in terms of "the convergence of people with compatible needs, desires, motivations, and emotions" (Forsyth, 1983, p. 311). Le Bon (1895) held otherwise and put forth the view that deindividuated behavior in crowds and mobs was due to a process of contagion. He observed that riotous behavior, not unlike the spread of a physical disease, began at one point in the larger group and then involuntarily spread throughout it. Yet a third explanation of deindividuation is the emergent-norm theory (Turner & Killian, 1972), in which a variety of group phenomena combine to foster anew the emergence of an array of arousal-associated and often antisocial behaviors. Forsyth (1983) correctly points out that all three explanations may fit a given instance of deindividuated collective behavior:

> The three perspectives on collective behavior—convergence, contagion, and emergent-norm theory—are in no sense compatible with one another . . . For example, consider the behavior of baiting crowds—groups of people who urge on a person threatening to jump from a building, bridge, or tower . . . Applying the three theories, the convergence approach suggests that only a certain "type" of person would be likely to bait the victim to leap to his or her death. Those shouts could then spread to other bystanders through a process of contagion until the onlookers were infected by a norm of callousness and cynicism. (p. 315)

What is known about the deindividuation process? Zimbardo (1969) has described the conditions purportedly promoting it, the cognitive states reflecting it, and the overt behaviors characterizing it (see Figure 1.2).

In the almost 35 years since Zimbardo's (1969) valuable summary statement regarding the causes, concomitants, and behavioral consequences of deindividuation, a substantial number of proposition-testing studies have been reported. Postmes and Spears (1998) have provided a useful meta-analysis of this body of work. Much of this research may be described as modestly supportive of the role in the deindividuation process of arousal, loss of individual responsibility, sensory overload, reduced public self-awareness, and anonymity—especially when this last is anonymity from potential sanctioning authorities, rather than from fellow members of one's group—all of which combine to yield a deindividuated state characterized by disinhibited and antinormative behavior. In this last regard, it is important to note that while the behavior displayed may indeed be antinormative (e.g., aggression) vis a vis general societal norms, the very same behaviors may be quite normative with respect to the norms or demands operating in situ with the particular group of which the person is a member.

Groupthink

A different, if related, influence of the group on individual member behavior has been termed groupthink. Forsyth (1983) defines this influence as

> A strong concurrence-seeking tendency that interferes with effective decision making . . . At the core of the process is the tendency for group members to strive for solidarity and cohesiveness to such an extent that they carefully avoid any

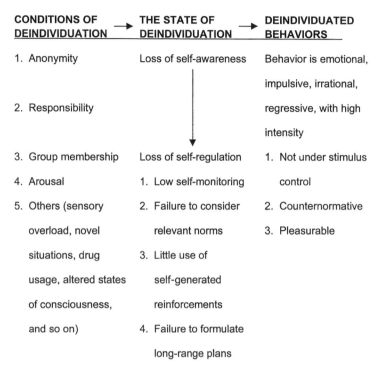

CONDITIONS OF → DEINDIVIDUATION	THE STATE OF → DEINDIVIDUATION	DEINDIVIDUATED BEHAVIORS
1. Anonymity	Loss of self-awareness	Behavior is emotional, impulsive, irrational, regressive, with high intensity
2. Responsibility		
3. Group membership	Loss of self-regulation	1. Not under stimulus control
4. Arousal	1. Low self-monitoring	
5. Others (sensory overload, novel situations, drug usage, altered states of consciousness, and so on)	2. Failure to consider relevant norms	2. Counternormative
	3. Little use of self-generated reinforcements	3. Pleasurable
	4. Failure to formulate long-range plans	

Figure 1.2   The process of deindividuation (Reproduced with permission from Zimbardo (1970) in *Nebraska symposium on motivation*, edited by W. J. Arnold and D. Levine. Copyright © 1970 by the University of Nebraska Press, Lincoln. Reprinted from Forsyth 1983.)

> questions or topics that could lead to disputes. If members anticipate arguments over an issue, they never raise it. If they are unable to answer a question, they never ask it. If they can find shortcuts and reach simplistic solutions, they take them. Thus, as a result of an irrational emphasis on maintaining unanimity and cohesiveness, the group's decisions are ill-considered, impractical, and unrealistic. (p. 341)

Groupthink is purported to be a not uncommon phenomenon. According to Janis (1972, 1979, 1982) who first labeled the process, it surfaces to varying degrees in groups that are highly cohesive, insulated, headed by a powerful leader, and under pressure to make important decisions. Gangs, certain committees, policy-making groups, industrial planning teams, and adolescent peer groups are all examples of potential groupthink settings. Groupthink is more likely to occur when two sets of conditions are operating. This first is premature concurrence seeking or excessive in-group pressure early in the group's decision-making deliberations. Premature concurrence seeking occurs if certain factors exist: (a) high pressure to conform to norms that support compliance and rule out disagreement; (b) self-censorship of dissenting ideas; (c) "mindguards" diverting controversial information away from group consideration by "losing it, forgetting to mention it, or deeming it irrelevant and thus unworthy of the group's attentions" (Forsyth, 1983, p. 345); and (d) apparent unanimity, in which group members focus on their areas of agreement and deemphasize divergencies. The second set of conditions promoting groupthink involves illusions and misperceptions. These include illusions of invulnerability, illusions of morality, biased perceptions of the out-group, and collective rationalizing (Forsyth, 1983; Janis, 1972). (Janis [1972] provides an interesting case study of the causes, development, and reduction of groupthink as it occurred with President Kennedy and his panel of advisors at the time of the Cuban Bay of Pigs invasion.)

Correspondingly, groupthink can be reduced or eliminated by steps that limit premature concurrence seeking and that correct illusions and misperceptions. Premature concurrence seeking can be thwarted by promoting open inquiry and welcoming new ideas and perspectives, by moderating the directiveness of leader behavior, and by having the leader (a) delay stating his or her own beliefs until late in the group's discussion, (b) request that all pros and cons of an issue be presented and explored, (c) reward criticism and dissent, and (d) arrange for the group to meet without the leader on a number of occasions. Errors in perception can be corrected if (a) members acknowledge their own lack of knowledge on given topics and seek expert consultation, (b) an effort is made to understand the out-group's view and feelings, and (c) "second chance" meetings are held after the group reaches a tentative decision in order for residual doubts and questions to be raised and considered.

While case study examinations of the groupthink phenomenon provide general support for its existence and functions (Esser & Lindoerfer, 1989; Hensley & Griffin, 1986; Tetlock, 1979), experimental evaluations have met with mixed success. Hodson and Sorrentino (1997), W. Park (1990) and others report little support in this work for group cohesiveness alone as a groupthink antecedent. It does, however, appear to contribute to the constellation of behaviors constituting the groupthink phenomenon when it operates in combination with other precursors, such as directive leadership (Mullen et al., 1994). Directive leadership operating alone, in partial contrast, has been shown to be a substantially more likely precursor. Peterson (1997) has shown this effect to be particularly more likely when the target of the directive leadership is the group's decision-making *process*, rather than its decisional outcome. Further, Hodson and Sorrentino (1997) have more finely reported that the effects of direct or closed group leadership on groupthink are most likely to appear for group members high in an information-processing quality; this they term "uncertainty orientation." Much like low tolerance for ambiguity, these are persons highly motivated in situations whose closure requires the resolution of uncertainty. In addition to concern with group member characteristics, such as the foregoing, as moderator variables, Aldag and Fuller (1993) add that the antecedent conditions promoting and inhibiting the occurrence of groupthink ought be augmented further by consideration of group norms, leader power, the nature of the group's task, and the stage of the group's development.

Adjourning

The group has established itself, dealt with areas of conflict, developed its norms of leader behavior and member roles, performed its task, and thus reached its goal. It is therefore time for the group to adjourn.

Group Aggression: An Initial Perspective

Aggression by or towards groups of persons is the central topic of this book. In the chapters that follow, I explore its major concretizations at its diverse levels of intensity. However, group dynamicists have also addressed this topic, and so in this chapter's concluding section I wish to share a sense of their views on the antecedents, concomitants, and consequences of group aggression.

I visited perhaps the over-riding precursor to group aggression at the outset of this chapter in the implicit and explicit examination of a particularly pervasive, enduring and consequential human quality, 'us versus them' thinking and perception. Such a stance lies at the heart of Realistic Conflict Theory's emphasis upon the creation and maintenance of a vast array of social hierarchies. Volkan (1988) has described such thinking as reflecting a basic "need for allies and enemies." Barash (1991) puts it even more pointedly:

> There is nothing so disorienting as the loss of a good friend, except perhaps the loss of a good enemy. Try to imagine: Captain Ahab without Moby Dick, the Hatfields without the McCoys, the Montagues without the Capulets, Belfast Catholics without Protestants, Israelis without Arabs, the United States without the Soviet Union or vice versa. Each has long been defined by the other. And, in the process, enmity has subtly been transformed into dependence...Sometimes these enemies go away, leaving us frustrated, empty, and strangely alone. (p. 9)

Many other psychologists, sociologists, political scientists, and commentators on the human scene have targeted the significance of such overdetermined need for in-group versus out-group demarcation (Bar-Tal, 1990; Frei, 1986; Keen, 1986; Kramer & Messick, 1998; Staub, 1993; Streufert & Streufert, 1986; Webb & Worchel, 1986). Though Streufert and Streufert (1986) are correct in urging caution when extrapolating laboratory-based 'us versus them' findings to larger, real-world collectives, as there remains much relevant value in assertions such as Brewer's (1979) that the expression of hostility toward an out-group reflects, among other influences, such factors as the similarity–dissimilarity of in-group and out-group members, their anticipated future interaction, and especially the competitive or cooperative nature of their relationship. Baron, Kerr, and Miller (1992) argue that aggression by human groups follows from a sequence that begins with the presence of arousal, situational cues, and modeling influences. Arousal may stem from frustration or anger, or even from sources not closely tied to aggression concerns at all per se, such as ambient temperature, crowding, noise, or other environmental discomforts. Situational cues helping to set the stage for overt aggression may also be of several types. These are objects or other cues which seemingly prime aggression-related thinking in the person, as was demonstrated by Berkowitz and LePage (1967) and by Carlson, Marcus-Newhall and Miller (1990) in their research on the "weapons effect." As they put it, the "gun may pull the trigger," i.e., the sheer presence of a weapon may, by association with aggression, help promote just such behavior. Modeling influences, suggest Baron et al. (1992) may serve as a third precursor and potentiator of group aggression. Especially under conditions of uncertainty, stress, high arousal (which itself may impair reasoning ability), and a social comparisons tendency under such conditions to look to others for direction, may encourage imitation to occur.

Three additional factors characterized the now-primed group aggression sequence. One is deindividuation, as discussed earlier in this chapter. A second is emergent norms favoring aggression developing within the group. And finally, an aggression-triggering event. These are

> ...events that are a vivid, dramatic, and specific instance of unfairness or instigation. Such triggering events may not, if taken in isolation, justify [aggression], but rather they mobilize action that is based on a combination of the other factors... Finally, they must also occur at a time when collective action... seems feasible or likely to succeed. (p. 148)

Much of Baron et al.'s (1992) proposed sequence for the initiation, development, and expression of group aggression appears to fit well the unfolding of such behavior in small groups, e.g., the rumor-mongering clique (see Chapter 2, the bullying cohort (Chapter 3), or the urban youth gang (Chapter 4). Aggression by groups of individuals also occurs, and does so dismayingly often, on a substantially larger scale—the mob, the riot, the rebellion. Such macro-level group aggression will be examined in depth in Chapter 5. Here, in group dynamic overview, I wish simply to summarize a second proposed grouping of factors, held by Staub (1993) to reflect the unfolding sequence leading to aggressive behavior in and by such larger collectives. Staub (1993) observes:

> Briefly, difficult social or life conditions, like intense and prolonged economic problems, intense political conflict in a society, or rapid and substantial social change, create social chaos and disorganization and give rise to intense needs in whole groups of people. These needs include the need for security, a positive identity... and hope for a better life. Certain characteristics of a group's culture make it likely that members deal with the needs that arise by elevating the group relative to other groups, scapegoating these other groups, and adopting ideologies that promise a better future while identifying enemies who stand in the way of the ideology's fulfillment. The cultural characteristics include a history of devaluation of a subgroup of society, a monolithic culture... a history of aggression in dealing with conflict, strong respect for authority... and certain group self-concepts. As the perpetrator group turns against the victims, often a subgroup of society, and begins to harm the victim group, an evolution begins. Acts that harm the victims change the perpetrators, and make more harmful acts possible and probable. These 'steps along a continuum of destruction' can lead to extreme violence. (p. 283)

I have in this chapter sought to provide a sense of much of the core literature in group dynamics, emphasizing in particular those topics of demonstrated or potential relevance to group aggression. These materials are offered here as a template for better understanding the several specific forms that group aggression may take. I do so in the aspiration of ultimately aiding our ability to reduce, control, and manage such harmful collective behavior.

Part II

FORMS AND FORMULATIONS

Chapter 2

LOW-LEVEL AGGRESSION

Aggression is typically defined as intentional physical or psychological injury to another person. It varies in both kind and intensity. The concerns of this chapter are ostracism, gossip, hazing, teasing, baiting and cursing, each of which are examples of what may be termed low-level aggression (Goldstein, 1999b). Each of these behaviors may be perpetrated by and towards either individuals or groups, and thus rightly become our concern in a discourse on group aggression. Each may, in its impact on the target persons, be experienced as noxious and hurtful, and hence each is an aggressive concern in its own right. Yet all forms of low-level aggression may, if successful in the eyes of its perpetrator, also thereby be encouraged to escalate to higher and more injurious forms of aggression. It is for both of these reasons, that is, their impact in low-intensity form and their incremental tendency, that we address them here.

JUST WHAT IS LOW-LEVEL AGGRESSION?

Definitions of Low-Level Aggression

Perhaps it should be defined as intentional physical or psychological injury that is only mildly or moderately injurious to another person. Yet serious definitional questions immediately arise. Whose perspectives—the perpetrators', the targets', third-party observers'—should be called upon to provide such seriousness or severity ratings or rankings. Shall we take the perpetrators' view and define it along a scale of expressive intensity, or that of target victim and seek a measure of injuriousness or harm done? If we opt for a harm-based definition, how shall injury or harm to the target be measured, and when, and again by whom? Just as we noted objections to defining group cohesiveness as an average of the attraction-to-group of individual members, shall severity of aggression perpetuated by or toward a group be defined as some arithmetic function of that held by its individual members? Or would it better be conceptualized as a group-level phenomenon, as Hogg (1992) sought to propose for group cohesiveness? And what of frequency or repetitiveness? Is a steady diet of cutting insults from a peer group a higher- or lower-level experience of aggression than a single hard smack to the face by one of them? Though ultimately, low-level aggression must be defined subjectively, must be defined by its target, and is incident specific, a number of definitional approximations are appropriate.

Across Incidents Chronology

The tracing of aggression pathways is one contributing approach to the task of defining low-level aggression since, generally, less harmful (target's perspective) or less intense (perpetrator's perspective) aggressive behaviors precede their more harmful and/or intense expression. (Such a sequence, while typical, is by no means invariant. One can imagine, for example, incidents in which members of a rival gang first shoot a target person, and only *then* curse him or her.)

Loeber et al. (1993) have identified three common developmental pathways, from "less-serious manifestations" to "more-serious manifestations", followed by a large percentage of the boys they studied as subjects progressed from disruptiveness to delinquency.

The Authority Conflict pathway is the earliest in terms of age. It begins with stubborn behavior, proceeds to defiance such as refusal and disobedience, and is followed by authority avoidance, as concretized by truancy and running away from home. The Covert pathway starts with frequent lying, shoplifting, and other "minor covert behaviors", moves on to property damage as incurred by vandalism or firesetting, and culminates in moderate to serious covert delinquency, such as fraud or burglary. The Overt pathway commences with minor overt behaviors such as annoying others or bullying, proceeds to individual or gang physical fighting, and reaches its severity extreme in assault, rape, or other violent behavior.

Other pathway models have been offered to depict common routes of escalation from minor to serious levels of aggression or delinquency (Elliott, 1994; Farrington, 1991; LeBlanc, 1996; Moffitt, 1993; Nagin, Farrington & Moffitt, 1995). It is proposed that the timing (age of onset) of aggressive acts, their variety, their rate of escalation and their chronicity each relate to their eventual level of seriousness.

Within Incidents Chronology

Low-level aggression may be further concretized, again by examining the sequencing of behavior, but in this instance within the temporal confines of single aggressive incidents. The opening moves made by individual and group perpetrators toward targets in violent incidents occurring in school settings may include unprovoked offensive touching (shove, grab, push, slap), insults, challenges, threats, or other provocations.

Aggressive opening moves are often followed by an escalating sequence, termed by some "character contests." These are retaliatory progressions of verbal and, eventually, physical attempts to harm, to save face and, ultimately, to defeat one's protagonist. The likelihood of such a contesting move from initial provocation to high-level aggression is apparently all the greater when it occurs in a group context, i.e., when a contest-viewing (or encouraging) audience is present (Borden, 1975; Cratty, 1981).

In addition to character contests, other researchers have described this very same process of escalation of aggression as resulting from disinhibition (J. H. Goldstein, Davis & Herman, 1975), amplification (Berkowitz, Lepinski, & Angulo, 1969), positive feedback (Marsh, Rosser & Harre, 1978), interaction sequencing (Rausch, 1965), affronts (Tuppern & Gaitan, 1989), and posturing (Grossman, 1995).

Ratings and Rankings

Warr (1989) reported a national survey on fear of crime, and found that the degree of citizen fear was a joint outcome of how serious each given crime was, combined with how likely it was to happen. Forgas, Brown and Menyhart (1980) also found probability of occurrence to be a significant influence upon seriousness ratings, along with the perceived justifiability of the act and the degree to which the act was sanctioned or not by those in authority. Alternatively, the seriousness level of an aggressive act may be judged based jointly on its wrongfulness and harmfulness (Thomas & Bilchik 1985).

Goldstein, A. P., et al. (1995) took a complementary approach to defining aggression levels. Their national survey of American teachers yielded a pool of 1000 descriptions of in-school aggressive incidents perpetrated either by individual students or groups of students, along with the details of how each incident was resolved. By what may best be described as an intuitive cluster analysis, these investigators grouped the 1000 incident reports into 13 categories arrayed from low level, through moderate, to high level aggression, as depicted in Table 2.1.

Goldstein et al. (1995) state:

> ... any act of aggression can escalate quickly into a serious situation. In fact, it is only possible to judge the level of severity of an aggressive incident in the specific context in which it occurs. What we can say, however, is that poor management of aggression at the lower levels facilitate its high level expression. Conversely, the teacher skilled at maintaining compliance or thwarting student disruptiveness is, we believe, considerably less likely to be faced with vandalistic, out-of-control, or armed students. 'Catch it low, to prevent it high' is a productive intervention strategy (pp. 19–20).

In a different context, but in the same spirit, Kelling and Coles (1996) assert that for many citizens and communities:

Table 2.1 Incident categories

1. Horseplay	8. Sexual harassment
2. Rules violation	9. Physical threats
3. Disruptiveness	10. Out-of-control behavior
4. Refusal	11. Fights
5. Cursing	12. Attacks on teachers
6. Vandalism	13. Group aggression
7. Bullying	

> ...criminal behavior is meaningful to all of us not merely because it involves an act of violence against a person or property. Any act becomes more serious if the setting in which it is carried out heightens the act's intensity, the resulting fear, and propensity for damaging the community as a whole (p. 30).

In their view, five qualities of the context in which (rated) low level disorder occurs can, individually and collectively transform such disorder into an (experienced) high-level, serious act. These elements are time (when it occurs), place (where it occurs), previous orderly or disorderly behavior by the perpetrator, the condition of the target person(s), and the specific disorderly act itself. Noisy boisterousness in one of their back yards by a group of neighbors on a Saturday or holiday evening that prevents one from going to sleep at 10:30 p.m. is experienced as a much less serious disorder than noise from unknown others at the same decibel level at 3:00 a.m. on a Tuesday, especially when the same disorderliness has occurred three other workdays in the past two weeks.

To repeat our chapter-opening query: what then is low-level aggression? We have examined its diverse operational definitions in aggression-seriousness research conducted both across and within incidents, and employing either rating or ranking methodologies. While one can pull from this body of research a general consensus regarding which particular behaviors are deemed to be "low level," it must be quickly acknowledged that judgments about the level of intensity of an aggressive act must remain very much in the eyes of its target: different people will experience the same aggressive act quite differently. For example, Sparks, Genn and Dodd (1977) found that given acts of aggression are perceived to be more serious with increasing age of the rater. Walker (1978) reported that men rate violent offenses more seriously than women do, and persons of higher social class also perceive violent offenses as significantly more serious than do raters from lower social class backgrounds. The reverse social class finding emerged in work by Sparks et al. (1977) for property offenses. Rose and Prell (1955) found that women tended to rate child-beaters, bigamists, forgers, and drunk drivers as significantly more serious than did men. Levi and Jones (1985) report that while ordinary citizens and police officers share similar rankings of crime seriousness, the citizens gave most offenses higher absolute ratings than did the police.

Though there exists some research reporting no effect of age, sex, or income on crime seriousness ratings (Cullen, Clark & Polanzi, 1982), the thrust of the studies just reviewed is of considerable individual variation in such ratings. Thus, while a broad consensus is reachable regarding which behavior may be categorized as "low level", it remains none the less true that what constitutes low-level aggression in any given incident must be defined via the subjective experience of the person(s) to whom it is directed.

Escalation to Higher Aggression Levels

That it is prone to escalate, that use of the "f" word can grow to use of fists, that teasing can grow to bullying and to punching, that gossip, rumor-mongering, and ostracism, as well as numerous other incarnations of low-level aggression, can grow to seriously injurious behavior is well supported by several lines of research. A body of laboratory studies of disinhibition and escalation of aggression do so (Goldstein, J. H., et al., 1981; Taylor, Shuntich & Greenberg, 1979). Perhaps of particular interest in this regard is the possible role of deindividuation—Jaffe and Yinon (1979) and Jaffe, Shapiro, and Yinon (1981) examined the escalation of individual- versus group-administered aggression, as measured by the pace and intensity of (apparent) shock administered by study participants. On both criteria, persons in groups significantly exceeded individuals acting alone, thus suggesting an aggression-escalation facilitating effect of hypothesized deindividuation.

Out of the laboratory, and in the streets and delinquency centers, the study of criminal pathways further confirms the commonality of the escalation process. Loeber et al.'s (1993) developmental pathways model, described earlier, is one such example. A second is Loeber and LeBlanc's (1990) tracing of criminal careers through stages of emergence, exploration, explosion, conflagration, and outburst. Finally, the escalation of aggression has also been well demonstrated in field studies of the consequences of physical and social incivilities. Physical incivilities include litter, graffiti, abandoned or burned-out stores, houses, and automobiles, dirt, broken windows, vandalism. Social incivilities may include presence of aggressive gangs, drug users, prostitutes, bench or street sleepers, "skid row" alcoholics. Skogan (1990), R. B. Taylor and Gottfredson (1986) and J. Q. Wilson and Kelling (1982) have all shown that the levels of such incivility relate to, and perhaps actually help cause, the escalation to higher levels of crime.

I have sought to define what constitutes low-level aggression, and urged that it demands our increased attention both for its immediate noxiousness as well as its frequent incremental growth via diversely motivated escalation processes to more seriously injurious aggressive behavior. In the sections which follow, I explore what is known about five specific types of low-level aggression, an exploration informed by both research findings and the perceptions and speculations of skilled practitioners.

OSTRACISM

Being isolated, ignored, avoided, excluded, rejected, shunned, exiled, banished, cut off, frozen out, made invisible—all are experiences that give the sense of ostracism. K. D. Williams (1997) suggests four types of ostracism, the first two of which I view as low-level aggression by what is not said. One is *physical ostracism*, which includes expulsion, banishment, exile, time-out, and, more generally, physically arranging a person's absence, departure, or isolation. In the second type, *social isolation*, the person remains visible to them but is ignored, given the silent treatment or the cold shoulder, frozen out. *Defensive ostracism* is a self-protective, preemptive self-isolation in anticipation of negative, threatening feedback (including ostracism from others). Finally, Williams notes, *oblivious ostracism* is the perhaps unintentional ignoring of certain people or types of people one views as not somehow worthy of one's time and energy—the elderly, people from low-income environments, people from particular ethnic groups. Each type of ostracism, Williams (1997) suggests, may vary as to motive, visibility, quantity, and causal clarity. Ostracism varies also by intensity. Such low-level aggression may vary in degree from coldness of tone and denial of eye contact to total ignoring—no speaking, looking, or attending.

K. D. Williams, Sherman-Williams, and Faulkner (1996) conducted a survey of over 2000 men and women in the United States regarding their personal experiences of the "silent treatment." Three-quarters of those surveyed reported that they had used this approach with loved ones; the same percentage revealed that it had been used on them. In a second such survey of long-term users and victims of the silent treatment, Williams (1997) found that "almost all of the victims we interviewed reported that the effects of long-term ostracism have been devastating... chronic or repeated exposure to the silent treatment elicited many negative emotions, such as anger, frustration, sadness, and despair" (p. 158).

Buss et al. (1987) found the use of ostracism to be common between married couples in conflict. Cairns and Cairns (1991) found that over a third of the conflicts among girls of middle-school age involved ostracism. Similar heavy use of such peer rejection behavior has also been reported among elementary-age children (Asher & Coie, 1990). Evans and Eder (1993) draw the distinction between neglected children, who tend to be viewed neutrally by their peers, and rejected children, who are actively disliked. Both are, in a sense, ostracized, but for the former it is "oblivious ostracism" and for the latter it is a much more active social rejection. Coie and Dodge (1983) found that youngsters rejected during one school year were quite likely to be rejected in subsequent years. A number of studies note that youngsters with mental handicaps or learning disabilities are disproportionately prone to receive such ostracism from their schoolmates.

Evans and Eder (1993) conducted a lengthy observational study of peer behavior among middle-school students. Observations took place in the school cafeteria. Students who were negatively evaluated by peers for appearance, gender behavior, or mental maturity were most prone to be ostracized—to be ridiculed, to be rejected, to sit alone at lunch. In a sense, such youngsters took a double hit. Not only were they ridiculed and ignored by peers who initiated such behavior, but other youngsters seeking to avoid a sort of stigma by association similarly ostracized them for fear of also becoming victims. The investigators followed up this observational study by interviewing many of the observed youths some time later, when they had left middle school and were in high school. In a statement that offers a strong argument for smaller schools in which every student can find a school-associated role and none or few are marginalized, Evans and Eder note:

> They reported that the middle school status hierarchy was so rigid and so limited that only a few students felt successful, whereas the rest perceived themselves as "dweebs" or "nerds." By giving only a few students positive visibility through select extracurricular activities such as basketball and cheerleading, a school tends to increase all students' concern with social status and peer acceptance. (p. 166)

Though I deal in this section with ostracism as low-level aggression, there is a constructive side to its use in some contexts. In the terminology of behavior modification, ostracism might be viewed as a sort of "extreme extinction" and employed as such to alter difficult-to-change inappropriate behaviors—including aggression. Barner-Barry (1986), for example, reports a case study in which a group of children, acting on their own, collectively and successfully used ostracism to reduce the chronic bullying behavior of one of their peers. In the same behavior modification spirit, De Angelis (1998) notes the tribal banishment of those who commit crimes against the community and the prison use of solitary confinement to punish and, it is hoped, correct serious acting-out behaviors in the correctional context.

Ostracism has also been the focus of a small number of laboratory investigations. Geller et al. (1974) found that young women ignored during a conversation by two female confederates of the experimenters reported feeling anxious, withdrawn, frustrated, and bored compared to included participants. Similar feelings— rejection, unworthiness, anger—were reported by participants in a second study who were simply asked to imagine that they were being ignored, whereas other participants were asked to image inclusion (Craighead, Kimball, & Rehak, 1979). In a third investigation (K. D. Williams & Sommer, 1997), one of two confederate participants, while supposedly waiting for the procedure to begin, noticed and began bouncing a racquetball, first alone, and then to others waiting (one of whom was another confederate, the other the real participant). After 1 minute of three-way play, and continuing for a 4-minute period, the two confederates then bounced and tossed the ball only between themselves, while totally ignoring the real participant. In this and a follow-on study that employed exclusive, two-person conversation and not ball bouncing, ostracized participants displayed substantial levels of disengagement and discomfort. Study findings also revealed reliable male–female differences. Ostracized women worked harder than did ostracized males on a subsequent collective task, perhaps as a means of gaining acceptance by the others involved. Women were also more likely to blame themselves for being excluded. Male participants neither compensated by working harder nor blamed themselves for being ostracized. K. D. Williams, Shore and Grahe (1998) report one further study of the impact of being the target of ostracism. In this instance, ostracism was operationally defined as the silent treatment (i.e., social isolation) carried out by avoidance of eye contact and absence of verbal communication. As the investigators had hypothesized, those targeted for such behaviors experienced threat to their sense of belonging, self-esteem, control, and meaningfulness. Interestingly, some of the same negative consequences were also experienced by those giving (not receiving) the silent treatment. The power of ostracism to engender negative feelings about oneself and one's place in a group was further demonstrated even more dramatically by Williams, Cheung, and Choi (2000) in a study somewhat reminiscent of the minimal group research described in Chapter 1. Rather than experiencing ostracism of one or another kind in actual face-to-face interaction in a real or research accomplice group, ostracism in this investigation was operationalized via "mental visualization" (of being ostracized). The study, titled "Cyberostracism: Effects of being ignored over the Internet" found that "Despite the minimal nature of their experience, the more participants were ostracized [in their imaginations] the more they reported feeling bad, having less control, and losing a sense of belonging." (p. 748)

Ostracism, K. D. Williams (1997) concludes, deprives people of a feeling of belonging, threatens their self-esteem, robs them of a sense of control, and reminds them of the fragility of their sense of worth. Clearly, it is a form of low-level aggression or, as Lewin (2000) terms it "disguised violence", worthy of continuing, serious attention.

GOSSIP

> In some cultures . . . we stick pins into the effigies of an unliked object; in modern society, gossiping is practiced in place of this mechanism of aggressive hostility and retaliation. (Fine & Rosnow, 1978, p. 166)

A good deal has been written about gossip, and, perhaps surprisingly, most of it is positive. *Webster's Third International Dictionary* defines it as "rumor, report, tattle, or behind-the-scene information, especially of an intimate or personal nature." Gossip is both process and content, verb and noun. In common parlance, it is "idle talk," but a number of writers emphasize its constructive functions. Fine and Rosnow (1978), for example, speak of gossip as purposeful communication that serves the function of information, influence, and entertainment. It is information in "its transmission of culture and illumination of ambiguous areas of behavior, [that] maps the social environment" (p. 162). It is a means for persons at all ages to become informed about norms for appropriate social behavior. As Szwed (1966) observed, gossip is "a sort of tally sheet of public opinion" (p. 435). It is a means of informal communication that can serve as an information grapevine. Gossip serves its information transfer function especially in those situations, personal or impersonal, in which the need for news is great. Gossip also serves an influence purpose. It is an opportunity not only for social comparison (Suls, 1977) but also for social control (Levin & Kimmel, 1977). Gossiping provides the opportunity to both receive and send opinions and evaluations. It is not about the weather that gossiper and gossipee exchange information; it is about norm-relevant standards and departures therefrom—about "improper" behavior, "inappropriate" dress, "inopportune" timing, and the like by one or more third parties. Gossip may also entertain, be a "satisfying diversion" (Fine & Rosnow, 1978, p. 164) or "intellectual chewing gum" (Lumley, 1925, p. 215).

In addition to its informational, influence, and entertainment purposes, gossip has been noted to provide the pleasure of simply talking to other people (Morreall, 1994), promote a sense of solidarity or closeness with others (Levin & Arluke, 1987), and maintain the dividing line between in-group members (who share the gossip) and out-group members (who do not) (Hannerz, 1967). If the substance of the gossip proposes that its targets are somehow inferior or immoral, then gossiping may enhance one's own sense of self-worth and respectability (Levin & Arluke, 1987). In children, Fine (1977) suggests that gossip serves four functions: socialization, evaluation, impression management, and competency development. Indeed, as noted earlier, the collective "take" on gossip by social and behavioral scientists is indeed a positive one.

There is, however, a darker side to gossip, a side that brings it into the realm of low-level aggression. Gossip can be malicious, demeaning, degrading, and in other ways harmful not only to absent third parties, but even indirectly to its participants. Levin and Arluke (1987) conducted two studies, one in a college student lounge and the other in a nearby bar, and found that between 25 and 30 % of student-to-student gossip was about negative personal habits, manners, appearance, or behavior. As Jaeger, Skleder, and Rosnow (1994) suggest, "Although it is described as a pleasurable activity, its consequences may be anything but pleasurable for its targets" (p. 154). These researchers examined gossip patterns and contents over time among members of a university sorority and found that a full half of remarks made emphasized negative themes and target characteristics. Kinney (1994) reports similar outcomes among high school students. Over a 2-year period, observations and interviews were conducted involving a large sample of female students attending an urban high school. Kinney notes that "the pervasive and intense gossip incited fights in the hallways, altered friendship patterns, and sustained separation between crowds" (p. 42).

In describing the public reputation of gossip, Emler (1994) observes:

> It has a reputation for triviality, for preoccupation with the thoroughly super-ficial and ephemeral in human affairs ... It is an unreliable and inaccurate, and entirely fallible source of information about other people. Its motivations are disreputable; tellers are motivated by mischief, rancor, or spite, listeners by prurient and improper interest in matters that are not of their business. Gos-sipers are often guilty of despicable violations of trust. The effects of gossip are frequently damaging—and sometimes catastrophically destructive—to the lives and livelihoods of those who are gossiped about. (p. 177)

Gossiping in the form of what Kowalski (2001) calls "managing rumors" may be a particularly incendiary form of low-level aggression. Kerner's Report of the National Advisory Commission on Civil Disorder (Kerner et al., 1968) concluded that such rumors had appreciably aggravated racial tensions in more than 65 % of the civil disorders they investigated. Others have drawn similar conclusions re-garding the pernicious influence of such rumoring in the stimulation and spread of group aggression in riot circumstances (Forbes, 1997; Horowitz, 2001). In both these extreme circumstances, as well with everyday "over the fence" gossiping, the process of message transmission has incorporated both leveling (the elimination of certain details) and sharpening (the emphasis and elaboration of certain details) along the chain of communication (Allport & Postman, 1947). Gossip in the form of rumor transmission becomes more likely, according to Kowalski (2001) to the degree that four conditions are operating. The first is *uncertainty*. When events are ambiguous, and especially when they are widespread, the inherent doubt, confu-sion, or unpredictability is rumor-promoting. When the ambiguous events' conse-quences are important to the effected persons, a condition Kowalski (2001) terms *outcome-relevant involvement*, rumor generation and transmission is more likely. *Personal anxiety* is the third proposed spur to the start and spread of rumor, refer-ring here to apprehension regarding the probable outcome of the ambiguous event. Finally, *credulity*, refers to the likelihood that rumor transmission also depends on whether the teller finds its contents to be plausible or trustworthy.

Who gossips? Perhaps almost everyone. Folklore has it that women do so more than men, but there is little evidence to support this view. Being generally more relationship oriented, women tend more than men to engage in gossip about friends and family members, whereas men focus on celebrities, sports figures, and the like

(Levin & Arluke, 1987). People who are more anxious tend to gossip more (Jaeger, Skleder, & Rosnow, 1994), as do individuals in people-oriented versus non-people-oriented professions (Nevo, Nevo, & Derech-Zehavi, 1994). Because participation in gossiping may place the individual at the center of the created communication network, it may temporarily enhance the gossiper's status. Thus, Levin and Arluke propose, it is the most isolated, least popular member of a group who may be most prone to gossip.

In evaluating the positivity or negativity of gossip, it is well to remember, as G. Taylor (1994) points out, that there are two quite different sorts of relationships associated with any act of gossip. For the several reasons described at the beginning of this section, the relationship between gossiper and gossipee may be positive to start with and become even more so as a result of the gossip communication act. However, the relationship between the parties sharing the gossip on the one hand, and the person(s) being gossiped about on the other, may well be made substantially more negative because of this same gossip action. In this sense gossip is indeed a verbal abuse example of low-level aggression. As Levin and Arluke (1987) note, "it permits the gossiper to communicate negative, even nasty, information about other people with impunity, regardless of its consequences for the well-being of the targets" (p. 21).

HAZING

Hazing is an organizational initiation ritual consisting in large part of low-level verbal and physical aggression directed to the initiate. It may take concrete form in "on-the-job pranking" (Satino, 1990), "sink or swim" experiences (Schein, 1978), the "blood pinning" in the US Marine Corp, where a paratrooper pin is pounded into the recruit's chest (Richter & Kempster, 1997) or, as L. A. Davis (1997) cites, asking the new shop employee to find a non-existent tool (wild-goose-chase hazing), having the navy recruit on an aircraft carrier look for the on-board McDonald's restaurant, arranging experiences whereby a new employee will be startled, frightened, or appalled (shock hazing), subjecting an employee to a situation from which he or she must extricate himself or herself (test hazing), not providing a newcomer with all the steps necessary to complete a task (hazing by omission), or harsh or cruel practices intended to cause physical discomfort or pain (barbarous hazing)— such as the historical practices of the printing industry, according to Davis (1997) of painting the genitals of newly accepted apprentices with printer's ink. This small sampling of specific hazing practices, as noted earlier as being true for gossip, is a mixture of practices that appear harmless and playful, but with injurious acts clearly qualifying as low-level aggression. Also, as this sampling makes clear, hazing is often used by those who are already members of a group for rites of initiation purposes directed toward recruits, newcomers, applicants, or novices in order to "tear them down" before accepting them into an organizational culture (Deal & Kennedy, 1982; Sweet, 1999), thus helping to build a "collective group identity" (Freeman, 1993). L. A. Davis (1997) discusses the use of such rites as a means of transmission from outgroup to ingroup, of crossing group boundaries. Davis (1997) comments:

Table 2.2   Fraternity hazing activities

1. Calisthenics	12. Non-fraternity-related memorizing
2. Nudity	13. Kidnaps, road trips, walks
3. Wearing/carrying unusual items	14. Confining in uncomfortable room
4. Dropping food into mouth	15. Repeated disturbances of sleep
5. Paddle swats	16. Pranks against other groups
6. Throwing substances on pledges	17. Misleading about initiation chances
7. Loud or repetitious music	18. Pledges used for entertainment
8. Pushing, shoving, tackling	19. House duties not shared by actives
9. Yelling, name-calling	20. Any assignment actives won't also do
10. Forced drinking of alcohol	21. Unusual, embarrassing, uncomfortable clothing
11. Pledge class lineups	22. Eating unpalatable foods

Reproduced with permission from Baier and P. Williams (1983), *Journal of College Student Personnel*, **24**, p. 301.

> Boundaries in groups exist that indicate who belongs and who does not ... The testing of new employees by hazing can determine, for the hazers, whether or not the newcomer will be accepted to the group. Once the newcomer gains acceptance the boundary still exists but the hazer would be on the 'inside.' (p. 98)

As early as 1908, Van Gennep in his *The Rites of Passage*, spoke of hazing and initiation practices as unfolding in three phases: separation, transition, and incorporation. After examining a litany of aggressive manifestations of hazing practices employed by college fraternities, such as those listed in Table 2.2 Raphael (1988) concludes that "The process, as bizarre and possibly degrading as it is, in reality does seem to accomplish the desired goals: integration and socialization of new members and solidarity of the group." (p. 91) Such rites have long been employed within civic organizations, industrial companies, military services, professional schools, high schools, and, especially, college fraternities. The occurrence of hazing in this last context is the focus of this section.

Baier and Williams (1983) identified a representative sample of specific member behaviors, directed toward pledges or applicants for membership, that constitute hazing. They are presented in Table 2.2.

Hazing may be perceived as playful by its perpetrators, but in far too many instances it is experienced as anything but play by its recipients. Its nasty nature ("collective stupidity, insensitivity, and irresponsibility," according to Buchanan et al., 1982, p. 57) is captured in the abstract by the Texas and Florida antihazing statutes that use legal definitions similar to those employed in antihazing statutes now in effect in most states.

The Texas statute (cited by Buchanan et al., 1982) defines hazing as follows:

1. Any willful act by one student alone or acting with others, directed against any other student of such educational institution, done for the purpose of submitting the student made the subject of the attack committed, to indignity or humiliation, without his consent;
2. Any willful act of any one student alone, or acting with others, directed against any other student of such educational institution, done for the purpose of intimidating the student attacked by threatening such student with social or other

ostracism, or of submitting such student to ignominy, shame, or disgrace among his fellow students, and acts calculated to produce such results.

3. Any willful act of any one student alone, or acting with others, directed against any other student of such educational institution, done for the purpose of humbling, or that is reasonably calculated to humble the pride, stifle the ambition, or blight the courage of the student attacked, or to discourage any such student from longer remaining at such educational institution or reasonably to cause him to leave the institution rather than submit to such acts; or

4. Any willful act by any one student alone, or acting with others, in striking, beating, bruising, or maiming; or seriously offering, threatening, or attempting to strike, beat, bruise, or maim, or to do or seriously offer, threaten, or attempt to do physical violence to any student of any such educational institution or any assault upon any such student made for the purpose of committing any of the acts, or producing any of the result, to such student as defined in this section. (Texas Code Annotated, Section 4.19)

In the Florida statute (cited by Buchanan et al., 1982), hazing is defined as follows:

> As used in this section, "hazing" means any action or situation which recklessly or intentionally endangers the mental or physical health or safety of a student for the purpose of initiation or admission into or affiliation with any organization operating under the sanction of a university, hereinafter referred to as "university organization." Such term shall include, but not be limited to, any brutality of a physical nature, such as whipping, beating, branding, forced calisthenics, exposure to the elements, forced consumption of any food, liquor, drug, or other substance, or any other forced physical activity which could adversely affect the physical health or safety of the individual, and shall include any activity which would subject the individual to extreme mental stress, such as sleep deprivation, forced exclusion from social contact, forced conduct which could result in extreme embarrassment, or any other forced activity which could adversely affect the mental health or dignity of the individual. For purposes of this section, any activity as described above upon which the initiation or admission into or affiliation with a university organization is directly or indirectly conditioned shall be presumed to be a "forced" activity, the willingness of an individual to participate in such activity notwithstanding. (Florida code 240.262)

The aggressive nature of hazing may also be concretized by the fact that, state antihazing statutes and university antihazing policy statements notwithstanding, a substantial number of pledges each year are seriously injured, and some killed, as direct result of hazing experiences (Bryan, 1987; Buchanan et al., 1982; Hammond, 1981).

Baier and Williams (1983) and Ramey (1981) have also noted that a large proportion of the attempts to limit or eliminate hazing on the university campus have been unsuccessful. Only twice in the more than 100 years that university fraternities have existed, has there been a decline in the incidence of hazing—in the late 1940s as a result of the large influx into university life of more mature returning veterans, and in the 1960s when student activist movements caused the Greek system to become less popular on campus and fraternity membership declined (Richmond, 1987). A survey of current and past fraternity members conducted by Baier and Williams

(1983) revealed strong attachment to a series of justifications for the continuance of hazing, including (a) building pledge class unity, (b) instilling humility, (c) perpetuating chapter tradition, (d) proving the pledge can "be a man," (e) maintaining campus respect for the chapter, and (f) fulfilling the expectations of pledges, who "enjoy it." With such a broad wall of rationalization, it is no wonder that hazing continues. These rationalizations are further buttressed by belief that if hazing is a problem, it is a problem for other fraternities, not one's own, as a survey of current and past fraternity members by Baier and Williams revealed:

> Despite the fact that a large percentage of both active and alumni members acknowledge that certain activities are hazing, that their chapters occasionally or usually engage in these activities, and that hazing is a problem nationally and at their university, only 10 % of the active members and 13 % of the alumni members believe hazing is a problem in their own chapters. The "it's somebody's else's problem" syndrome that is prominent in most fraternal organizations also appears to be a primary hindrance to the reduction or elimination of hazing in college fraternities. (p. 304)

Hazing as an initiation rite clearly seems to qualify as low-level aggression, sometimes innocuous and playful, at other times serious and harmful. Continued legal and administrative sanctioning to reduce and eliminate its use appears wise and worth encouraging.

TEASING

Although with the hindsight of adulthood it may seem that the teasing often directed toward adolescents and younger children by their peers is merely harmless kidding, ask the adolescents and children themselves. For many, teasing can be painful, even traumatizing, aggression directed toward them. True, in the grand scheme of things, it typically is not the most damaging type of aggression. None the less, it has been shown by a number of investigators to function not infrequently as the first step on an escalation process culminating in serous displays of aggression (Abrahams, 1962; Fry, 1992; P. Miller, 1986; Murphy, 1983; Shantz, 1987). Teasing is by far not an uncommon event. School surveys at several grade levels reveal that at least two-thirds of students are at times, and sometimes frequently, teasing targets (Kelly & Cohn, 1988; Mooney, Creeser, & Blatchford, 1991).

Teasing embodies three qualities: aggression, humor, and ambiguity about its seriousness (Shapiro, Baumeister, & Kessler, 1991). It may mask criticism and insult and thus actually be aggressive, or it may be gentle and friendly and thus contain little or no aggression. Research shows that its most common form entails making fun of someone or something. Delivering sarcasm, tricking the target person into believing something, using exaggerated imitation, pointing, making faces, physically pestering, taking an item such as the target's hat and refusing to give it back—these are among the several forms that teasing can take (Kowalski, 2000; Shapiro, Baumeister, & Kessler, 1991).

What are children and adolescents teased about? Mostly physical appearance (especially being overweight), but also intellectual performance (being either too slow or too smart), physical and athletic performance, family members, interest in the opposite or the same sex, personal hygiene, race, fearfulness, promiscuity, psychological problems, handicapping conditions, and more (Cash, 1995; Kelly & Cohn, 1988; Tizard et al., 1988). Pearce (1997) adds that teasing is frequently directed at children with unusual names, people who stutter, individuals with strong accents, and those who in other ways are "different." The list is long: a youngster seeking to tease another indeed has many choices.

When asked, young people say they tease others because someone teased them first, as a joke, because they disliked the other person, because they were in a bad mood, or because the rest of their group was teasing someone (Mooney, Creeser, & Blatchford, 1991; Shapiro, Baumeister, & Kessler, 1991). Much teasing also seems to be motivated by an effort to rein in any behaviors that are too different from the group norm. Thus, not only are unpopular, obese, or intellectually slow children teased a lot, but so also are those who are popular, good-looking, and intellectually advanced. Teasing may be an effort to communicate aggression in a safe way, as happens when two youths engage in verbal dueling. It may also, in its more benign expressions, communicate affection and do so in a way that is less embarrassing to the teaser than its direct expression would be. Kowalski, Howerton and McKenzie (2001) add that it also is a means for establishing social dominance, promoting group conformity, and disguising one's true intentions vis a vis feelings in addition to affection. Teasing may also be veiled criticism, self-disclosure, or even self-teasing.

The person being teased must decode the message, must figure out how much is humor and how much is aggression, as well as determine exactly what the teaser was intending to say. The parties' relationship, the teaser's tone of voice and facial expression, and what was going on just before the tease all go into this decoding effort (Warm, 1997).

In families, especially early in children's lives, teasing is more a paternal than either a maternal or a sibling behavior (Labrell, 1994). Fathers tease by blocking their infants' ongoing actions, by pretend fighting or roughhouse play, and by sudden surprise (as in peek-a-boo games or "magic"). Such introduction of upended expectancies, challenge, and novelty, Labrell (1994) proposes, may contribute in positive ways to a youngster's emotional and cognitive development. Warm (1997) takes a quite similar position. When teasing moves beyond mild play, however, its consequences seem to be anything but benign.

When asked how being teased made them feel, 97 % of the elementary school students in one survey said angry, embarrassed, hurt, or sad (Shapiro, Baumeister, & Kessler, 1991). The teaser may be creating what he or she thinks is harmless fun, but for the target person it may be anything but fun. Of those surveyed, 10 % respond by fighting, 40 % by teasing back, and 25 % by trying to ignore the teasing; only 12 % said they usually laughed along with the teaser. Child judges in the study by Warm (1997) rated humor as the most effective response to being teased, followed by ignoring, and followed in turn by the method they judged least effective, aggression. Teasing is a common event. Mooney et al. (1991) report that two-thirds of both their child and adolescent samples reported being the targets of teasing, and about 30 % of each group admitted to doing it. Alberts (1996) reports that males tease others more frequently than do females. When teasing, men are more likely to do so about the targets' physical appearance, while women tend to tease about relationship matters or personal habits. The adverse effects of teasing are enhanced by its frequency, by the support or concurrence it receives from the victim's peers, if the perpetrator is a significant person in the victim's life, and by the manner in which the victim evaluates the tease and his or her ability to deal with it (Keltner et al., 1998). Gleason, Alexander and Somers (2000) have, confirmed the speculation of numerous other observers that teasing may have substantial negative long-term consequences for the chronic target's self-esteem and body image.

Consistent with our earlier emphasis on the manner in which low-level aggression often escalates to more serious violence, Feldman and Dodge (1987) report that adolescents who felt insulted by teasing and who had trouble responding thereto verbally, were the ones most likely to respond in a physically aggressive manner to the teasers. Not only may teasing lead to (responsive) aggression by the victim, but as we describe in the following chapter, teasing often grows into overt bullying behaviors by its perpetrators. Words can and do hurt. Teasing, especially teasing with a bite to it, is not playful behavior to be ignored. It is low-level aggression, to be actively discouraged.

BAITING

Harris Brown was very depressed. His marriage had slowly been going sour for many months, and he had begun to suspect that his wife had a lover. Today at work he had been given a first-hand lesson in the meaning of the word *downsizing*. He'd spent 22 years at the company, 22 faithful, hard-working years. And now a note: "Not needed anymore. Good-bye. Clean out your desk by Friday." He crossed the street to the office building he had seen from his office for years but never entered. Took the elevator to the 12th floor. Entered the men's room, opened the window, and crawled out on the ledge.

Harris stood there, gazing down but not really seeing. He looked across the street to his own office and thought about the memo. "Not needed anymore. Good-bye. Clean out your desk by Friday." Words broke through his fog of depression. They seemed to be coming from below, from the street.

"Jump! Jump! . . . Jump! Jump!"

This strange and repugnant expression of low level aggression, the suicide-baiting crowd has been studied by Mann (1981). His data consist of 21 cases in which a crowd was present when a person threatened to jump off a building, bridge, or tower. Crowd reaction, he suggests, may be primarily concern, curiosity, or callousness. This last group quality, he proposes, is what characterizes the suicide-baiting crowd whose members jeer, taunt, and urge the victim to jump.

What conditions give rise to such behavior? Mann (1981) hypothesized that a callous crowd would be characterized by deindividuation—the condition of diminished self-awareness examined in Chapter 1, a condition in which, in a sense, one's identity is lost in, and merges with, the crowd. Deindividuation is more likely to occur under some circumstances than others, and the research sought to find out if these circumstances were present when baiting occurred and absent when it did not. Here is what Mann (1981) found.

Crowd size. People should feel more anonymous in large crowds than in smaller groupings. In fact, there was significantly more baiting of the victim in crowds of more than 300 persons than in smaller ones.

Cover of darkness. Dim lighting should also contribute to deindividuation for the same reason as does crowd size: It increases anonymity. Again, analyses showed more taunting, jeering, and encouragement to jump in incidents occurring after 6 p.m. than before.

Physical distance between crowd and victim. Where the potential suicide is close to the crowd, making it difficult for crowd members to remain anonymous, little baiting should occur. Further, when so much distance intervenes that the victim would be unable to hear the taunts and jeers, it is also true that little baiting should occur. Most baiting should take place at an intermediate distance, when victim and crowd are far enough apart for crowd members to lose their identity, yet close enough for shouted communications to be heard. This is just what the research found: Baiting occurred only when the person threatening to jump was on the 6th to 12th floors of the building involved, not at a lower or a higher level.

Duration of the incident. It has been proposed that deindividuation is more likely when crowd members are tired and perhaps irritable. Consistent with this idea, baiting was substantially more frequent in those incidents lasting more than 2 hours as compared to briefer ones.

Baiting is an uncommon event. However, when it does take place, it may function as a type of low-level aggression that may encourage seriously self-injurious behavior in its target. It is therefore desirable that such crowd reaction be better understood and minimized.

CURSING

Cursing is a form of low-level aggression that begins quite early in life and grows in frequency over childhood and adolescence. Jay (1992) reports that by age 2, children typically know about four words that can be categorized as curse words. By age 4, the number is about 20, and it grows from there—with boys learning both more, and more offensive, words than girls. By age 10, children can produce between 30 and 40 different expressions containing dirty word. (For adults, the comparable number is 60 to 70.) Much of the content of curse words early in life concerns the rituals of toilet training and elimination. As the child grows to and through adolescence, terms focused on body processes and parts associated with sexual behavior become the most frequently used curse words (e.g., *shit, motherfucker, cocksucker*), as do those targeted to ancestral allusions (e.g., *bastard, son of a bitch*).

Vetter (1969) suggests that all curse words are related to either sex and excretion, blasphemy, or animal abuse. What words are in fact used, and how frequently? A survey conducted by Foote and Woodward (1973) revealed, for the male and female adults they sampled, the 20 most frequently used obscenities, listed in order of frequency in Table 2.3.

Categories of curse words, this survey reveals, are more diverse than Vetter (1969) proposed; they include body processes, parts, and products, ancestral

Table 2.3   Most frequently produced obscenities

Word	Denotative classification	Word	Denotative classification
Fuck	Body process	Damn	Religious blasphemy
Shit	Body product	Whore	Social deviation
Bastard	Ancestral allusion	Hell	Religious blasphemy
Cunt	Body part	Asshole	Body part
Motherfucker	Body process/ancestral allusion	Cock	Body part/animal
Cocksucker	Body process	Piss	Body product
Son-of-a-bitch	Animal/ancestral allusion	Tit(s)	Body part
Bitch	Animal	Suck	Body process
God damn	Religious blasphemy	Bullshit	Animal/body product
Prick	Body part	Nigger	Ethnic-racial slur

From Foote and Woodward, *Journal of Psychology*, **83**, 263–275 (1973). Reprinted with permission of the Helen Dwight Reid Educational Foundation. Published by Heldref Publications, 1319 Eighteenth St., NW, Washington, DC 20036-1802. Copyright © 1973.

allusions, blasphemy, social deviation, and ethnic and racial slurs. Essentially similar frequency-of-use results emerged in a second survey, reported by Jay (1992), with the added information that the rated frequency of use and the rated tabooness of terms were closely and positively associated.

Of interest for this book's primary focus, low-level aggression, Driscoll (1981) obtained level-of-aggression and frequency-of-use ratings from successive samples of adult raters, a process yielding the level-of-frequency data reported in Table 2.4.

Like all other forms of low-level aggression, cursing is very much a person–environment event. What is said is determined not only by who is saying it but also by where the person is and when. Cameron (1969) found that curse words constituted 3 % of adult conversation on the job but 13 % of what they said during leisure conversations. A college student sample (Jay, 1992) estimated the likelihood (0 to 100) of hearing a dirty word to vary considerably by campus location: dormitory (90), parking lot (54), bookstore (33), copy center (21), admissions office (7), dean's office (7), day-care center (1). More generally, the contextual examination of cursing has revealed that their frequency of use is effected by one's conversational partner's social identity, status, role, relationship, and gender (Bailey & Timm, 1996; DeKlerk, 1991; Winters, 1993), as well as the topic of discussion, the intimacy of the physical setting, and the private or public character of the conversation (Graham, 1986; Hartford, 1972). Some have suggested that cursing is more frequent in America's large cities than in other venues, perhaps because of higher stress levels, greater anonymity, and higher levels of tolerance (Goldstein, 1996).

Why do people curse? At an intergroup level, Winters and Duck (2001) suggest that cursing may serve to derogate or stigmatize out-groups, express prejudice via racial or other slurs, or by the act itself symbolize one's membership in a given group and rejection of membership in another. Hughes (1991) has also asserted that a primary purpose of cursing is just such social differentiation. Its other functions, according to Winters and Duck (2001) may be to indicate familiarity, informality, and acceptance of others, to create relational boundaries, and for cathartic purposes as a means of expressing frustration. Gilliam, Stough, and Fad

Table 2.4   Level of aggression and frequency-of-use ratings for cursing

	Aggression ratings	Frequency-of-aggressive-use ratings
Asshole	4.90	4.80
Ball-buster	3.67	1.34
Bastard	4.81	4.17
Beast	2.26	2.85
Bitch	5.35	5.13
Blubberhead	2.09	1.56
Brown-noser	3.17	2.95
Bullshitter	4.02	4.32
Chicken	2.79	3.32
Chump	2.47	2.60
Clown	1.77	3.38
Cock	4.52	2.53
Cocksucker	5.31	3.65
Crazy	1.77	3.50
Dimwit	2.35	2.74
Dipshit	3.81	2.98
Dope	2.20	3.44
Dork	2.87	2.96
Fart	3.26	3.64
Fathead	2.65	3.04
Fuck off	5.27	3.77
Goon	2.48	2.45
Ham	1.61	2.55
Hothead	2.95	3.22
Jackass	4.34	4.21
Liar	4.39	4.47
Maniac	2.97	3.00
Motherfucker	5.65	4.82
Nag	2.34	2.97
Numbskull	2.34	2.97
Prick	4.73	3.70
Punk	2.95	4.15
Sap	2.39	2.24
Schlemiel	2.29	.44
Schmo	2.00	.59
Screwball	2.57	2.82
Shit	4.44	4.00
Skunk	2.00	1.92
Slut	5.33	3.79
Snake	2.11	1.52
Son-of-a-bitch	5.45	5.08
Stink	3.38	3.10
Sucker	4.18	3.75
Turkey	1.99	4.22
Wacko	2.06	1.82
Weirdo	2.78	3.59
Windbag	2.49	2.16
Wise-ass	4.02	2.91

From Driscoll, *Journal of Social Psychology*, **104**, 111–126 (1981). Reprinted with permission of the Helen Dwight Reid Educational Foundation. Published by Heldref Publications, 1319 Eighteenth St., NW, Washington, DC 20036-1802. Copyright © 1981.

(1991) propose several additional reasons for cursing: expression of anger, attention seeking, impression management (i.e., to appear "tough"), imitation, rebellion, and preoccupation with bodily organs and sexual acts. Attention seeking may be particularly significant. The youngster who says "fuck" or "shit" in class is immediately and unequivocally rewarded with teacher and classmate attention. Such attention, even if it takes the form of teacher alarm, anger, and criticism, is likely to serve as a positive reward that encourages further cursing. For this reason, one of the frequently recommended tactics for reducing the likelihood of such inappropriate behavior is to withhold such attention (i.e., extinction or ignoring). Unfortunately, even when the teacher can refrain from attending to cursing (itself not an easy task), the perpetrator's peers are unlikely to do so. Behaviors rewarded are behaviors that continue. Beyond this concern, although extinction may work to diminish the frequency of some inappropriate behaviors, teacher-ignored cursing (just like ignored bullying, vandalism, or any other low-level aggressive act) is quite likely to both continue and escalate as a result of the attentional or other rewards it elicits from other persons.

Epstein, Repp, and Cullinan (1978) offer an alternative attention-providing perspective, one targeted toward encouraging progressively diminishing levels of cursing. Rather than withholding attention, in this study each time a student used obscene language, a mark was placed on his or her individual "obscene language chart," displayed on the classroom bulletin board. If the student was able to stay below a given level, token reinforcements exchangeable for tangible rewards were provided. Employing a gradually lowering criterion of acceptability, three obscenities per day were permitted initially, diminishing to two, one, and none as the study's phases progressed. Study results demonstrated such differential reinforcement of progressively lower rates of cursing to be successful.

Certain non-violent punishments may also work: time-out, response cost, overcorrection, and contingency contracting are viable possibilities. Beyond these methods, I have three additional suggestions. One is negative practice, also known as satiation or instructed repetition. Here, the student is asked to go to a location where others cannot hear him or her (perhaps a time-out room) and repeatedly say the curse word used in public. The repetitions should continue until saying the word becomes not only non-rewarding but even unpleasant. As Gilliam, Stough, and Fad (1991) observe, "Satiation . . . involves presenting a reinforcing stimulus at such a high rate that its reinforcing properties are lost" (p. 368). In addition to the use of such a "swear-down," Novelli (1993) proposes that youth be encouraged to substitute non-offensive words, acceptable slang, or nonsense syllables for curse words. To be sure, if youngsters can follow this suggestion, "glug you" has a markedly different interpersonal effect than "fuck you" does. However, perhaps the most potent means for altering cursing (or any other form of low-level aggression) is the long-recommended but far too infrequently employed recommendation: "Catch them being good." Stated simply, it is a recommendation, based upon literally hundreds of studies of the consequences of positive reinforcement, to reward the youngster with praise, approval, and/or something tangible if he or she refrains from cursing in a situation in which he or she has cursed in the past—or even if the youngster curses but does so less often, less intensely, or more briefly. Cursing is a common and challenging form of low-level aggression. Considerable energy, creativity, and consistency on the part of the teacher, parent, or other change agent will be necessary to eliminate or even reduce it.

In the present chapter I have examined the existing research and speculative literature concerned with ostracism, gossip, hazing, teasing, baiting, and cursing. Each are forms of low-level aggression that, as noted, are noxious in their own right and have potential to escalate to higher, more injurious, levels of aggression. Yet the continua from low to high levels of harm-doing are long ones and, in this chapter's focus on low-level aggression, it is useful to suggest that the several behaviors I have thus examined as frequent precursors to higher levels of aggression may well have precursors themselves. Stated otherwise, the forms of low-level aggression considered here may be preceded by yet lower forms of such behavior—lower in intensity, explicitness, or other qualities. I mention these here for the precisely same purposes as our look at ostracism, gossip, and so forth, namely increased attention to such pre-precursors offers the opportunity to reduce both their immediate impacts as well as their escalatory potential. Hence, I wish to conclude this chapter by urging greater reader attention to threats (Baron & Richardson, 1994), insults (Bond & Venus, 1991), meanness (Mills, 1997), incivility (Carter, 1998), argumentativeness (Tannen, 1998), and humiliation (W. I. Miller, 1993). In the spirit of my favorite intervention prescription, "catch it low to prevent it high" (Goldstein, 1999), I add the subtext, "and catch it as low as possible."

Chapter 3

BULLYING AND HARASSMENT

BULLYING

Definitions and Escalation

Bullying is harm-intending behavior of a verbal and/or physical character that is typically both unprovoked and repeated. In Schuster's (1999) definition:

> Bullying is said to take place when an individual, unable to defend him- or herself, is exposed repeatedly (e.g., at least once a week) and over a long period of time (e.g., at least half a year) to intentional harm by one or several others, either directly (e.g., through physical assaults) or indirectly (e.g., through spreading rumors).

As Stephenson and Smith (1997) note, it is aggressive behavior that is intended to and frequently does cause distress to its targeted victim. More than one bully and more than one victim are quite often involved in any given bullying incident. Olweus (1993) has employed a definitional distinction between direct and indirect bullying. The former entails face-to-face confrontations, open physical attacks by bully on victim, and the use in such contexts of threats and intimidating gestures. Indirect bullying is exemplified by social exclusion and isolation, scapegoating, the spreading of rumors, and similar behaviors, more akin to the forms of aggression examined in Chapter 2.

Bullying has received relatively little attention in the United States (Hoover & Hazler, 1991). Its early recognition and research examination as it occurs in school settings occurred primarily in Scandinavian countries (Olweus, 1993) and in Great Britain (M. Elliott, 1997a; Smith & Sharp, 1994a). The little that has appeared in American publications is largely anecdotal—opinion pieces and not useful research. One might even say we have been bully-shy in the United States. In spite of the substantial frequency with which bullying occurs, it is often the school's best-kept secret. Teachers and administrators may be preoccupied with acts reflecting higher levels of aggression, or they may simply ignore bullying because most victims, as we shall see, elect not to call it to their attention. When it does occur, it is more likely on the playground or in the school corridors between classes rather than in the classroom, so it usually doesn't disrupt the class. Further, even when its reality is acknowledged, it may still be ignored, given the belief of many school personnel (and parents) that bullying is a "natural" part of growing up and perhaps even a positive contributor to the toughening-up purported to be so useful in a competitive society. Thus, school staff may be unaware that bullying is taking place or, if aware, may ignore it. Others, too, may be blind or mute to its occurrence. The bully won't tell; why should he or she volunteer to get in trouble? The victim won't tell for fear of bringing on further and perhaps more severe episodes of the very behavior he or she wishes to avoid. Other students more often than not elect not to speak up, out of concern about becoming targets themselves and reluctance to break the code of silence that far too frequently prevails among students regarding such matters. The victim's parents are also likely to be unaware that bullying is taking place. They may wonder why their child comes home during the school day to use the bathroom, or how his clothing gets torn, or why she seems so hungry at supper time.

In consequence, like all other forms of aggression similarly ignored, bullying continues and grows more frequent, and its sequelae emerge and escalate in intensity. Greenbaum, Turner, and Stephens (1989) report that adults who were childhood bullies are five times more likely to have serious criminal records by age 30 than are peers who were not bullies. In a longitudinal study conducted by Olweus (1993), 60 % of the boys identified as bullies in grades 6 through 9 had, by age 24, at least one criminal conviction, and 40 % of them had three or more arrests. That was true for only 10 % of boys who earlier were neither bullies nor victims. Eron et al. (1987) found that youths who bullied at age 8 had a 1-in-4 chance of having a criminal record by age 30, as compared to the 1-in-20 chance most children have. It is not only early adult arrest records that illustrate the escalation potential of physical maltreatment via bullying. So also do school dropout, spouse abuse, drug dealing, and vandalism (Eron et al., 1987; Rigby & Cox, 1996). Findings concerning the escalation of bullying directly confirm the concern, expressed in Chapter 2, about developmental pathways begun with low-level aggression. Bullying escalation findings also provide strong evidence of the collective need both to better understand its causes and to remediate its consequences.

Bullying as a Group Phenomenon

Bullying has been examined as an event or series of events occurring in the context of social dominance hierarchies (D. E. Williams & Schaller, 1993) or pecking orders (Vermande et al., 2000) whose intended goals may be group exclusion (Owens, Shute & Slee, 2000). Craig and Pepler (1995), O'Connell, Pepler & Craig (1999), and Salmivalli et al. (1996) each independently found that approximately 85 % of the bullying behaviors that they observed occurred in a (mostly peer) group context. Indeed, bullying (often called "mobbing" in European research) is very often a group phenomenon.

However, for the most part, the "others" at a bullying episode are typically not mere spectators, idly observing the event unfold. While some are, most witnesses contribute in large or small ways to the continuance or cessation of the bullying. Salmivalli et al. (1996) describe the actors at a bullying episode, besides the primary bully and the targeted victim, as youngsters taking on the roles of (1) assistant, who actually participates physically, and may help escalate the attack from an individual to a group physical encounter, (2) reinforcer, who encourages, shouts

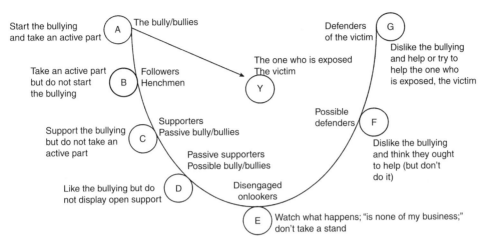

Figure 3.1 Participants in typical bullying event.

approval or "eggs on" the attack, (3) outsider, who does nothing either to end or to escalate it, and (4) the defender, who verbally or physically comes to the aid of the victim either directly or by seeking help from a responsible adult. Similarly, O'Connell, Pepler, and Craig (1999) identified the peer roles of co-bullies (23 % of the sample observed), supporters (of the bully), audience (non-participators), and seldom intervenors (who on occasion helped the victim).

Olweus (2001) concurs with this range of bullying event roles and their behavioral manifestations, as depicted in Figure 3.1.

The net influence of the several actors at the typical bullying event is clearly to sustain and perhaps escalate the bullying. Based upon analysis of large samples of middle school youths, Salmivalli (2001) reports, for example, that

> In all age groups, the percentage of children who act either as bullies, assis-
> tants, or reinforcers—that is, clearly in 'pro-bullying' roles, is about 35 to 40 %.
> Furthermore, if those in the role of outsider are taken into account, there are as
> many as 60 to 70 % of students who do nothing to stop bullying. (p. 405)

Age differences also emerge in such pro-bullying complicity, with such behavior being least common in preschool and the early grades of elementary school, and becoming more common toward later grades and into and through middle school (Whitney & Smith, 1993). More boys than girls characteristically take on the assistant and reinforcer roles, girls more frequently elect to serve as defenders (Salmivalli et al., 1996).

Olweus (1999) suggests that the assistant and reinforcer roles emerge via such group dynamic processes as modeling, disinhibition, social contagion, and guilt mitigation consequent to the diffusion or dilution of responsibility.

Salmivalli (2001) proposes that these diverse bullying event roles and their associated behaviors are optimally viewed as norm-governed phenomena. Norms, defined as "what the persons think the important others think they should do." (p. 409), most certainly operate in the school context.

> A school class in itself is, for most students, a group of important others. What a student thinks others think he or she should do (subjective norms) and what kind of behaviors a student thinks will be punished or rewarded in the group (group norms) probably have an impact on behavior. This is what the group mechanisms in bullyng are about. (Salmivalli, 2001, p. 409)

Bukowski and Sippola (2001) provide a more finely grained analysis of the influence of group norms on bullying behavior—particularly the kinds of bullying leading to exclusion from the peer group. They propose that to function effectively and maintain their existence, groups must achieve three goals: (1) cohesion, (2) homogeneity, and (3) evolution. Cohesion in their view refers to the structural integration within the group, linking group members; homogeneity concerns the degree of inter-member agreement on group-relevant issues, and evolution refers to change. They comment:

> We propose to explain victimization as a result of the potential conflict between particular characteristics of individuals and a group's need to achieve cohesion, homogeneity, and evolution . . . Persons who facilitate the achievement of these goals are given special rights and privileges; those who impede their achievement are treated in ways that minimize their participation in the group. In fact, we believe that such individuals are actively forced out of the group. We regard this latter process as peer group victimization. (p. 361)

Bullying, it seems clear, is most certainly appropriately viewed as a group process, with group structural and functional properties shaping its initiation, course, and consequences.

Frequency and Forms

Because bullying, for the reasons noted, is often a hidden, ignored, or unreported event, its frequency is difficult to estimate. Further, as Hoover and Juul (1993) note, the various survey attempts to do this employ differing definitions of bullying as well as differing sample selection and data collection procedures. Thus, estimates of frequency differ widely and are at best approximations. Perhaps the safest answer to the question "How much bullying is there?" is "A lot!" The results of actual surveys vary widely, but they are invariably substantial. Bullying, these surveys reveal, is regularly perpetrated by 5 % (Smith & Sharp, 1994a), 7 % (Pearce, 1997), 12 % (Hoover & Hazler, 1991), 13 % (Boulton & Smith, 1994), 15 % (Olweus, 1993), and 17 % (Boulton & Underwood, 1992) of all children surveyed. Victims were 9 % (Olweus, 1989), 11 % (Pearce, 1997), 17 % (Boulton & Smith, 1994), 18 % (Rigby & O'Brien, 1992), 27 % (Smith & Sharp, 1994a), 40 % (Elliott & Kilpatrick, 1994), 68 % (Elliott, 1997b), and 80 % (Hoover & Juul, 1993) of youth surveyed. P. K. Smith and Brian (2000) found it to be clearly present in all 16 of the countries they studied. Beyond the quantifier "a lot," it is not easy to bring order into these arrays of outcomes. As noted, denial, indifference, reluctance to report, diversity of reporting formats, and exaggeration, all play indeterminate roles in shaping the numbers. The two ranges are sufficiently broad that central tendency data (means, medians) are largely uninformative. Perhaps greater comfort with, and openness of, reporting in the future will combine with greater standardization of survey methodology to yield closer approximations to actual frequency of occurrence. With regard to frequency, though its occurrence in school settings is the major focus of this chapter, bullying in the workplace, family homes, old people's homes, prisons and other settings has also recently become the concern of the intervention community (see, for example, the special issue of the *Journal of Community and Applied Psychology*, **7**, No. 3, 1997).

Beyond frequency, and with somewhat greater confidence, however, one can assert that boys bully more frequently than do girls (Olweus, 1993; Ross, 1996), that frequency of bullying peaks in the middle school/junior high school years (Boulton & Underwood, 1992), and that bullying is not uncommon even in preschool (Manning, Heron, & Marshall, 1978) and the earliest years of elementary school (P. K. Smith & Levan, 1995). It is directed with particular frequency at special needs children (O'Moore, 1995). A final consideration regarding frequency concerns repetition. Once initiated, bullying behaviors are often prone to continue, depending on victim and contextual response. In M. Elliott's (1997b) survey of 4000 children in the United Kingdom, for example, almost 40 % of victims were victimized multiple times. In Stephenson and Smith's (1997) survey of 1000 Cleveland school children, 80 % of those bullied report being targeted for a year or longer. Boulton and Smith (1994) report similar continuity of victimization.

A small body of literature has accumulated regarding types of bullying behavior as well as types of bullies and victims. The major behavioral distinction to be identified (alluded to earlier) is direct versus indirect bullying. Direct bullying, also termed *overt bullying* (Ahmed & Smith, 1994), consists of hitting, kicking, taking things, pushing, tripping, and shoving as well as yelling, cursing, and threatening. Direct bullying, more generally, is observable physical or verbal aggression. Indirect bullying consists of covert processes, typically conducted via a third party and concretized by spreading of rumors, backbiting, persuading of others not to associate with target person, and similar behaviors. Such behaviors are examples of the social manipulation and relational aggression that characterize indirect aggression, that is, behavior intended to harm someone without confronting the target, via actions through other people.

Lagerspetz, Bjorkqvist, and Peltonen (1988) found that preadolescent girls made greater use of indirect means of bullying, whereas 11- to 12-year-old boys more frequently used direct bullying behaviors. Boys and girls differ little in means employed until about age 8. Starting around this age, girls become more indirect in bullying behaviors, a trend peaking, as just noted, around age 11 or 12. This trend is not apparent in boys until age 15 or older (Rivers & Smith, 1994). A number of investigators have verified these trends (Bjorkqvist, Lagerspetz, & Kaukiainen, 1992; Lane, 1989; Owens, Shute & Slee, 2000; Roland, 1993; Smith & Levan, 1995) and suggested that their bases lie both in the greater orientations to affiliation and interpersonal relationships in girls and to power assertion in boys, as well as in safety considerations.

> When in conflict, the individual makes his/her choice of aggressive strategy after an assessment based on the effect/danger ratio...The object is to find a strategy as effective as possible, while at the same time exposing the individual to

as little danger as possible. Therefore the usefulness of covert, indirect strategies. [They] put distance to the opponent, and they are accordingly less dangerous than physical aggression. Therefore, when verbal skills develop, verbal means of aggression tend to replace physical ones whenever possible. Since females are physically weaker than males, they may early in life learn to avoid physical aggression. (Roland, 1993, p. 185)

Although the study of bullying in schools spotlights the aggressive behavior of individual and groups of students, it has also been estimated that 10 % of teachers regularly engage in bullying behavior.

In addition to different types of bullying, Olweus (1978) has suggested that there are different types of bullies. The *aggressive bully* is largely as stereotypically imagined—belligerent, coercive, and impulsive, with little tolerance for frustration. Ross (1996) describes such youngsters: "Their salient characteristics are an inflammatory combination of physical strength . . . a concern with power fueled by a strong need to dominate others, and a tendency to overreact aggressively in ambiguous confrontations" (p. 42). Bentley and Li (1994) report these to be youths who believe aggression is an appropriate, legitimate response to others. Miedzian (1992) describes the aggressive bully as one who views the world as made up of two kinds of people: those who dominate and those who submit. The bully is the former, inflicting pain with little remorse upon the latter.

The *passive* or *anxious bully* rarely takes the initiative in provoking a bullying incident but is rather an eagerly waiting lieutenant to the aggressive bully. This bully-helper may not start the action, but once it commences, he or she jumps on board. As Ross (1996) observes:

The actions of the aggressive bully have a disinhibitory effect by appearing to legitimize the bullying and this effect is strengthened in the anxious bullies by seeing the aggressive bully rewarded. . . . They appear to buy the approach of the aggressive bullies with intense loyalty. (p. 6)

Bullies, of either subtype, hold more positive attitudes towards aggression (Lagerspetz et al., 1982), are more impulsive (Olweus, 1978), possess strong dominance needs (Boldizar, Perry & Perry, 1989), tend to misinterpret others' emotions (Fonzi, 1997), are low in empathy, feel little guilt for their aggression, and tend to claim it was provoked by the victim (Smorti & Criraci, 2000).

Batsche and Knoff (1994) suggest that bullying is an intergenerational phenomenon in that the bully at school is often a bullying victim at home. Bullies typically come from home environments relying heavily on physical discipline, offering little warmth, evincing poor problem-solving skills, and reflecting a belief that it is appropriate for children to use physical means for settling conflict situations (Floyd, 1985; Greenbaum, 1989).

All acts of aggression, we would stress, are perpetrator–victim transactions. Among young children, under age 5, victims have been described as sensitive and gentle youngsters, often unused to and confused by conflict (Elliott, 1997). Bernstein and Watson (1997) suggest a victim pattern, a constellation of qualities that predispose certain children to be chronically bullied. As evidence in support of this assertion, they point first to the several qualities that these youngsters often have in common and that differentiate them from children not victimized—for example, passivity, poor motor coordination, odd mannerisms, lower self-esteem, and poorer social information processing skills. Second, they note, children who are victimized early in life tend to remain victims for a long time, even though they may change schools and neighborhoods of residence. Finally, other children, such as classmates, are able to identify potential victims with high reliability.

Although some victims of bullying have themselves been described as provocative for their ineffectual but none the less aggressive behaviors, most are more likely to be social isolates (Ross, 1996). These are youngsters of poor social competence, with little social support, often caught in a downward spiral of growing rejection as non bullying peers elect to ignore them for fear of a sort of stigma by association that might diffuse to their becoming targets for bullying themselves. Olweus (1993) has described this group mechanism as one in which peers undergo gradual cognitive changes in perceptions of the victim. As it continues, classmates or other peers increasingly see the victim as deviant, worthless, and—as Lerner's (1980) "just world" perspective would suggest—almost deserving of being bullied. The victim becomes progressively less popular. As Salmivalli et al. (1996) note, "It becomes a social norm of the group not to like him or her" (p. 12). D. G. Perry, Kusel and Perry (1988) have in their sociometric studies indeed found significant negative correlations between social preference scores and frequency of peer victimization.

Given what I have said about bullying frequently being a secret, hidden act, how might we identify which youngsters are in fact being victimized? According to Elliott (1997a), school officials, teachers, and other responsible adults ought to look for the following array of "telltale signs":

- Being frightened of walking to or from school
- Being unwilling to go to school
- Changing the route to school every day
- Showing a marked drop in quality of school work
- Having torn or destroyed clothes, books, or school work
- Returning home from school very hungry
- Beginning bed wetting
- Crying frequently
- Developing stomach aches, headaches
- Frequently "losing" pocket money
- Refusing to describe what is wrong
- Giving improbable excuses for behavior

I have in this section examined the diverse forms that bullying takes and explored a number of salient characteristics of both bullies and victims. In the following section, I offer some beginning notions of the reasons for such behavior.

Causes of Bullying: Person and Environment

At several points throughout this book, I speak of low-level aggression as behavior that grows from characteristics of its perpetrators as they interact with qualities of the social and physical environments in which they live and function. That is, aggression grows from a person–environment duet. Bullying grows not only from the several cognitive, dispositional, and behavioral qualities I described earlier as typical of the schoolhouse bully, but also from characteristics of the other persons and places both surrounding the bullying event and antecedent to it.

At the bullying event there is, first of all, the victim. D. G. Perry, Willard, and Perry (1990) found that the signs of distress emitted by victimized children often function as the very type of reinforcement to the perpetrator that encourages further bullying. Salmivalli, Karhunen, and Lagerspetz's (1996) study of bullying victims identified three common responses:

1. Counteraggression: The victim speaks up to the bully, tries to get others on his/her side, makes faces at the bully, attacks the bully, calls the bully names, calls to others for help, laughs or shouts at the bully.
2. Helplessness: The victim does or says nothing, starts to cry, stays home from school the next day, leaves in the middle of the day, tells his or her parents and/or teacher.
3. Nonchalance. The victim stays calm, acts as if he or she doesn't care, ignores the bully.

Salmivalli, Karhunen, and Lagerspetz (1969) found that 70 % of all victims, even if they are repeatedly bullied, react with helplessness or nonchalance. S. Sharp (1995) reports concurring passivity findings. Coie et al. (1991) found that youths in their investigation employed escalation of the aggression, self-defense, conflict resolution, ignoring, and submission in response to bullying. Almost 50 % of the time, as Salmivalli, Karhunen and Lagerspetz (1996) had found, the alternative chosen was submission. Counter-aggression-avoiding strategies also emerged predominantly in an inquiry by Smith and Sharp (1994a). Their respondents employed avoiding the perpetrator (67 %), staying close to other students (57 %), or staying home from school (20 %).

What of the contribution of the school staff? I have already noted the manner in which some teachers and administrators may directly increase the frequency of student bullying by modeling it. Staff may also encourage bullying by what they fail to do: I refer here to the need for adequate surveillance and timely intervention. O'Moore and Hillery (1991) found that teachers in their study were able to identify only 24 % of the youths who had engaged in bullying. Further, research in three nations, the United Kingdom (Whitney & Smith, 1993), Italy (Menesini et al., 1997), and Ireland (O'Moore, Kirkham, & Smith, 1997) reveals that about half of primary school teachers and less than half of secondary school teachers try to intervene when a student is being bullied. Prime venues for bullying are the playground and school corridors, both locations often without adequate numbers of watching and supervising staff. As Higgins (1994) notes, the playground is often a site of overcrowding, exclusion, marginalization, and boredom. As such, it is a prime setting for bullying to take root. So, too, are school corridors and other locations often understaffed and thus under observed (Ahmed & Smith, 1994). When insufficiency of monitoring is combined, as it too often is in the bully-friendly school, with an indifferent administration and staff prone to ignore bullying incidents or to blame the victim, or when students are taught not to "tell tales," bullying easily escalates.

To be sure, school budgets for supervising personnel are perpetually tight. In addition, as Besag (1997) notes, in the bustle of a large playground it is often quite difficult to distinguish bullying behavior from rough-and-tumble play. Yet, is it really too expensive to upgrade the *quality* of supervision? In one school, for very few additional dollars:

> Teachers are now in class at least five minutes before pupils enter the building. The corridors are supervised on a rotating basis by teachers informally chatting to pupils or among themselves. The outside play areas are observed from second-story classroom windows so that the bird's-eye view supports the supervision of staff in the playground. (p. 43)

A second school, whose playground lies behind the building, has inexpensively re-configured its front-of-building area into a "trial playground," a sort of practice and transition venue in which both chronic bullies and chronic bullying victims can have modeled for them by staff appropriate playground behaviors, which the youths then practice at this semi-protective site. In this context, it is relevant that Olweus (1987) found a negative correlation of 0.50 between the relative density of teacher supervision at playtime and the number of bullying incidents.

Stephenson and Smith (1997) illuminate the great importance of school characteristics with their recommendations on "how to *encourage* bullying":

1. The school should have many areas that are difficult for staff to supervise.
2. Students should be placed in these areas at times of least supervision—break time, lunch time, the beginning and end of the school day.
3. If supervision is provided at these times, it should be by untrained and underpaid staff.
4. The school day should be arranged so that the entire age range of the school arrives and leaves the school at the same time.
5. There should be no designated places of respite for students, and the majority of areas in which the students do gather should be dominated by fast and furious games.
6. Arrangements should be made that contribute to large numbers of students having to move around the school in different directions at the same time.
7. The school should be designed so that the corridors used at class transition time are narrow.
8. There should be only one door into and out of each classroom.
9. Teachers should be encouraged to arrive at class late.
10. There should be no agreed, clear, and consistent way to record incidents of bullying.
11. There should be a lack of any clear policy on the use of sanctions.
12. Bullying should be viewed by school administrators and staff as part of the normal growing-up process.

13. The school should promote the view that high achievement rather than relative achievement or effort is valued. This should ensure that many students will feel inadequate and marginalized at school.
14. Administrators should avoid developing a whole-school antibullying policy.

(Reproduced by permission of Pitman Publishing from Stephenson & Smith, 1997).

Intervention

Beginning with the pioneering school bullying program developed by Olweus (1993) and progressing through the similarly comprehensive interventions offered by A. Duncan (1996), Elliott (1997a), Garrity et al. (1994), Pepler et al. (1994), Roland (1993), Stephenson and Smith (1997), and Tattum (1997), it has become clear that the optimal intervention strategy for dealing effectively with bullying by and of students is a whole-school approach. I made much at the beginning of this chapter of the ways in which the initiation and maintenance of bullying are so very frequently *group* phenomena. Ideally, so too will its successful intervention be. This is our concretization of a "whole-school" approach. Optimally it should contain major elements involving peers of the involved students—such as a buddy system, creating a "circle of friends," cooperative learning activities, support and peer mediation programs (Cowie & Sharp, 1996; Naylor & Cowie, 1999; Newman, Horne & Bartolomucci, 2000; Peterson & Rigby, 1999)—and also much more. Involvement of the whole school demands serious and responsible participation by *all* school and school-relevant persons—students, teachers, administrators, security, custodians, cafeteria staff, secretaries, school bus drivers, school board, and parents (Goldstein & Conoley, 1997; Limper, 2000; Olweus, 1993; S. Sharp & Thompson, 1994).

Drawing upon and merging the several such comprehensive programs cited earlier, a menu (below) or pool of useful school-based antibullying procedures is provided and I urge school-based readers to select and sequence whichever elements appear to fit their school's particular institutional climate, readiness, and resources. Following Olweus (1993) but expanding substantially on his specific offerings, program intervention components are grouped at the school, class, and individual levels. To flesh out the contents of components selected from this pool of alternatives, I especially recommend the training manuals of Garrity et al. (1994) and Olweus (1993).

School-level interventions
- Schoolwide survey to determine amount, frequency, and locus of bullying
- Discussion of bullying (nature, sources, signs, prevention) at whole-school and by-grade assemblies
- Increased quantity and quality of student surveillance and supervision
- Establishment of school antibullying policy concretized by mission statement distributed to all staff, students, and parents
- Creation of a schoolwide "telling" climate legitimizing informing about bullying and concretized in a phone hot line, an anonymous mail drop, or other means

- Regular staff meetings to exchange bullying-relevant information and to monitor intervention effectiveness
- Development and dissemination of antibullying rules via posters, memos, and other means
- Restructuring of high-bullying school locations
- Separate break times for younger and older students

Class-level interventions

- Discussions of bullying (nature, sources, signs, prevention) at class meetings
- Regular role-plays of bullying response measures
- Announcement of use of non-violent sanctions in response to bullying behavior
- Training of students to be helpful bystanders/informers when bullying occurs
- Formation of victim support groups
- Increased use of cooperative learning for curriculum delivery
- Use of student-run "bully courts" to adjudicate incidents
- Avoidance of use of bullying behavior by teachers
- Monitoring of student understanding of and compliance with schoolwide antibullying policy and rules
- Contracting with students for compliance with antibullying rules
- Use of stories, art, and activities to communicate and reinforce antibullying policy and rules
- Announcement and use of positive consequences for rule-following behavior in regard to bullying

Individual-level interventions

- With bullies:
  - Social skills training
  - Sanctions for bullying behavior
  - Employment as cross-age tutors
  - Individual counseling
  - Anger control training
  - Empathy training
- With victims:
  - Assertiveness training
  - Martial arts training
  - Social skills training
  - Changes of class or school
  - Encouragement of association with new peers
  - Individual counseling

Whole-school antibullying programs employing varied combinations of these several school-, class-, and individual-level components have been systematically evaluated by a number of investigators in widely dispersed locations and have consistently yielded substantial bullying-reduction outcomes (Arora, 1994; Olweus, 1993; Pepler et al., 1994; Roland, 1989; P. K. Smith & Sharp, 1994b). Whole-school intervention programming is a comprehensive strategy well deserving of implementation.

A final note regarding bullying is worth entering. As the contents of the present chapter upto this point make clear, almost all of the existing theorizing and research regarding bullying concerns school-based phenomena. Indeed, given the magnitude of its occurrence and consequences in that context, such a level of attention is fitting. Bullying behavior and its negative sequelae are far from being only a schoolhouse concern, however. Though relevant literature is sparse, it should be noted that at least a small beginning of attention to this same phenomenon as it occurs in adult workplace settings has quite recently emerged. Rayner and Hoel (1997) reflect this (mostly anecdotal) literature by reporting that workplace bullying may manifest itself in

> ... threat to professional status (e.g., belittling opinion, public professional humiliation, accusation regarding lack of effort); threat to personal standing (e.g., name-calling, insults, intimidation, devaluing with reference to age); isolation (e.g., preventing access to opportunities, physical or social isolation, withholding of information); overwork (e.g., undue pressure, impossible deadlines, unnecessary descriptions); and destabilization (e.g., failure to give credit when due, meaningless tasks, removal of responsibility, repeated reminders of blunders, setting up to fail). (p. 183)

A useful review and evaluation of this initial body of work on bullying in the workplace is provided by Einarsen (2000), who offers and examines what is available to date regarding frequency, antecedents, consequences, and amelioration. In this last regard, given our above emphasis on the need for whole-school programming as the preferred strategy for bullying remediation in that context, Einarsen (2000) strongly urges better understanding and management of the work environment, and its full participation, as primary means to workplace bullying reduction.

SEXUAL HARASSMENT

> Of the times I was sexually harassed at school, one of them made me feel really bad. I was in class and the teacher was looking right at me when this guy grabbed my butt. The teacher saw it happen. I slapped the guy and told him not to do that. The teacher didn't say anything and looked away and went on with the lesson like nothing out of the ordinary had happened. It really confused me because I knew guys weren't supposed to do that, but the teacher didn't do anything. I felt like the teacher (who was a man) betrayed me and thought I was making a big deal out of nothing. But most of all, I felt really bad about myself because it made me feel slutty and cheap. It made me feel mad too because we shouldn't have to put up with that stuff, but no one will do anything to stop it. Now sexual harassment doesn't bother me as much because it happens so much it almost seems normal. I know that sounds awful, but the longer it goes on without any one doing anything, the more I think of it as just one of those things that I have to put up with.—14-year-old girl

The lines between bullying and sexual harassment are often blurred in the research and applied literature, with some seeing the latter as an example of the former with sexual content (Batsche & Knoff, 1994), and others suggesting that bullying is a common antecedent of sexual harassment (Stein, 1995). In either event, the two are close cousins and are frequently adjacent steps in a sequence of verbal and physical maltreatment. A number of investigators have offered typologies of sexual harassment, in each case arraying subtypes according to one or another view of severity. In considering these typologies, it is well to recall the assertion in Chapter 2 that the level of severity rests in the perceptions of the maltreatment target. Hence, as Fitzgerald and Shullman (1993) observe regarding sexual harassment, "Severity of the stressor is not considered to inhere in the event itself; rather it is an individual's evaluation of the situation, as influenced by such factors as ambiguity, perceived threat, loss and so forth that is determinative" (p. 15).

Classification Typologies

The earliest attempt at classification in the domain of sexual harassment was made by Till (1980), who worked with a female college student population. Till ordered behaviors from least to most severe as follows:

1. Generalized sexist remarks: These are insulting, degrading comments about women in general, and are not intended to elicit sexual cooperation.
2. Sanction-free sexual advances: These are solicitations for sexual activity, but with no penalty proposed for the woman's refusal to comply.
3. Solicitation of sexual activity: Here the proposal is accompanied by promise of reward for acquiescence.
4. Coercion of sexual activity: The proposal in this instance is accompanied by threat of punishment for refusal.
5. Sexual crimes: such as rape and sexual assault.

Fitzgerald, Swan, and Magley (1997) offer a three-category classification scheme. The first category, *gender harassment* (similar to Till's generalized sexist remarks), refers to verbal, non-verbal, and physical acts intended to convey hostility or insult to women rather than to solicit sexual cooperation. Acts of *unwanted sexual attention* are solicitations for sexual activity that are unwanted, offensive, and unreciprocated. Finally, *sexual coercion* is extortion of sexual cooperation in return for promised reward or threatened punishment. In addition to the intent of the perpetrator(s) and content of the harassing communications, Fitzgerald, Swan and Magley suggest that the severity of harassment experienced by the victim will also be a function of (a) characteristics of the victim herself; (b) characteristics of the context in which the harassment occurs, such as whether complaints are taken seriously, the victim may incur risks in reporting, or meaningful sanctions for perpetrators exist; and (c) qualities of the harassing behavior—for example, physical versus verbal, single versus multiple perpetrators, frightening versus annoying, focused on victim only or others also, status of the perpetrator, and possibilities for escape.

A final, finer grain category system for concretely defining sexual harassment has been offered by Gruber (1992). Within each of three main classifications—verbal requests, verbal comments, and non-verbal displays—the specific subtypes of sexually harassing behavior are arrayed from most to least severe (Table 3.1).

Table 3.1 Gruber typology of sexual harassment

A. Verbal requests (more to less severe)
    1. Sexual bribery—with threat and/or promise of reward (quid pro quo)
    2. Sexual advances—no threat, seeking sexual intimacy
    3. Relational advances—no threat, repetitively seeking social relationship
    4. Subtle pressures/advances—no threat, implicit or ambiguous goal or target
B. Verbal comments (more to less severe)
    1. Personal rem1arks—unsolicited and directed *to* a woman
    2. Subjective objectification—rumors and/or comments made about a woman
    3. Sexual categorical remarks—about women "in general"
C. Non-verbal displays (more to less severe)
    1. Sexual assault—aggressive contact involving coercion
    2. Sexual touching—brief sexual or contextually sexualized
    3. Sexual posturing—violations of personal space or attempts at personal contact
    4. Sexual materials—pornographic materials, sexually demeaning objects, profanation of women's sexuality

Reproduced by permission of Kluwer Academic (Plenum, from Gruber (1992), *Sex Roles*, **26**, 447–464).

Like the classification system of Fitzgerald, Swan and Murphy (1997), Gruber's (1992) severity rankings as reported in Table 3.1 derive from multiple criteria. An act of sexual harassment will be judged more severe the higher the status of its source, the more frequent its occurrence, the longer its duration, the more explicit and direct its contents, the greater its aversiveness or offensiveness, and the more threatening its quality.

Frequency of Occurrence

The diverse forms of sexual harassment indicated in Table 3.1 are far from uncommon. The first nationwide survey seeking to identify the prevalence of sexual harassment was conducted in 1981 by the US Merit Systems Protection Board (1981). It collected relevant data from a sample of more than 20,000 federal employees, and it showed that 42 % of female respondents reported having experienced at least one of the six forms of sexual harassment presented in the survey. Substantially similar findings have subsequently been reported by others—53 % (Gutek, 1985), 50 % (Fitzgerald & Shullman, 1993), and, in a review of 18 such surveys, a range of 28 to 75 % with a median rate of 44 % (Gruber, 1992). Particularly dismaying are the frequency data among school children. A national survey of middle school children reported that 85 % of girls and 76 % of boys had experience unwelcome behavior of a sexual nature at school (American Association of University Women, 1993). Table 3.2 provides frequency percentages from this survey by type of harassment for both girls and boys.

An independent survey, also targeted to middle school youth and conducted in 79 schools by Lee et al. (1996), found directly comparable victimization outcomes— 83 % of the girls, 60 % of the boys. One might guess, given the hormonal pressures of puberty, that sexual harassment of children by children begins at about his middle school age. Not so. The American Association of University Women (1993)

Table 3.2 Survey of students' sexual harassment in schools

	Girls (%)	Boys (%)
Sexual comments, jokes gestures, or looks	76	56
Touched, grabbed, or pinched in a sexual way	65	42
Intentionally brushed up against in a sexual way	57	36
Flashed or mooned	49	41
Had sexual rumors spread about them	42	34

Reproduced with permission from *Hostile Hallways: The AAUW Survey on Sexual Harassment in America's Schools,* American Association of University Women Educational Foundation (1993).

school survey further reports that 32 % of students surveyed had been harassed by grade 6 or lower, and 6 % were before grade 3! What are the behaviors that concretize sexual harassment in elementary school? Strauss (1994) reports those listed in Table 3.3, based upon a survey of a large sample of Midwestern US teachers.

These findings combine with those of other surveys of sexual harassment at elementary-school age (Paludi, 1997) to suggest, as Strauss (1994) has proposed, that the age for onset of sexually harassing behavior is moving from adolescence to early childhood. Our growing "adultification" of children in the United States vis-à-vis clothing, cosmetics, media exposure, and much more is apparently increasingly extending to realms of sexuality, including sexual harassment. Data on the frequency of sexual harassment at all school levels deserve wide and repeated dissemination to help us overcome denial of its reality and implement effective interventions. As was true of bullying per se (noted earlier), such denial by both parents and school authorities is far from rare. Sabella and Myrick (1995) concur:

Table 3.3 Elementary school sexual harassment behaviors

Spiking (forcibly pulling down pants)
Snuggies (forcibly pulling up pants)
Flipping up skirts
Forcing kisses
Grabbing/touching another's genitals
Calling others sexually offensive names
Asking others to perform sexual acts
Threatening rape
Perpetrating sexual assault
Passing sexually explicit notes
Making gender-demeaning comments
Commenting on body parts
Using sexual profanity
Exposing genitals
Circulating pornography

From Strauss (1994). Reproduced by permission of National Association of Elementary School Principals. Copyright 1974. All rights reserved.

> Many parents resist the idea of their children discussing such delicate issues and, thus, have denied permission for systematic intervention and data collection among their children. To appease parents and others, administration may ignore or deny the problem and conclude that it rarely occurs in their schools. (p. 18)

Sexual harassment is intentional physical or psychological injury to another person, that is, aggression. As such, it must be acknowledged to exist, identified when it occurs, and consequated to reduce or eliminate it. By the same token, it is equally important that we avoid a "moral panic" and that both children and adults learn not only what harassment is but also what it is not. For children (in this case adolescents), Sandler and Paludi (1993) offer guidelines to help distinguish flirtation from sexual harassment. Flirting feels good, makes one feel attractive, is a compliment, is two-way, and is positive. Sexual harassment feels bad, is degrading, makes one feel cheap, is one-way, and is negative. For teachers, the in-school behavior strategy for themselves, "Teach, don't touch," has become the gross overreaction. As Delisle (1994,) admonishes:

> Every pat on the back has become suspect, each congratulatory squeeze to the shoulder a source of potential problems. Hugs have been demoted to handshakes. Private meetings with students have regressed to public forums.... In adopting this new philosophy our profession has quietly but surely taken a step back. (p. 10)

Although a significant portion of students experiencing sexual harassment—25 % of harassed girls and 10 % of boys—are victimized by school staff and rather than by students (Paludi, 1997) and such behavior must be vigorously discouraged and sanctioned, it is equally important to warn teachers and administrators against becoming overly cautious and forgetting the power of appropriate touching.

Response to Sexual Harassment

Fitzgerald, Gold, and Brock (1990, cited in Paludi, 1997) constructed a valuable classification system for categorizing student response to sexual harassment, as reflected in Table 3.4.

Other responses to and impacts of sexual harassment have been demonstrated. In the previously noted American Association of University Women (1993) survey, a number of negative academic or emotional sequelae to harassment were reported. In manifestations of the former, victims often wished to stop attending school (33 % girls, 12 % boys), found it more difficult to pay attention in class (28 % girls, 13 % boys), and preferred not to talk at all in class (32 % girls, 13 % boys). Negative emotional responses, of girls and boys respectively, included embarassment (64 %, 36 %), loss of self-confidence (43 %, 14 %), increased self-consciousness (52 %, 21 %) and increased fearfulness (39 %, 8 %).

In adult work settings, as in schools, the consequences for victims of repeated sexual harassment can be both broad and deep. Paludi (1997) points to decreased

Table 3.4 Student responses to sexual harassment

Internally focused strategies	
Detachment	Minimizes situation; treats it like a joke
Denial	Denies it occurred; attempts to ignore/forget it
Relabeling	Reappraises event as less threatening; offers excuses for harasser's behavior
Illusory control	Takes responsibility for the harassment
Endurance	Puts up with harassment, believing help is unavailable or fearing retaliation
Externally focused strategies	
Avoidance	Avoids situation by staying away from harasser
Assertion/confrontation	Refuses sexual offer, verbally confronts harasser
Seeks organizational relief	Reports the incident and files a complaint
Seeks social support	Seeks support of others to validate perceptions
Appeasement	Attempts to evade or placate the harasser

morale, damaged interpersonal relations, a sense of helplessness, depression, sleep and eating disturbances, and a host of additional psychological and physiological reactions. Dansky and Kilpatrick (1997) note decreased job satisfaction and performance, lessened motivation and morale, increased absenteeism, heightened anxiety, irritability, and sense of vulnerability, fatigue, loss of appetite, and more. C. B. Gardner (1995) reports similar untoward consequences of harassment victimization on America's streets in his provocative study of such behavior and its impact in an array of public venues. Clearly, sexual harassment is a form of aggression whose negative consequences can be, and are, considerable.

Intervention

Whether in school, office, factory, or elsewhere, intervention designed to control, reduce, and eliminate sexual harassment—as with interventions for all other forms of aggression—must consist of comprehensive, whole-facility, total-push approaches. In close parallel to my recommendation of multilevel intervention for bullying (school, class, individual), Strauss (1994) recommends administration, teacher, staff, parent, and student involvement in an ongoing intervention process that begins with a broad, frequency-determining survey, development and dissemination of policy statements and establishment of reporting procedures, moves to personnel awareness and intervention training, establishment of grievance procedures, and monitoring for violations, and seeks evaluation of efficacy and feedback at each level on a continuing basis. Roscoe, Strause, and Goodwin (1992) suggest that a comprehensive intervention for sexual harassment directed to (early adolescent) students optimally will include the following components:

1. Definitions of sexual harassment.
2. Specific behaviors that constitute sexual harassment.
3. Information about who can be perpetrators and victims.
4. Potential effects of sexual harassment on the victim.

5. Consequences of sexual harassment for the perpetrator.
6. Reasons why sexual harassment occurs.
7. Steps students should take if sexually harassed.

Valuable manuals detailing comprehensive intervention programming for dealing effectively with sexual harassment have been prepared by O'Donohue (1997) and Ross (1996). Strauss's (1994) and Roscoe, Strause and Goodwin's (1992) recommendations are school oriented, but with minimal alteration fit quite well any work or organizational setting, whether for children, adolescents, or adults.

Bullying and sexual harassment are both pervasive forms of aggression. Considerably more often than not, they are hidden abuses. Our schools and work sites, propelled by law and good conscience, have increasingly begun to acknowledge their existence more fully, to identify their causes, consequate their perpetrators, support their victims, and to offer intervention programming intense enough to contribute meaningfully to their prevention and elimination. I applaud these healthy developments, while acknowledging that we as a society have a long road ahead, and urge that the effort continues.

Chapter 4

DELINQUENT GANGS

Youth gangs in the United States, as a social (or, better, anti-social) phenomenon, ebb and flow in terms of both their numbers and societal impact. As America enters the 2000s, there seem to be, and are, more of them, more gang youth drug involvement, and greater levels of violence being perpetrated by such youths. The present chapter seeks to describe the sources and substance of this phenomenon by first defining the diverse meanings of "gang" in America, examining its history and current demographics, exploring the internal and extra-gang phenomena which promote within-gang solidarity and "in-groupness," as well as out-group discrimination and hostility, and in particular considering the foregoing information as it relates to the scope, intensity, and targeting of aggression perpetrated by such collectives.

Let us begin by defining the domain of this chapter. What is a gang? This seemingly straightforward question of definition masks concerns of considerable complexity. There is not, nor should there be, a single, acceptable definition of "gang," any more than a single definition would suffice over the course of many years, settings, and subcultures for other types of human groups. Many definitions have been put forward during the past 90 years, and in a real sense *all* are correct. What constitutes a gang has varied with time and place, with political and economic conditions, with community tolerance and community conservatism, with level and nature of police and citizen concern, with cultural and subcultural traditions and mores, and with media-generated sensationalism or indifference to law-violating youth groups. The answer to "What is a gang?" has varied chronologically from a play group formed out of unconscious pressures:

> . . . for the boy one of the three primary social groups. These three are, the family, the neighborhood, and the play group; but for the normal boy the play group is the gang. All three are restrictive human groupings, formed like pack and flock and hive, in response to deep-seated but unconscious need. (Puffer, 1912, p. 7)

to an interstitial group derived from conflict:

> An interstitial group originally formed spontaneously, and then integrated through conflict. It is characterized by the following types of behavior: meeting face to face, milling, movement through space as a unit, conflict, and planning. The result of this collective behavior is the development of tradition, unreflective internal structure, esprit de corps, solidarity, morale, group awareness, and attachment to a local territory. (Thrasher, 1936, p. 46)

an aggregation demarcated as "a gang" via community and then self-labeling processes:

> Any denotable adolescent group of youngsters who (a) are generally perceived as a distinct aggregation by others in their neighborhood, (b) recognize themselves as a denotable group (almost invariably with a group name), and (c) have been involved in a sufficient number of delinquent incidents to call forth a consistent negative response from neighborhood residents and/or law enforcement agencies. (Klein, 1971, p.111)

a singular definitional emphasis on delinquent behavior:

> An organization of young people usually between their early teens and early twenties, which has a group name, claims a territory, or neighborhood as its own, meets with its members on a regular basis, and has recognizable leadership. The key element that distinguishes a gang from other organizations of young people is delinquency: its members regularly participate in activities that violate the law. (S. Gardner, 1983, p. 5)

And, most recently, a particular definitional focus on violence and drug involvement:

> The most frequently cited elements of a definition for gang [in their national survey] was certain group or organizational characteristics, symbols, a range of specific and general criminal activities, particularly violence, drug use and sales. The most frequent elements used to define a gang member were symbols or symbolic behavior, self-admission, identification by others, especially the police, and association with gang members. (Spergel et al., 1989, p. 206)

Spergel et al. (1989) comment with regard to this definitional progression:

> Definitions in the 1950s and 1960s were related to issues of etiology as well as based on liberal, social reform assumptions. Definitions in the 1970s and 1980s are more descriptive, emphasize violent and criminal characteristics, and possibly a more conservative philosophy of social control and deterrence (Klein and Maxson 1989). The most recent trend may be to view gangs as more pathological than functional and to restrict usage of the term to a narrow set of violent and criminal groups. (p. 13)

The contemporary American juvenile gang may have structured organization, identifiable leadership, territorial identification, continuous association, specific purpose, and engage in illegal behavior—as many of the current youth gangs in California, Illinois and elsewhere in America are largely characterized. Or, rather less characteristic of the typical, contemporary gang, they may—as is largely the case in New York City—be loosely organized, of changeable leadership, be criminal activity and not territorially oriented, associate irregularly, pursue amorphous purposes, and engage not only in illegal, but also legal activities. Nevertheless, they are more violent and more drug involved, and these two characteristics must also be included in establishing an accurate, contemporary definition of "gang" in America.

How else may the nature of youth gangs in the United States best be clarified? In the sections which follow we will seek to do so by examining their history, sketching both early and more recent theories of why groups of youths engage in criminal behavior, and describing the core demographics of America's contemporary gang. We will then turn to a consideration in depth of the forces that build and maintain their strong sense of ingroup solidarity and outgroup hostility.

HISTORY

Ganging in twentieth century America did not emerge de novo, but grew from a long and varied American tradition of group violence. Between 1760 and 1900, 500 vigilante groups—the Ku Klux Klan, the White Cappers, the Black Legion prominent among them—appeared in the United States (Gurr, 1989). Whippings, bombings, arson, and murder were among their violent tools for terrorizing ethnic and religious minorities, and other targets of their hate. Less organized, but directed toward similar violent ends, were lynch mobs, responsible for taking the lives of 3400 black Americans between 1882 and 1951 (Gurr, 1989). Piracy, banditry, feuding, labor, agrarian and race riots, and the frequently glamorized marauding bands of frontier outlaws, such as Butch Cassidy's High Five and the Jesse James gang, are each in their own ways ancestors of the contemporary American gang (Brown, 1989). The Forty Thieves, an Irish-American immigrant gang formed in 1820 in the Five Points District of New York City is cited by the Illinois State Police (1989) as the first modern (adult) criminal gang. It gave rise, as did many of the adult gangs which followed, to an "auxiliary" or "sub-gang" of juveniles, in this first instance called the Forty Little Thieves. Other such adult and juvenile gangs quickly followed, the Kerryonians, the Dusters, the Plug Uglies, the Dead Rabbits, and others (Asbury, 1971).

Thinking about causation, that is, *why* gangs form changed over the course of this period of early gang interest. In its beginning, reflecting the heavy reliance on both Darwinian theorizing and *instinct* as the core explanatory construct in the behavioral science of the day, Puffer (1912) asserted:

> We must, then, so far as we are good evolutionists, look upon the boy's gang as the result of a group of instincts inherited from a distant past...we must suppose that these gang instincts arose in the first because they were useful once, and that they have been preserved to the present day because they are, on the whole, useful still. (p. 83)

Thrasher (1927/1963) looked for causative explanation both within the youths themselves and in the community of which the youths were a part. The typical gang member, in his view, was "...a rather healthy, well-adjusted, red-blooded American boy seeking an outlet for normal adolescent drives for adventure and expression." (Hardman, 1967, p. 7). Yet, the youth's environment was equally important to Thrasher. Inadequacies in family functioning, schools, housing, sanitation, employment and other community characteristics combined to help motivate youth to turn elsewhere—to his gang—for life satisfactions and rewards. This focus on social causation blossomed fully during the next era of gang research, the 1930s into the early 1940s, which Hardman (1967) appropriately labeled "the depression studies." It was an era in which social scientists sought explanation for many of America's ills—including delinquent ganging—in "... social causation, social failure, social breakdown." (Hardman, 1967, p. 9). Landesco (1932) emphasized the effects of conflicting immigrant and American cultures. Shaw and McKay (1942) more complexly stressed a combination of slum area deterioration, poverty, family dissolution, and organized crime. Tannenbaum (1938) analogously proposed that the gang forms not because of its attractiveness per se, but because "positive socio-cultural forces" such as family, school, church—that might train a youth into more socially acceptable behaviors are weak or unavailable. Wattenberg and Balistrieri (1950) similarly stressed socioeconomically substandard neighborhoods and lax parental supervision. In the same contextual explanatory spirit, Bogardus (1943)—in one of the first West-Coast gang studies—emphasized the war and war-like climate in America as underpinning the aggressive gangs forming at that time. Dumpson (1949), more multicausal, but still contextual in his causative thinking, identified the war, racism, and diverse political and economic sources.

While the social problems of the day have over the decades largely formed the basis for explaining why youths form gangs, W. B. Miller (1982) has offered a more fully inclusive perspective, which appears to us to capture more adequately the likely complex determinants of gang formation. He observes:

> Youth gangs persist because they are a product of conditions basic to our social order. Among these are a division of labor between the family and the peer group in the socialization of adolescents, and emphasis on masculinity and collective action in the male subculture; a stress on excitement, congregation, and mating in the adolescent subculture; the importance of toughness and smartness in the subcultures of lower-status populations; and the density conditions and territoriality patterns affecting the subcultures of urban and urbanized locales. (p. 320)

A somewhat different, but equally comprehensive view of gang formation determinants is offered by Edgerton (1988), and reflects a causal emphasis on the construct of multiple marginality. He proposes that the factors contributing importantly to the formation of gangs include:

> ... residential segregation in low-income areas, poverty, poor school performance, little parental supervision, discrimination, and distrust of law enforcement. In these conditions, young people spent much of their lives together on the streets where a gang served them ... as surrogate family, school, and police. We also hear from gang members ... about the appeal that gang membership has for them—friendship, pride, prestige, belongingness, identity, self-esteem, and a desire to emulate their uncles and older brothers who were gang members before them. (p. x)

DELINQUENT GANG THEORY

The early periods in the history of social science interest in delinquent gangs were largely descriptive. What gangs were and the societal/familial conditions that were their antecedents and concomitants were the focus of concern. Little emerged during this time in the way of formal gang theory, i.e., conceptualizations of the structural and dynamic variables underlying gang formation, organization and, especially, the delinquent behavior which characterized a substantial amount of gang functioning. This theoretical lacuna was filled, and then some, beginning in the 1950s. By far the majority of this theory development effort was sociological in nature. Note below how two of the theoretical positions are especially relevant to the establishment and maintenance of in-groups, and associated in-group versus out-group phenomena. Specifically, subcultural theory offers a reasonable, if partial, basis for the initial formation of youth in-groups, and labeling theory provides a probable basis for their continuance.

Strain Theory

The discrepancy between economic aspiration and opportunity lies at the heart of strain theory, as do such discrepancy-induced reactions as frustration, deprivation, and discontent. Strain theoretical notions first appeared in Merton's article "Social structure and anomie," (Merton, 1938) in which he observed:

> It is only when a system of cultural values extols, virtually above all else, certain common symbols of success for the population at large, while its social structure rigorously restricts or completely eliminates access to approved modes of acquiring these symbols for a considerable part of the same population that antisocial behavior ensues on a considerable scale. (p. 673)

A. K. Cohen's (1955) reactance theory, and Cloward and Ohlin's (1960) differential opportunity theory are both elaborations of strain theory. Each seems to enhance its explanatory power, especially with regard to delinquent behavior by low income youth. Yet such social class–delinquency association is inconsistent (Linden, 1978; Rutter & Giller, 1983). Furthermore, though their economic status often remains unchanged, most low-income delinquent youths eventually become law-abiding adults. Hirshi (1969) also marshals evidence indicating that many delinquent youths do not experience the sense of deprivation-induced motivation central to strain theory, and R. E. Johnson (1979) suggests that strain theory holds little explanatory relevance for delinquent acts committed by middle-class youths. These and related caveats not withstanding, strain theory appropriately survives to this day, its more contemporary versions seeking to be responsive to both changed societal economic forces and evidence indicating that middle-class youths are just as likely as those from low income environments to aspire beyond their means (D. S. Elliott & Voss, 1979). It survives not as an all-encompassing explanation of juvenile delinquency in its individual and group/gang manifestations, but as one component of integrative theoretical views on delinquency that consider it to be complex behavior derived from a complex of causes.

Subculture Theory

Subcultural or cultural deviance theory holds that delinquent behavior grows from conformity to the prevailing social norms experienced by the youth in his or her particular subcultural group, norms largely at variance with those held by society at large and including, according to Cohen (A. K. Cohen, 1966), gratuitous hostility, group autonomy, intolerance of restraint, short-run hedonism, the seeking of recognition via antisocial behavior, little interest in planning for long-term goals, and related behavioral preferences. W. B. Miller (1958) describes these subcultural norms or "focal concerns" as centering around trouble, toughness, (out)smartness, excitement, fate, and autonomy. In this view, the adolescent is ". . . drawn or socialized into law violation in an attempt to live up to the perceived expectations of his or her deviant associates." (R. E. Johnson, 1979, p. 2) Sutherland's (Sutherland & Cressey, 1974) differential association theory, W. B. Miller's (1958) notion of lower class culture as a "generating milieu" for gang delinquency, differential identification theory (Glaser, 1956), culture conflict theory (Shaw & McKay, 1942), illicit means theory (Shaw & McKay, 1942), and what might be termed structural determinism theory (Clarke, 1977) are the major concretizations of subcultural theory. Of these, differential association theory has clearly been most influential. Delinquent behavior, according to this view, is learned behavior.

A substantial diversity of findings lends considerable credence to the likely role of such association-engendered learning in the etiology of delinquency, especially gang delinquency. Most delinquent acts are committed in the company of other youths (Farrington, Gundry & West, 1975), youngsters attending a school or living in a neighborhood with high rates of delinquency are more likely to commit delinquency acts than are similar youths attending schools or living in areas with low rates of delinquency (Rutter & Giller, 1983). Males who admit to having delinquent friends are more likely than those who claim not to have such friends also to admit to delinquent acts (R. E. Johnson, 1979; Voss, 1963). The likelihood of committing a specific type of delinquent act is significantly correlated with the likelihood of commission of the same acts by members of one's peer group (Reiss & Rhodes, 1964). The number of delinquent acts committed by a boy's friends are predictive of his own future convictions (West & Farrington, 1977), and self-report data indicate that across alternative etiological bases for delinquency (delinquent associates, delinquent values, attachment to school, school performance, parental love, attachment to parents, occupational expectations, perceived risk of apprehension), the strongest covariate by far was delinquent associates (R. E. Johnson, 1979). Sutherland and Cressey (1974) have criticized differential association theory for omitting consideration of personality traits. Nettler (1974) has noted its disregard for situational determinants of criminal behavior. Nietzel (1979) asserts that it reflects on overly simplified view of the learning process, and J. Q. Wilson and Hernstein (1985) observe that it provides no explanation for individual differences and hence fails to account for the fact that within a given neighborhood, for example, some youth adopt deviant values and others adopt more conventional ones. Thus, as with aspiration–opportunity induced strain, it is appropriate to view subcultural influences as but part of the etiological picture but, in this instance, an especially important part.

Control Theory

While both strain and subcultural theories seek to explain why some youngsters commit delinquent acts, control theory operationalizes its concern with the etiology of delinquency by positing reasons why some youngsters do not. Everyone, it is assumed by this position, has a predisposition to commit delinquent acts, and the theory concerns itself with how individuals learn not to offend. The central construct of control theory, the major mediator of such learning not to offend, is the social bond (Hirschi, 1969). Social bonds grow from both direct social controls (e.g., externally imposed restrictions and punishments) and internal controls (resulting primarily from affectional identification with one's parents). Social bonds find overt expression, it is held, in attachment to other people, commitment to organized society, involvement in conventional activities, and belief in a common value system. Hirschi (1969) proposes, for example, that

> ...the prospects of delinquent behavior decline as the adolescent is controlled by such bonds as affective ties to parents, success in school, involvement in school activities, high occupational and educational aspirations, and belief in the moral validity of conventional norms. (Johnson, 1979, p. 2)

The weaker the social bonding thus defined, the greater is the purported likelihood of delinquent behavior. Both Hirschi (1969) and D. S. Elliott, Ageton and Canter (1979) have reported evidence in support of this control theory hypothesis. Control theory and its variations (Hewitt, 1970; Matza, 1964; Nye 1958; Reckless, 1961; Sykes & Matza, 1957) find particular support in the very substantial empirical literature that convincingly demonstrates the broad and deep influence of family factors upon the likelihood of delinquent behavior, e.g., parental criminality (Osborn & West, 1979; Robins, West & Herjanic, 1975), parental social difficulties (excessive drinking, frequent unemployment, etc.) (Robins & Lewis, 1966), poor parental supervision and monitoring (Patterson, 1982; Wilson and Hernstein, 1985), poor disciplining practices—excessive, erotic or harsh (Deur & Parke, 1970; Sawin & Parke, 1979; Snyder & Patterson, 1987), and, as compared to parents of non-delinquent youths, greater parental reward for deviant behavior, greater likelihood of becoming involved in coercive interchanges, more frequent modeling of aggressive behavior, and the provision of less support and affection (Bandura, 1973; Patterson, 1982; Snyder & Patterson, 1987). Families of delinquent youth also often display a lack of shared leisure time (Gold, 1963; West & Farrington, 1977), a lack of intimate parent–child communication (Hirschi, 1969), a lack of parental warmth (McCord & McCord, 1959; Rutter, 1980), and parental reports of lack of attachment to their children and poor identification with the role of parent (Patterson, 1982).

Labeling Theory

In 1938, Tannenbaum described an escalating process of stigmatization or labeling which, he asserted, can occur between the delinquent individual or group and the community of which it is a part. Minor transgressions are responded to with admonitions, chastisements, and perhaps initial exposure to the police and court components of the criminal justice system. As the transgressive behavior escalates, community response hardens into a demand for suppression.

> There is a gradual shift from the definition of the specific acts as evil to a definition of the individual as evil, and that all his acts come to be looked upon with suspicion... From the individual's point of view there has taken place a similar change. He has gone slowly from a sense of grievance and injustice, of being unduly mistreated and punished, to a recognition that the definition of him as a human being is different from that of other boys in his neighborhood, his school, street, community. The young delinquent becomes bad because he is defined as bad.
>
> The process of making the criminal, therefore, is a process of tagging, defining, identifying, segregating, describing, emphasizing, making conscious and self-conscious. The person becomes the thing he is described as being. (Tannenbaum, 1938, pp. 87–88)

Note how closely this statement accords with the very definition of "gang" by M. W. Klein (1971), cited at the beginning of this chapter, with its focus on neighborhood perception of the youth group as "a distinct aggregation" and self-labeling by the group itself "as a denotable group." Mead's (1934) earlier notion that one's self-concept derives in large part from how others define us lies at the heart of labeling theory. Becker (1963), Hawkins and Tiedman (1975), Lemert (1967), and Schur (1971) have each explored this notion as it applies to diverse behaviors— including individual and group delinquency—which society at large labels as deviant. It is not the initial act(s) of delinquent behavior ("primary deviance") that labeling theory seeks to explain, but delinquent acts subsequent to society's official response to these initial act(s) ("secondary deviance"). According to Nietzel (1979), "...persons are pushed to accept and enact these roles because of social expectations which are very difficult to disconfirm. Individuals, ultimately, conform to the stereotypes which have been applied to them." (p. 111). Once the labeling process is underway, Krohn, Massey and Skinner (1987) note, conventional behaviors performed by the labeled individual may be less likely to be reinforced, opportunities to engage in such behaviors may diminish, and impetus to associate increasingly with other persons so-labeled may increase. While labeling theory fails to attempt any causative explanation of prelabeling delinquent acts (primary deviance), and completely externalizes responsibility for the types of delinquent behavior it does seek to explain, it nevertheless quite appropriately sensitizes us to the likely substantial role of the stigmatizing process in encouraging the very behavior society wishes to reduce. Decriminalization and diversion programs are positive responses by America's criminal justice system to this heightened awareness.

Radical Theory

Radical theory, sometimes termed "the new criminology" by its proponents (Abadinsky, 1979; Meier, 1976), is a sociopolitical perspective on crime and delinquency. Its focus is the political meanings and motivations underlying society's definitions of crime and its control. In this view, crime is a phenomenon largely created by those who possess wealth and power in the United States. America's laws, it is held, are the laws of the ruling elite, used to subjugate the poor, minorities and the powerless. The specific propositions which constitute radical theory (Quinney, 1974) concretize its sociopolitical thrust.

1. American society is based on an advanced capitalist economy.
2. The state is organized to serve the interests of the dominant economic class, the capitalist ruling class.
3. Criminal law is an instrument of the state and the ruling class, and is used by them to maintain and perpetuate the existing social and economic order.
4. Crime control in capitalist society is accomplished through a variety of institutions and agencies established and administered by a government elite, representing ruling class interests, for the purpose of establishing domestic order.
5. The contradictions of advanced capitalism require that the subordinate classes remain oppressed by whatever seems necessary, especially through the coercion and violence of the legal system.
6. Only with the collapse of capitalist society and the creation of a new society, based on socialist principles, will there be a solution to the crime problem.

As can be seen, radical theory goes very far beyond mere matters of social labeling, differential opportunity, or like concerns. Its target is no less than the social and economic structure of American society. While its preferred solutions appear to have little likelihood of becoming reality, the promotion of radical theory has rendered a not unimportant "consciousness-raising" service resulting in increased awareness within the criminal justice system, and perhaps in society at large, of the degree to which social conflict, racism, exploitation, and related social ills are relevant to the etiology and remediation of criminal behavior.

CURRENT GANG DEMOGRAPHICS

Accurate data on the number, nature, structure and functioning of delinquent gangs are hard to come by. While individual investigators have over the years sought to mount large-scale national gang surveys (Miller, 1975; Spergel et al., 1989; Curry & Spergel,1992), a major government effort of this type was not initiated until 1997. Even in the context of the recently begun National Youth Gang Survey (National Youth Gang Center, 2000) of police and sheriffs' departments in the United States, each city or region is free to, and does, formulate its own definition of "gang", and decides what gang-relevant data to collect. Police, public service agencies, schools, mass media representatives, and others regularly exposed to gang youth not infrequently exaggerate or minimize their numbers and illegal behaviors as a function of political, financial or other impression management needs. Compounding the difficulty in obtaining adequate, accurate, objective and relevant information are gang youths themselves. Hagedorn & Macon (1988) comment:

> . . . be wary of your information. Gang members are quite adept at telling social workers and policemen self-serving lies. Glib misinformation is, in fact, a survival tool for many gang members. It is easy for outside people (and that is practically everybody) to believe social workers and policemen because they

have direct contact with gang members. Yet this direct contact is often managed by the gang members themselves, sometimes for survival, sometimes even for self-glorifying exaggeration, and police and gang workers also have some self-interest in the images they purvey. (p. 4)

Thus, caution in accepting the available data, and conservatism in its interpretation are requisite. Given these provisos, what is currently known about the structure and demographics of the contemporary delinquent gang?

In 1974, W. B. Miller conducted a major national survey seeking gang-relevant information from a spectrum of public and private service agencies, police departments, probation offices, courts, juvenile bureaus and similar sources. Particular attention was paid in this effort to the six American cities reporting the highest levels of gang activity. Philadelphia and Los Angeles reported the highest proportion of gang members to their respective male adolescent populations (6 per 100). For the other survey cities, comparable ratios were New York (4 per 100), Chicago (2 per 100), Detroit and San Francisco (less than 1 per 100). The combined rate for all six cities was 37 per 1000, or approximately 4 %. As has consistently been reported in earlier decades, gang members in the (1974) surveyed cities were predominantly male, age 12 to 21, residing in the poorer, usually central city areas, and came from families at the lower occupational and educational levels. Gang youth were African American (1/2), Hispanic (1/6), Asian (1/10) and non-Hispanic White (1/10), and strongly tended to form themselves into ethnically homogeneous gangs.

Needle and Stapleton (1982) surveyed police departments in 60 American cities of various sizes. Half of the cities with populations between a quarter and a half million, and more than a third of the cities with between 100,000 and a quarter million people reported gang problems. Delinquent youth gangs were no longer to be seen as only a big city problem. Though the popular mythology of this spread is that most such non-big city gangs are branches intentionally exported to such locations by big city gangs or mega-gangs (especially Los Angeles' Crips and Bloods), reality appears a bit more complex. While a modest amount of such "franchising," "branching," or "hiving off" may occur, most middle sized- and smaller-city gangs either originate in such locations or are started by non-resident gang members via kinship, alliance, the expansion of turf boundaries, or the movement of gang members' families into new areas (Moore, Vigil & Garcia, 1983). Whether leaving and setting up anew elsewhere is a gang or a family decision, the departure city holds a number of real or perceived pressures (from law enforcement agencies, rival gangs, saturated drug market, family pressures), and the destination city portends certain real or perceived opportunities (such as family relocation, distance from aforementioned pressures, drug market opportunities, legitimate employment opportunities).

By 1989, according to yet another, and particularly extensive, survey conducted by Spergel et al., delinquent gangs were located in almost all 50 states. As a group, 35 surveyed cities reported 1439 gangs. California, Illinois and Florida had (and still have) substantial gang concentrations. Spergel et al., report that three jurisdictions in particular have especially high numbers of youth gangs: Los Angeles county (600), Los Angeles City (280), and Chicago (128). Of the total of 120,636 gang members that were reported to exist in all the surveyed cities combined, 70,000 were estimated to be in Los Angeles County, including 26,000 in Los Angeles,

Figure 4.1   Gang Distribution in the US.

and 12,000 in Chicago.[1] However, it is clearly not only these three jurisdictions expressing concern. Spergel et al. (1989) report that while 14 % of their survey's law enforcement respondents and 8 % of other respondents believed that the gang situation in their respective jurisdictions had improved since 1980, 56 % of the police and 68 % of the non-law enforcement respondents claim that their situation had worsened.

As cited earlier, in recent years a National Youth Gang Survey has been conducted and reported by the US Department of Justices' National Youth Gang Center. In 1998, this survey of police and sheriff's departments in 1385 US cities reported 28,7000 street gangs with a total membership of 780,000 youths. Their geographic distribution is depicted in Figure 4.1 (Klein, 1995), with California (by far), Illinois, Texas, Ohio, and Indiana being its numerical leaders. By ethnic group, these youngsters were Latino (44 %), African-American (35 %), Caucasian (14 %), Asian (5 %), and other (2 %). Given that the US Bureau of the Census (1993) predicts an increase of 15 % in the population of juveniles in the years America from 1990 to 2010 (from 64,185,000 to 73,617,000), the number of gang youths in the United States may well similarly increase. Males continue to outnumber female gang members, most recently at a ratio of approximately 9 to 1. Gang size is a variable function of a number of determinants, including density of the youth population in a given

---

[1] This numerical litany of youth participation in gangs should be tempered with the reminder that most youths, even in areas in which gangs are common, do not join gangs. Vigil (1983), for example, estimates that only 4 to 10 % of Chicano youth are affiliated with gangs.

geographical or psychological area (i.e., the pool to draw upon), the nature of the gang's activities, police pressures, season of the year, gang recruitment efforts, relevant agency activity, and additional factors (Spergel, 1965). Only 5 % or less of gang crime is committed by females. Females join gangs later than do males, and leave earlier. Hagedorn (1998) reports that 98 % of the women who were founding members of six all-female Milwaukee gangs had left the gang by the end of their teen years, in contrast to only 25 % of the men in male gangs. Though female gang members can and do fight, and appear increasingly likely to do so, they are less likely than their male counterparts to use guns or other weapons when doing so. The age range of gang membership appears to have expanded, to from 9 to 30, as gang involvement in drug dealing has increased. Younger members are often used as lookouts, runners, etc., with the knowledge that if caught, judges and juvenile law tend to be more lenient when the perpetrator is younger. Older members tend to remain in the gang as a result of both the profitability of drug dealing, and the paucity of employment opportunities for disadvantaged populations in the legitimate economy.

Why do they join? Largely to obtain what all adolescents appropriately seek— peer friendship, pride, identity development, self-esteem enhancement, excitement, the acquisition of resources and, in response to family and community tradition, goals that often are not available through legitimate means in the disorganized and low-income environments from which most gang youth derive. In part the answer parallels why any groups form. Why do people need, seek, and appear to derive benefit from the company of others? In Chapter 1, I offered answers to this question that appear to apply well to that particular type of group called the gang. These included need similarity and complementarity, increased positive distinctiveness via social comparison, social exchange benefits, and decreased costs of these types. Popular mythology holds that once a member, the youth is a member forever ("down for life"). While some youths indeed are long term, even very long term members of their gangs—well into adulthood—a recent survey of three major American cities revealed a surprising percentage of new members leaving their gangs after less than a year of membership: Rochester (54 %), Denver (67 %), Seattle (69 %).

COHESIVENESS

Starting early in its formation, and continuing throughout its life, the group develops a sense of cohesiveness. As described in Chapter 1, this centrally important quality of groups has been defined in terms of (a) the attraction members feel toward other actual and prototypical group members as well as toward the group as a unit, (b) member motivation to participate in the group's activities and contribute to the group's goals, and (c) the coordination of group member effort.

There already exists a considerable literature on group cohesiveness as it relates both to gang formation and to gang behavior. It will aid our effort to understand this literature as it applies to youth gangs if we keep in mind that gangs can and do differ in substantial ways from one another, both over time, and across locations at the same time. Thus, in an obvious example, Thrasher's gangs of 1927 typically differ in several ways, including cohesiveness, from the modern American gang of today. Also, as we have noted elsewhere (Goldstein, 1991), California gangs clearly tend to cohere more fully than do those in New York. These caveats in place, what is known about gang cohesiveness? Two major issues have been addressed. The first concerns the central in-group matter of how cohesive gangs are. The second seeks to discern the relationship between gang cohesiveness and delinquent behavior. Klein (1968b) comments with regard to the first of these matters:

> ...earlier writers stressed the esprit de corps, face-to-face relations, and general camaraderie to be found in juvenile gangs. More recently, however, gangs...are found to be rather loosely structured with varying but generally low cohesiveness. (p. 103)

Klein (1968b) offers several bases for this decline in intermember attraction,[2] including the very size of many contemporary gangs, and their vertical (age-graded) structure—both of which decrease interaction opportunities—and the fact, that, as we shall see below, many gang youth are drawn to gang membership not so much by the positive pull of the gang as the negative push of their own communities, combined with their own, individual social disabilities.

Klein and Crawford (1968) draw the valuable distinction between internal and external sources of cohesiveness, providing further bases for possible diminution in gang cohesiveness. Cohesiveness for many groups, they observe, rests on a within-group foundation of attraction and positive interaction, group-wide goals, membership stability, group norms, and role differentiation. For gangs, however, they assert that such internal sources of cohesiveness are non-existent or substantially less potent today than are sources external to the group itself (e.g., poverty, educational deficits, poor job opportunity, dysfunctional family relations, the antipathy of community adults, and hostility from rival gangs). These external realities, according to Klein (1968b) help drive the youths together, via a sense of deprivation, dissatisfaction, and an effort to make the most of an unhappy life situation.

> When a number of boys in a neighborhood withdraw from similar sets of environmental frustrations and interact with one another enough to recognize, and perhaps generate, common attitudes, the group has begun to form. Added to threats of rival groups are the many ways in which society reinforces this tendency—police behavior, teacher reactions, lack of acceptance by adults on playgrounds and in local business establishments, and so on. (Klein, 1968b, p. 106).

In addition to such external sources of cohesiveness, intermember attraction may also be enhanced in gangs, according to Cartwright, Howard & Reuterman (1970), via selective recruitment, shared neighborhood residence, and the diverse conformity pressures within the group. Yet a further source of within-group cohesiveness, in the spirit of realistic conflict theory, Short and Strodtbeck (1965) found that gang leaders in their research often sought to capitalize on external threat from rival gangs by encouraging a gang-wide violent response. As armies everywhere have

---

[2] Cartwright (1975) correctly observes that while gang-wide cohesiveness may be lower than is popularly believed, there often exist highly cohesive within-gang cliques, especially among core gang members.

found, fighting together serves as a major spur to in-group solidarity. At times, Jansyn (1966) adds, the initiation of aggression toward an outgroup for explicit in group cohesiveness enhancement will be forthcoming from the gang as a whole, not just its leadership.

The position that cohesiveness in delinquent gangs is often modest or low, perhaps a surprise to the reader given the popular writings about such youth acting in concert and with esprit, also has intervention implications:

> Because gang cohesiveness is not generally high, by and large gangs do not act as gangs; rather, temporary groups and cliques are normally the functional units of activity beyond the individual level. For control and prevention efforts, this means that 'the' gang presents a shifting, elusive target, permeable and elastic, and thus inherently resistant to outside intervention. It presents not a cohesive force but, rather, a spongelike resilience. (Klein & Maxson, 1989, p. 211)

Our second concern is the relationship between gang cohesiveness and delinquent behavior. Quicker (1983) asserts that gangs do not need to be cohesive to be delinquent. In fact, he proposes that the more cohesive the gang, the less property and conflict offenses it perpetrates. Tognacci's (1975) understanding of the relevant data is similar. Thrasher (1927/1963) early suggested otherwise, and Klein (1968b), Lucore (1975) and Spergel et al. (1989) more recently concur. Our understanding of this phenomenon does suggest that gang cohesiveness and gang delinquency appear to be positively related, though it must quickly be added that the causal direction(s) of this association is unclear. Does cohesiveness cause delinquency, does delinquency enhance cohesiveness, do both phenomena occur, or is a third variable responsible? We strongly suspect that cohesiveness and delinquency reciprocally influence one another. Lucore (1975) agrees, but wonders if the relationship may be more complicated, perhaps curvilinear:

> In this discussion about which comes first, the cohesive behavior or the delinquent behavior, it is at least clear that delinquent behavior and cohesive behavior increase and decrease together, whether in response to each other or in response to an outside force. A circular, dependent relationship seems to exist: delinquent behavior increases with more contact among gang members, and gang solidarity also increases with common involvement in delinquent activity. There may some optimal level of attitudinal gang cohesiveness at which most delinquent activity occurs. Certainly some minimum level of mutual trust and loyalty is needed to enable the gang to act together. On the other hand, very high levels of attitudinal cohesiveness seem to preclude delinquent action. (p. 96)

Attempts to discern the nature of possible cohesiveness–delinquency relationships will be furthered by efforts directed at understanding the dynamics of how these phenomena might directionally or reciprocally operate to influence one another. In a manner consistent with Tannenbaum's (1938) social labeling theory of delinquency examined earlier, Klein and Crawford (1967) provide helpful direction for this effort:

> Most gang theorists presently concur that, if offenses are affected by mutual gang membership, it is because the antecedent deviant values, the requisite skills, and the opportunities for misbehavior are learned and reinforced through

association with other members ... these processes can occur and persist because the external sources of cohesion continually throw the gang members together, forcing the kinds of interactions which are preliminary to increased gang-related offenses. These interactions become secondary sources of cohesion in conjunction with offense behavior, each reinforcing the other as the members mingle and verbalize the deviance which labels them as different. (p. 264)

Cohesiveness appears to be an especially important group dynamic for better understanding of why gangs form, why they persist, and what they do while they exist. Why else do they join?

We have elsewhere stressed in particular two other sources of attractiveness of gang membership, both of which strongly emphasize the ingroup quality of such belonging (Goldstein, 1991). The first concerns conformity to peer pressure:

...we have described an array of characteristics typical of the American adolescent, e.g., marginality, a chronic challenging of those in authority, the need to experiment with diverse adult-like roles, status seeking—especially vis a vis peers—concern with self-esteem enhancement, preoccupation with independence striving and, especially, deep involvement in the task of identity formation and, for this and many other reasons, also deeply involved in developing and maintaining peer relationships. For structural, compensatory, and esteem-enhancement purposes, conformity pressure in such adolescent peer groups is intense and, very often, successful. We hope that it is clear to the reader, as it is to us, that all of these qualities are fully descriptive not only of the hypothetical typical American adolescent, but also for the youth involved in delinquent gangs. In fact, we would assert, "even more so!" Youngsters who are members of delinquent gangs are not only—in all the sense described in this chapter—adolescents, they are more accurately *hyperadolescents*. (p. 73)

If peer pressure is a major part of the "push" to gang membership, the sense of family or community such membership often provides is in large measure the "pull." Here we wish to quote not our own earlier writings, but instead two gang youths, who communicate this pull very well:

Q.   What does being in a gang mean to you?
A.   Being in a gang to me means if I didn't have no family, I'd think that's where I'll be. If I didn't have no job, that's where I'd be. To me its like community help without all the community. They understand better than my mother and father. Its just like a community group, but its together you know. You don't see it but its there. (Hagedorn & Macon, 1988)

They're the only ones I can depend on, 'cause I know if I get into hassles, they'll help me ... The ones that are my friends, my real friends ... they are all from M (gang name). To us, we're like one big family. If they do wrong to my homegirl or homeboy, it's like they're doing wrong to me and it hurts me. (Gardner, 1983, p. 17)

Diverse types and levels of gang membership exist (Padilla, 1992). *Hard core* and *regular* members typically have been with the gang the longest. Some may be "OG", i.e., "original gangsters"—its founding members or at least long-term members. Their ages are usually 17 to 21, they tend to be the more lethally violent members of a gang and, when perpetrated, their violence is often directed towards material gain. Gang leadership will typically come from its hardcore members.

However, consistent with the view of group leadership presented in Chapter 1, as a situationally determined phenomenon emerging as a function of the given group's tasks and goals, Klein (1969) emphasizes "that gang leadership does not reside wholly within one or two individuals, but is in fact shared by many depending upon the group's activities and the context of the moment." (p. 1432) *Wannabes* and *peripherals* have joined more recently, are 12 to 16 in age, and, as noted earlier, often come in and out of gang membership: join, stay a while, leave, perhaps rejoin it or another gang. Their violence is often motivated by a desire for reputation-building. *Potentials* are youngsters residing in the gang's neighborhood who are not in the gang, but who will become members if invited. *Neutrons*, in contrast, do not desire gang affiliation. However, since they too live in the gang's neighborhood, and may count gang members among their friends, rival gang members may label them as if they were in fact neighborhood gang members, harass them accordingly and, in response, neutrons may feel considerable pressure to "join up." Finally *veterans* are young adults, ex-members of 21 and over, who have left, faded out from, or graduated out of the gang.

Gang recruitment, suggests Jankowski (1991), is primarily of three types. *Fraternity* type structurally resembles the "rush" recruiting activity of the college fraternity or sorority. Social and other "hang out" activities and experiences provide a number of opportunities for reciprocal, mutual inspection. If members like the target person, and he or she feels similarly, an invitation to join is forthcoming. *Obligation* recruitment is a message to the potential recruit that membership is a family and/or community tradition and expectation. Your father, two brothers, cousin are/were in the gang, you're in the family, we invite you to the gang." Finally, *coercive* recruitment transpires via a threat invitation, e.g., "They have 90 members; over there: 80 members; we have only 50. You live on this block. Join our gang or get your head cracked!"

Once recruited, in a manner not unlike our earlier examination of hazing, it is common that initiation rites will occur as a hurdle to get beyond as a precondition to gang membership. In female youth gangs, for example, initiation may take form in a *jump in*, which is a time-limited beating by a subgroup of gang members; a *sex in*, requiring the initiate to have sexual intercourse with any and all members of the male gang with whom the initiating female gang is associated; or a *job in*, demanding that the candidate commit a serious, often felony-level crime as a requirement of admission. It is of interest with regard to our earlier examination of group cohesiveness in the contemporary youth gang, that a number of investigators have demonstrated in experimental laboratory research that the more severe or effortful the initiation, the greater is the target person's attraction to the group he or she is seeking to join (Aronson, 1961; Aronson & Mills, 1959; Goldstein, 1971; Zimbardo, 1960).

Once in the gang, the new member finds that like other types of organizations, there exist rules and codes of membership behavior (Jankowski, 1991). These often include formal or informal understandings about fighting (e.g., hand-to-hand, no weapons for in-gang conflict), personal relations with relatives and lovers, consumption of drugs, meeting place behavior, leadership abuse of power, leadership change processes, offense-punishment specifications and, given their status as hyperadolescents, great concern with appropriate dress and appearance. As noted below, most of the time "ganging" is no more than typical adolescent hanging out. At not infrequent times, however, it is constituted of illegal behaviors—selling drugs, liquor, auto parts, guns, and electronic equipment, protection racketeering, arson or other demolition, running numbers, cockfights, and gambling, and as we discuss at length shortly, engaging as individuals or in subgroups in muggings, burglaries, assaults, murder, and other forms of criminal aggression. It is clear in these last regards that delinquent acts in general and violence in particular are made more frequent by gang membership. It is not the case (or it is not only the case) that the more aggression-prone youths are attracted to gang membership, hence explaining why individual delinquency rates are higher for gang-affiliated as compared to non-gang-affiliated youths. Instead, this escalation in criminal activity appears to occur *because* of gang membership, (Rutter, Giller & Hagell, 1998; Thornberry et al., 1993; Esbensen & Huizinga, 1993) in a manner quite consistent with the subcultural delinquent gang theories examined earlier in this chapter, and also in a manner consistent with the repeated finding that, unlike criminal acts perpetrated by adults—most of whom commit their crimes alone— crime by juveniles is in the large majority of instances a group phenomenon (Miller, 1975; Zimring, 1981). As Thornberry, et al. (1993) note, the core explanatory process appears to be one of "social facilitation." Howell (1995) comments in this connection:

> The social facilitation model also was supported in the examination of offense type categories . . . both transient and stable gang members showed higher rates only when they were active gang members. Violent offenders' rates were at least twice as high while they were gang members than before and after [their] gang participation. (p. 266)

Further, that such peer-mediated social facilitation may transpire via processes of modeling by peers of antisocial behavior, pressure from peers to engage in these actions, and differential reinforcement by peers when one has done so.

How do they leave? They may jump out, fade out, or relocate. They may marry-out, age-out, and find employment in the legitimate economy. They may shift to individual or organized crime. Many go to prison. Some die.

What do gangs do? Mostly they just "hang out," engaging in the diverse interpersonal behaviors characteristic of almost all adolescents. Approximately a third of them, those who are members of so-called "instrumental" gangs—rather than the more typical, neighborhood-protecting "cultural" gangs—will be involved in the illegal drug trade. Most often, the nature of such involvement will be at the lower, least profitable, and most dangerous levels of such business, e.g., street seller, runner, lookout. In order to claim and topographically define their turf or territory, members of "cultural" gangs may make (sometimes extensive) use of graffiti— often in the form of a wall painting of the gang's name, a member's name, or the gang's symbol. Graffiti may also be used to challenge or show contempt for a rival gang, by crossing out the latter's graffiti, or by drawing it oneself but backwards or upside-down. As part of its central effort to create both we-ness (within the gang) and difference (from other gangs), gang members will often incorporate distinctive colors or color combinations within their dress, make use of special hand signs as a means of communicating, and engage in representing, e.g., wearing one's clothes in such a manner that either the left or right side of one's body is emphasized. A report by the Illinois State Police (1989) captures well these (often highly elaborate) efforts at creating positive distinctiveness:

> The Discipline Nation and their affiliates...refer to themselves as the Folks, their major insignia is the Six Pointed Star, and their dress is 'right.' Their basic color is black and if they wear an earring it will be in the right ear. They wear their hat tilted to the right and one of their favorite hats is the blue Civil War cap, they will wear one glove on the right hand, they may have one pocket on the right side turned inside out and it will be dyed in the gang's color or colors, they will roll up the right pants leg, they may have two of the fingernails on the right hand colored with the gang's colors, the hood of their sweatshirt will be dyed with the gang's colors, their shoes will either be colored or the laces of the right shoe will be in the gang's color, their belt buckle will be loose on the right side, and they may wear a bandanna in the gang's colors anywhere on the right side of their body. (pp. 9–10)

What else do gangs do? On occasion they fight, act aggressively, behave violently. While the absolute amount of such behavior is small, its effect on the chain of media response, public perception of gang youth behavior, and police and public agency counter-measures is quite substantial. In the section which follows we will examine more fully the sources, scope and impact of such gang behavior.

GANG VIOLENCE

Violent behavior perpetrated by gang youth in the United States will be understood best if viewed first in the context of the larger American society. The levels, forms and distal, if not proximal causes of aggression by gang youth appear largely to parallel and reflect the levels, forms, and causes of aggression in general in the United States. Such societal aggression, it appears, has consistently risen in recent decades within each major facet of American society—its streets (Goldstein & Segall, 1983; Federal Bureau of Investigation 1998), its homes (Federation of Child Abuse & Neglect, 1990), its schools (Goldstein & Conoley, 1997), and its mass media (J. Goldstein, 1998). Acts of violence perpetrated by youths in gangs should be viewed not as a phenomenon apart but, instead, as yet one more manifestation of behavior trends which characterize so much of life in contemporary America.

The delinquent gang of yesteryear (Thrasher , 1927/1963) committed acts of theft, burglary and perhaps vandalism. While there occurred (very) occasional within- or between-gang fighting, such behaviors were markedly uncommon (Puffer, 1912; Thrasher, 1927/1963). It is no wonder that Thrasher termed such gangs, at their worst, to be "predatory play groups." At about mid-century, however, matters began to change. The 1950s were the years of the gang rumble and its variants. S. Gardner (1983) observes:

> The gangs of the 1950s engaged in big fights called rumbles, which had definite arrangements and rules to be followed. Times, places, and uses of weapons were agreed upon in advance by the war council or leadership of the two warring gangs. Usually, the location chosen would be a deserted area of the city, where the police were not likely to discover them. In those days, gangs fought each other

with bats, bricks, clubs, and chains. Occasionally, someone flashed a switchblade or used a homemade zip gun. (p. 23)

Their purposes were diverse:

> ...to inflict humiliation and insult on the opposing group...to increase the victor's reputation and status...to regain territory [and] sometimes to gain new territories...to re-establish discipline...[in response to] boredom and apathy. (New York City Youth Board, 1960, p. 83)

Such in-group versus out-group fighting between entire gangs or gang members did occur, though their frequency and resultant damage were often exaggerated by the mass media, and sometimes by the participating youth themselves. Not infrequently, gang members anticipated such experiences with considerable ambivalence but, under considerable peer pressure as well as an overriding need to maintain "rep," proceeded to fight nevertheless. Sometimes, under rep-maintaining circumstances, the rumble was avoided. Spergel (1964) notes:

> Youngsters may literally pray silently that something will occur to prevent them from reaching their destination. Consequently, almost any excuse to avoid contact with the opposing group may be utilized. The appearance of the worker, the arrival of the police, or a sudden flat tire on a car which was to take the group into enemy territory may be sufficient to prevent the spontaneous or planned attack. (p. 115)

Klein and Maxson (1989) similarly note: "In the 1950s and 1960s, gang members talked much about their fighting episodes, but [homicide] data from several projects revealed their bark to be worse than their bite." (p. 218)

Intergang-member fighting took a variety of forms. W. B. Miller (1975) offered the following subtyping of such assaultive gang member behaviors:

- Planned rumble, a prearranged encounter between sizeable rival groups
- Rumble, an encounter between sizeable rival groups
- Warfare, a continuing series of retaliatory engagements between members of rival groups
- Foray, in which smaller bands of youths engage rival bands
- Hit, in which smaller bands of youths engage one or two rivals
- Fair fight, in which a single gang member engages a single rival

Sometimes, fighting between two gangs extended over long time periods and several separate altercations. Horowitz (1987) comments;

> In seeking to protect and promote their reputations, gangs often engage in prolonged 'wars,' which are kept alive between larger fights by many small incidents and threats of violence. Following each incident one gang claims precedence, which means that the other group must challenge them if they want to retain their honor and reassert their reputation. (p. 94)

In a manner similarly tied to "honor," and just as Levine, Moreland and Ryan (1998) have shown that relationships *within* non-gang groups (conflict, cohesiveness, etc.) influence behavior toward outgroup members, Moore (1991) suggests that a portion of intergang violence originates in the efforts of one clique within a gang attempting to match or outdo the out-group-directed violence of another (often earlier) clique within their own gang.

Gradually into and through the 1970s and 1980s, the levels and forms of gang violence in the United States changed for the worse in parallel, as we noted earlier, with the levels and forms of violence elsewhere on the American scene. Whereas the Roxbury Project (Miller, 1958), Group Guidance Project (Klein, 1971), and Ladino Hills Project (Klein, 1971) gang intervention programs of the 1950s and 1960s collectively revealed almost no homicides and only modest amounts of other types of gang violence, there were 81 gang-related homicides in Chicago in 1981, 351 such deaths in Los Angeles in 1980, and over 1500 in Los Angeles during the 1985–89 period (Gott, 1989). Spergel et al. (1989) report that only about 1 % of all violent crime committed in Chicago was perpetrated by gang members. The seriousness of such figures, however, resides not only in their relative increase from past years, but also, and especially, in their nature—primarily homicide and aggravated assault. Such violent offences, Spergel et al. (1989) observe, are three times more likely to be committed by gang members than by non-gang delinquents, a finding also reported by Friedman, Mann, & Friedman (1975) and Tracy (1979).

In companion with this growth in the level or intensity of violence by gang youths, there appeared changes in its very forms as the United States moved into the 1990s. The rumble, warfare, and fair fight of earlier eras faded and largely disappeared, to be replaced by the:

- Show by, in which a clique or subgroup of a gang drives through a rival gang's neighborhood to flash their weapons intimidatingly
- Drive by, in which a clique or subgroup of a gang drives through a rival gang's neighborhood and actually uses (fires) their weapons
- Swarming, also known as home intrusion or push-in, in which a clique or subgroup of a gang forcefully invades a private home and threaten/assault its occupants while committing theft of their property
- Wilding, in which a loosely-organized subgroup of gang youths destroy property and assault unknown-to-them citizens in what appears to be random violence
- Bashing/slashing, in which unknown-to-them citizens are attacked by bat or razor, purportedly as part of a gang initiation ritual.

Reminiscent of the risky shift (Myers, 1978), group polarization (Lamm & Myers, 1978) and groupthink (Janis & Mann, 1977) phenomena identified in the context of group dynamics research, Klein (1969) suggests that the gang may *as a gang* engage in higher levels of aggression than desired by any of the individual members. He comments:

> The gang inadvertently leads to violence because of a 'shared misunderstanding' that leads each member to assume that peer norms call for greater involvement than he himself would undertake . . . combined with status anxiety that prevents members from testing the limits of the presumed group norms for fear of seeming 'chicken,' this may result in commitment to mutually undesired activities . . . As Spergel (1965) has described it, 'a dozen youngsters suddenly find themselves walking down the street to a fight, and eight or ten or even all of them, individually may be wondering why he is there.' (p. 115) (p. 1443)

Sanders (1994) describes a similar risky-shift emergent-norm event in his depiction of the evolution of a drive-by shooting that began with an innocent ride by a gang member and his girlfriend, gathered into the car additional gang members and weaponry, and evolved into a hunt for rival gang members, and culminated in a lethal shooting.

For most of the 1990s, gang-related homicides continued to increase precipitously. Block et al. (1996) reported a fivefold jump from 1987 to 1994 in Chicago, and such deaths doubled during this time span in Los Angeles. Along with a dip in crime in general, gang perpetrated homicides declined somewhat towards the end of this decade. It remains to be determined whether such a dip is spurious, or the beginnings of a mini-trend.

The weight of evidence combines to suggest that delinquent gangs in America are indeed behaving in a more violent manner in recent years (Block et al., 1996; National Youth Gang Center, 1998). Nevertheless, it is important to note that such an apparent increase may derive, at least in part, from artifactual sources. Media interest in youth gangs ebbs and flows, and tends to be accentuated in direct proportion to youth violence levels. The contemporary increase in such behaviors may partially be just such a media-interest effect. The likelihood of this possibility is enhanced by a second potential artifact, following from the fact that by far the majority of the current gang-relevant information that is available comes from police sources. It is possible that information regarding increased gang violence is, in part, also an artifact of more, and more intensive, police department gang intelligence unit activity.

None the less, even given its ebb and flow, violence by youth gangs is very much with us in the United States today. While most of it is directed by gang members toward persons or groups (gangs) outside of their own gang, considerable amounts of aggression occur on an intragang basis. Miller, Geertz & Cutter (1968) examined this phenomenon, and set its occurrence at 70 % of all gang member aggression. Of the 1395 aggressive acts recorded during their observational period, 7 % were physical attacks, and 65 % were derogations, devaluations or some other directly hostile statement. Such within-gang aggression may be part of the initiation to membership, when gang rules or codes are not followed, or as part of the resignation from the gang process.

Though the substantial literature on gang violence refers in the very large majority of instances to violence by male gang members, female members may also be of clenched fists and even blood on their hands. True, their rates of violent offending are consistently much lower than that of their male counterparts. Block et al. (1996) report that between 1965 and 1994, the male-to-female gang member arrest ratio was 15:1 for non-lethal violence, and that in only 1.1 % of gang-related homicides were the perpetrator(s) female. None the less, Moore and Hagedorn (2001) observe:

> Some might conclude from these data that female gang members are not violent enough to be of concern. However, an 11-city survey of eighth graders undertaken in the mid-1990s found that more than 90 % of both male and female gang members reported having engaged in one or more violent acts in the previous 12 months (Esbensen & Osgood, 1997). The researchers found that 78 % of female gang members reported being involved in gang fights, 65 % reported carrying a weapon for protection, and 39 % reported attacking someone with a weapon (Deschenes & Esbensen, 1999).

BASES FOR INCREASED VIOLENCE

Elsewhere we have presented an extended rationale for the value of conceptualizing of aggression, as a multicausal, complexly determined, primarily learned set of behaviors (Goldstein, 1989). Conceptualizing aggression in this manner, we believe, both more accurately captures its diverse origins, and provides substantially enhanced opportunity (since its source is not located in its entirety in the perpetrator) for its remediation. In the present section, which seeks to identify bases for the increased levels of contemporary gang violence in particular, we will seek to take a similarly complex, multicausal position. Thus, the bases enumerated and discussed below are to be seen more as an additive combination of likely sources, and less as alternative explanations. It will also be apparent that the sources offered here are, as a group, consistent with the interactionist philosophy growing in popularity in contemporary psychology, a philosophy which holds that human behavior springs co-jointly from characteristics of the individual actor and qualities of his or her environment.

Environmental Enhancers

Personal history

I earlier noted the broader societal context from which many youth come, namely the poorer, more disorganized, more chaotic, and more stressful areas of America's urban, suburban, and rural scenes. These are, as Klein (1969) observed, often neighborhoods and regions with minimal economic opportunity, and cultural norms supportive of gang involvement—particularly its aggressive component. This facilitation of gang member aggression by supportive cultural norms was shown in Spergel's (1964) comparison of "Haulberg" (theft-oriented norms), "Racketville" (racket-oriented norms), and "Slumtown" (conflict-oriented norms), as well as by R. Horowitz's (1987) study of community tolerance for such antisocial gang behavior. Their more immediate, familial, context is also frequently generative of aggressive gang involvement. Knox (1998) conducted a survey of over 1000 members of Chicago-area youth gangs, and found that 77 % of them had one or more family members who belonged to a gang. Forty-two percent had been physically assaulted by a family member, and a like number had perpetrated such assaults themselves. These youngsters averaged ten fights each year, experienced daily anger control problems, and 68 % claim to have shot at someone. The most basic tenets of contemporary psychological theory place prime emphasis on social learning, on the teachings one derives from one's environment. It is clear that for many gang youths, this environment is daily infused with both gang presence and high and repeated levels of violent behavior.

Drugs

The major environmental enhancers of contemporary gang violence—in addition to the heightened general levels of aggression in American society, as well as in the youths' immediate settings—appear to be drugs, territory, and guns. Approximately one-third of gang members are involved to greater or lesser degree in drug distribution (National Youth Gang Center, 2000). To an increasing degree, fighting is over drug selling and economic territory and less about turf ownership and physical territory, though the latter still fuel the majority of violent incidents. Hagedorn (1998) relevantly comments:

> ...many gangs now operate as well-armed economic units inside a vastly expanded informal economy, replacing factory work for young males with jobs selling drugs... The old turf or neighborhood, which was once a place to protect, has for some gangs become little more than a market. (p. 368)

Competition for drug markets, at least in some regions of the United States, appears in fact to be an especially important source of gangs as aggressors. Hagedorn (1998) notes further:

> With the introduction of cocaine into drug markets, guns were needed for self-protection, and an 'arms race' ensued... Fagan (1990) concurs, although he adds that gang drug-related violence may also be the result of the drug trade recruiting more individuals with a proclivity to violence. (p. 380)

Both Maxson, Gordon, and Klein (1989) and Miller (1975) have independently reported that approximately 10 % of drug trafficking crimes involve serious levels of violent behavior. Maxson and Klein (1996) found that depending upon how "gang-related" is defined, between 29 and 41 % of all gang-related homicides in Los Angeles had some drug involvement. Drugs, guns, gangs, and violence appear to be a common combination.

Territory

The traditional major source of gang violence—territoriality—continues to be a relevant concern. Physically, turf usually means one's neighborhood, but can translate as one's street, block, shopping mall, park, skating rink, or other entity or place. Though enhanced mobility off of one's turf via use of automobiles, dispersal of many school-age youths to schools out of their home areas as a result of desegregation efforts, and enhanced focus on economic rather than physical territory, have all taken place, many gangs continue to mark, define, claim, protect and fight over their turf. Vigil (1988) quotes one gang youth who powerfully makes this point:

> The only thing we can do is build our own little nation. We know that we have complete control in our community. Its like we're making our stand... We're all brothers and nobody fuck with us... We take pride in our little nation and if any intruders enter, we get panicked because we feel our community is being threatened. The only way is with violence. (p. 131)

With whom do they fight? Spergel et al. (1989) observe:

> Propinquity emerges as a critical factor in motivations for gang conflict. Of 188 gang incidents between 32 gangs in Philadelphia... (Homicides, stabbings, shootings and gang fights), 60 % occurred between gangs who shared a common

boundary and another 23 % between gangs whose territories were two blocks or less apart. Only two incidents occurred between groups whose turfs were separated by more than 10 blocks. (Ley, 1976, pp. 262–263)

Miller (1982) suggests that such territorial defense seeks to protect both identification and control, and can be manifested in three types of claimed rights by the defending (or attacking) gang members:

1. Ownership rights, in which gang members claim, and are willing to fight for, ownership of the entire property and all activity within it, including who may enter, and who may leave.
2. Occupancy rights, in which gangs engage in shared use of a given territory under specified conditions, e.g., when, for how long, for what purpose.
3. Enterprise monopoly rights, in which gangs claim exclusive rights to conduct certain criminal activities (theft, drug-selling, etc.) within a specified territory.

Among the several antecedents to gang violence considered here, territorial protection looms especially large. Block (1985), for example, found that over a recent 3-year period, the majority of the gang-related homicides they identified were over turf ownership and rights. Further, most such lethality occurred at or near disputed turf boundaries. Consistent with such finding, Sanders (1994) reports that 75 % of the victims of gang-related homicides were rival gang members.

Guns

There are 190 million privately owned guns in the United States including over 65 million handguns. Since 1900, over 750,000 American civilians have been killed by privately owned guns. Each year, there are 200,000 gun related injuries and approximately 20,000 gun related deaths: 3000 by accident, 7000 by homicide, 9000 by suicide. Guns are involved in two out of every three murders in America, one-third of all robberies, and one-fifth of all aggravated assaults. Such remarkable levels and use of gun weaponry have major implications for both the level and lethality of American gang violence. The gang rumbles of decades ago, whatever their group or individual expressions, typically involved utilization of fists, sticks, bricks, bats, pipes, knives, and an occasional home-made zip gun. The geometric proliferation of often sophisticated (automatic and semi-automatic) guns in America, and their ready availability have changed matters considerably. Klein and Maxson (1989) put it well:

> Does the ready access to guns explain much of the increase in violence? The notion here is that more weapons yield more shootings; these, in turn, lead to more 'hits'; and these, in turn, lead to more retaliations in a series of reciprocal actions defending honor and territory ... The theory is that firearms have been the teeth that transform bark into bite. (p. 219)

These several speculations associating gangs, guns, and violence are well buttressed by relevant data. Bjerregaard and Lizotte (1990, reported in Howell, 1993) found that gang members were significantly more likely to own a gun than were non-members, more likely to have peers who owned a gun, and more likely to carry a gun outside their home.

Gang Member Qualities

Demographics

There appears to be a number of characteristics of contemporary American gang members which, when combined with the environmental enhancers just described, contribute importantly to the observed increases in current gang violence. Two such characteristics are straightforwardly demographic—more gangs, and older gang members. Both Maxson, Gordon and Klein (1989) and Spergel et al. (1989) have speculated that these qualities may themselves help account for the apparently heightened levels of gang violence. There may also be a relevant weapons by gang member age interaction:

> The older age of gang members may also be responsible for greater use of sophis-
> ticated weaponry and consequent violence. More and better weaponry may be
> [more] available to older teenagers and young adults than to juveniles. The me-
> dian age of the gang homicide offender has been 19 years . . . in Chicago for the
> past ten years (Spergel, 1985). Los Angeles data (Maxson, Gordon & Klein, 1983)
> and San Diego police statistics (San Diego Association of State Governments,
> 1982) also indicate that older adolescents and young adults are mainly involved
> in gang homicide. Younger gang members are engaged in a pattern of gang
> assault which leads to less lethal consequences. (Spergel et al., 1989)

Honor

Honor, and its several related qualities—machismo, self-esteem, status, power, heart, rep-long gang youth characteristics purported to contribute importantly to overt aggression, perhaps does so even more so today. W. B. Miller (1982) wonders if honor has become less of a factor in the etiology of gang member aggression. As such aggression has changed in form and frequency, from intergang rumbles defending local turf to individual or small group acts of mugging, robbery or other "gain" or "control" behaviors, perhaps, he asserts, the protection and enhancement of "rep" becomes less focal. We would posit the opposite. Gardner (1983) has noted in this context, "With few resources available to poor urban young people, a repu-tation for being tough and a good fighter is one of the only ways to attain status" (p. 27). A. K. Cohen (1966) and W. B. Miller (1958) have offered concurring obser-vations. It is a sad commentary on America's priorities, but we believe that such resources have become even scarcer in the years since Gardner's observation, the potential status-enhancing avenues available to our low-income youth even fewer, and hence the need to seek such enhancement by means designated by the larger society as illegal or inappropriate—including overt aggression—even greater.

Sociopathy

One further gang-member characteristic that may be relevant in seeking to un-derstand increased levels of contemporary gang violence is sociopathy. While "sociopathy" is no longer used as an official DSM diagnostic category, it remains both a term extant in the criminology literature, and a label communicating trait and behavioral information. Thus, we have elected to employ it here. The sociopath has been variously described as an individual who is aggressive, reckless, cruel to others, impulsive, superficial, callous, irresponsible, cunning, self-assured (Magdid & McKelvey, 1987); who fails to learn by experience, is unable to form meaningful relationships, is chronically antisocial, unresponsive to punishment, unable to experience guilt, is self-centered, and lacks a moral sense (Gray & Hutchison, 1964); is unreliable, untruthful, shameless, shows poor judgement, is highly egocentric (Cleckly, 1964); is unable to show empathy or genuine concern for others, manipulates others toward satisfying his own needs, shows a glib sophistication and superficial sincerity (Hare, 1976); is loveless and guiltless (McCord & McCord, 1964); and shows a particular deficiency in perspective taking or taking the role of other persons (Gough, 1948). In 1967, Yablonsky asserted that "The violent gang structure recruits its participants from the more sociopathic youths living in the disorganized slum community." (p. 189) He adds that:

> The selection of violence by the sociopathic youth in his adjustment process is not difficult to understand. Violent behavior requires limited training, personal ability, or even physical strength. Because violence is a demonstration of easily achieved power, it becomes the paramount value of the gang. (Yablonsky, 1967, p. 199)

Reuterman (1975) has similarly observed that "adolescent residents of slum areas who exhibit these traits tend to constitute the membership of violent gangs." (p. 41). Thompson, Brownfield, and Sorenson (1998) in fact found that youths high on their "index of at-risk behaviors," based upon drug use, binge drinking, police contact, seatbelt non-use, and related criteria, are 20 times more likely to become engaged in gang fighting than are youths scoring low on this index. If Fahlberg (1979), Magdid and McKelvey (1987) and Rutter (1980) are correct in their contention that early childhood failures of bonding and attachment lie importantly at the roots of such sociopathy, and that societal conditions in America of the 1980s and 1990s are promotive of such failure, then there may now exist an increased likelihood of sociopathic individuals developing. We refer in particular here to the several manifestations of dysfunctional family life currently apparent.

> Because of necessity or desire, more and more mothers are returning to work, many just weeks after the birth of their babies. Parents need to know that this may be putting their children at risk for unattachment. Other factors can contribute to faulty infant attachment: high divorce rates, day-care problems, lack of a national parent leave policy, epidemic teenage pregnancies, too-late adoptions, the foster care system. (Magdid & McKelvey, 1987, p. 4)

We wish to avoid circularity here. If sociopathic individuals tend to behave aggressively, and more aggression by gang youth seems apparent, we do not by any means necessarily have evidence that sociopathy has itself increased. However, we are asserting, given the apparently increased presence of the conditions held to give rise to sociopathic youths, that such is not an improbable speculation. Yablonsky (1967) has often been criticized in the academic literature on gangs for purportedly

Table 4.1 Possible provocations to aggression

Exterior provocations	Interior provocations
Bad looks	Leader power needs
Rumors	Compensation for Inadequate self-esteem
Territorial boundary disputes	Acting-out to convince self of potency
Disputes over girls	Acting-out to obtain group affection
Out of neighborhood parties	Acting-out to retaliate against fantasized aggression
Drinking	
Narcotics	
Ethnic tensions	

holding that most gang youths and most gang violence have sociopathic roots. We are less declarative and more speculative here. It may be, we wonder, that his observations fit the contemporary American gang even better than the gang youth Yablonsky observed earlier and, some hold, (mis)described.

Immediate Provocations

We have examined both the contextual features (family, drugs, territory, weapons) and youth characteristics (number, age, honor, sociopathy) which collectively may function as the distal explanations of heightened gang violence in contemporary America. What of its proximal or immediate causes? What are the common provocations or triggers that spark the fuse? No doubt triggers change with culture, time and place, but Table 4.1 (a 1960 list from the New York City Youth Board) appears remarkably current. The reader should note that, not unlike the contextual versus youth causal dichotomy we have employed in this chapter, the Youth Board separately identified "exterior" and "interior" provocations.

These are, of course, but a sampling of possible provocations to aggression. Moore et al. (1978) demonstrated that gang youths are not infrequently hyper-vigilant in their attention to possible slights, and Dodge and Murphy have (1984) shown that such attention often leads to misperceptions of hostile intent and related misinterpretations of neutral events. As the New York City Youth Board (1960) observes:

> The possibilities [for provocation] are almost limitless since the act itself in many cases is relatively unimportant, but rather is seen in a total context of the past, the present, and the future. Further, the act is seen in a total context of its stated, implied, and imagined meanings, all of which are subject to distortion by the groups, individuals, and the gangs. (p. 69)

Having considered the nature, sources, and immediate provocations for aggressive behavior by gang youth and acknowledging, as have a number of gang researchers, that there will always be slight increases and decreases over time in the frequency of such behavior, it is appropriate to assert that, as is true for aggression in America at large, the overall trend is unfortunately quite probably upward. Howell (1995) observes in this regard:

> Is the violent youth gang problem growing? Yes. Surveys conducted over the past decade... have found gangs in more and more cities. The gang problem is also increasing from the standpoint of more violent offenses being committed by gang members, more serious injuries, and more lethal weapons employed. (p. 270)

Yet, its scope and impact ought not to be overstated. Some people, overwhelmingly other gang members, die at the hands of it, as does on occasion an innocent bystander. None the less, Klein's (1969) wise conclusion of over 30 years ago, still largely holds true today.

> Gang violence exists; it exists in almost every large urban area; it represents a continuing social problem and is curiously resistant to change efforts. However, it seems clear that the public view of gang violence as an ever present, widely threatening phenomenon simply does not fit the facts. The likeliest victim of gang violence is the gang member himself. The general public is bothered by the myth more than by the realities of gang behavior. Violence constitutes a small portion of gang activity and is commonly of low seriousness in its physical consequences. If the truth be known, the greatest damage caused by gang members is to their own futures as husbands, fathers, and breadwinners.... The gang member is the victim of his own gang membership. (p. 1449)

I have in this chapter examined a broad array of gang relevant concerns—the history of ganging in the United States, including: its diverse definitions and manifestations; the major theories of gang development and behavior; gang member demographics; youth motivations for joining and remaining a member; and typical gang member behaviors, highlighting here aggressive behaviors in particular. Across these several topics, we have sought to underscore the relevance of in-group versus out-group considerations. For many youths, the gang is "us," and everyone else is "them." Gangs and cliques within gangs often function as cohesive peer groups, family, and community combined. In-group favoritism and out-group discrimination biases are not only likely to operate under such circumstances, but their strength and both perceptual and behavioral consequences may be highly accentuated. Clearly, the study of the contemporary American youth gang offers a living laboratory for advancing our understanding of in-group–out-group processes and their consequences.

Chapter 5

THE MOB

...he was repeating the phrase, It's going off, it's going off. Everyone around him was excited. It was an excitement that verged on being something greater, an emotion more transcendent—joy at the very least, but more like ecstasy. There was an intense energy about it; it was impossible not to feel some of the thrill....There was more going on than I could assimilate: there were violent noises constantly—something breaking or crashing—and I could never tell where they were coming from. In every direction something was happening. I have no sense of sequence.

The group crossed a street, a major intersection. It had long abandoned the pretense of invisibility and had reverted to the arrogant identity of the violent crowd, walking, without hesitation, straight into the congested traffic, across the hoods of the cars, knowing they would stop. At the head of the traffic was a bus, and one of the supporters stepped up to the front of it, and from about six feet, hurled something with great force—it wasn't a stone, it was big and made of metal, like the manifold of a car engine—straight into the driver's windshield...The sound of the shattering windshield...was a powerful stimulant, physical and intrusive, and it had been the range of sounds, of things breaking and crashing, coming from somewhere in the darkness, unidentifiable, that was increasing steadily the strength of feeling of everyone around me.

...Someone came rushing at the bus with a pole...and smashed a passenger window. A second crashing sound. Others came running over and started throwing stones and bottles with great ferocity. They were, again, in a frenzy....A window shattered, and another shattered, and there was screaming inside....All around me people were throwing stones and bottles, and I felt afraid for my own eyes.

I looked behind me and I saw that a large vehicle had been overturned, and that further down the street flames were issuing from a building...there was now the sound of sirens, many sirens, different kinds, coming from several directions. The city is ours, Sammy said, and he repeated the possessive each time with greater intensity: It is ours, ours, ours. (From *Among the thugs*, Buford, 1991, pp. 89–92)

As size and emotional intensity grow, groups are redefined as mobs. For Chaplin (1985), a mob is a crowd acting under strong emotional conditions that often lead to violence or illegal acts. Milgram and Toch (1969) describe the actions of such a collective as "group behavior which originates in its course of development, and which depends on interstimulation among participants" (p. 507). For Staub and Rosenthal (1994), a crowd is a collection of people who share a common interest and whose emotions may be easily aroused; a mob is a crowd acting under strong emotional conditions that often lead to violence or illegal acts. A riot is an instance of mob violence, with the destruction of property or looting, or violence against people. Forsyth (1999) similarly defines a mob as an emotionally charged crowd. Staub and Rosenthal (1994) have drawn a distinction between conserving mobs, who fight to maintain the status quo, and reforming mobs, whose violence seeks to change it. Momboisse (1970) speaks of four types of mobs: escape, acquisitive, expressive, and aggressive. Thus a mob may be a panicked collective seeking safety by fleeing from some real or imagined threat. Or mob formation and expression may take such concrete benign forms as a congregation at an emotional religious meeting or an aroused audience at an athletic event or a rock concert. Far less benign mobs may emerge in the form of a collective: urging a potential jumper suicide; a loosely affiliated, ganglike group of adolescent males engaged in wilding, swarming, or other violent behavior, or a full-scale riot destructive of property and persons in a community, prison, or other setting.

In the United States, each era in its history helped shaped the particular forms of mob and related collective aggression that occurred. As the nation began moving westward in the late 1700s, frontier settlements and a frontier mentality prevailed. Independence, self-reliance, and impatience with the still poorly formulated civil and criminal laws of the nation were all characteristic. Justice was often "frontier justice" which meant "taking the law into one's own hands" by groups of local citizenry. Hanging for horse thievery, "riding undesirables out of town," and similar unorganized group aggressiveness may be viewed as the informal beginnings of what, especially immediately after the Civil War, became the vigilante movement. Frontier living, its purported glamor in the mass media notwithstanding, was often very difficult economically, giving rise not only to criminal gangs, bank robbers, counterfeiters, and other early forms of group and individual crime in America, but also to aggressive behavior by many of its non-criminal, rural citizens. Shay's Rebellion in the State of Massachusetts (1786–1787), the Whiskey Rebellion in Pennsylvania (1794), and the series of similar incidents initiated by such groups as the Grangers, the Greenbackers, and the Farmer's Alliance, are examples of the several economically engendered agrarian uprisings characteristic of the day.

Beginning in the early 1800s, and peaking during 1830–1860, a major new feature was added to the American scene, and to aggression in the United States. This was a lengthy period of great immigration, as thousands and then millions of persons from diverse national, religious, and ethnic backgrounds migrated to the United States. The ingredients in this great, human melting pot often mixed poorly, and high levels of individual and collective aggression were the frequent result— particularly in America's cities.

The Civil War took place in the United States during 1861–1865, pitting Northerner against Southerner and, at times, neighbor against neighbor and even cousin against cousin, in bitter, lethal conflict. Its price was high, and well beyond the actual war casualties (617,000 dead and 375,000 injured), for out of this war grew forces which engendered new and virulent forms of group aggression throughout the country. During the postwar reconstruction period, and stemming from war-related animosities, feuding, lynching, and high levels of vigilante activities occurred. The feud, primarily a phenomenon of the Southern mountain states, was a type of interfamily or interclan guerrilla warfare. Much more malignant in its effects was lynching. Here, unorganized, ephemeral mobs, in a deindividuated expression, usually of anti-Black aggression, would capture and hang usually guilt-less Black persons. It is the shame of America that 4850 recorded lynchings occurred during the period 1882–1927.

Vigilante aggression became more organized. Its targets included Blacks, but also many other (usually minority) groups. Among the 326 known vigilante groups recognized as having existed, perhaps the most infamous were the Ku Klux Klan, the Bald Knobbers, and the White Cappers. The cowboy gang, romanticized in book and movie, also became prominent during this post-Civil-War period. Their specialities, train and bank robberies, while consistently portrayed as flamboyant derring-do by the media, were plain and simple acts of criminal violence.

The Industrial Revolution came to America's burgeoning cities during the late 1800s. It was progress, and brought with it hope, modernization, and economic growth. However, it not infrequently also involved economic exploitation and management–labor violence. Strikes and boycotts grew to become riots, some of them among the bloodiest events in American history. The railroad strike in Pittsburgh in 1877, and the strife in the Pennsylvania coal fields around the Molly Maguire movement at about the same time are two prime examples. Industrial conflict continued at high levels as workers sought to unionize, and especially violent strikes occurred in the Colorado mining industry (1913–1914), and throughout the auto industry during the 1930s. During this extended period, there were 160 separate times in which state or federal troops were called out to intervene in industrial violence.

As has been found to be true in other nations, the level of individual and collective violence within the United States diminished considerably during the two world wars, and during the economic depression in the 1930s. Perhaps both events, war and depression, engender a sufficient sense of being joined against a common enemy, or at least of being caught in similar circumstances, that within-nation/out-group hostility diminishes.

In the middle of the Twentieth century, while labor violence, feuding, vigilante groups, lynching, and the aggression of the frontier West all became largely events of the past, America's affinity with violence continued in new forms. Crime, especially by juveniles, grew both in sheer amount and in its level of aggression. While conservative forces, the traditional instigators of group aggression in the United States, less frequently, or at least less obviously, initiated collective violence, radical forces took their place. In the 1960s, the United States was rocked time and again with student, racial, and antiwar riots, as well as a small number of terrorist events. This last incarnation of group aggression, but not other forms, continued to be evident at infrequent but costly times as the century drew to a close.

This litany of America's violent history would be much less than complete without mention of perhaps its saddest chapter. Starting in Tidewater, Virginia in 1607 and ending in 1890 in Wounded Knee, South Dakota, nearly 300 years of intermittent aggression was perpetrated against the American Indian. It is a history which can never be undone, but, hopefully, is partially being redressed in the America of today.

Indeed, the history of humankind is, in a very great many of its particulars, an accounting of collective aggression in its unending variety of incarnations—mob violence, ethnic cleansing, riots, rebellions, revolutions, torture, warfare, and more.

I focus here on mob aggression in particular, as a phenomenon of interest in its own right, and as a prototype of use for examining and better understanding the many other forms of aggression perpetrated by large groups of persons.

What does mob formation "feel" like? Momboisse (1970) provides a process-oriented sense of mob development and coalescence:

> Mobs are the product of a process of evolution . . . The first step in the transformation of a preconditional and responsive group of individuals into a mob is some climactic event . . . This is the period when the mob "mutters." . . . It [the event] causes a crowd to gather at the scene. Its members mill about like a herd of cattle. The gathering of a crowd automatically causes more onlookers to gather. These persons usually have little if any direct knowledge of the incident which gave rise to the mob . . . Rumors are numerous and spread rapidly . . . As an incident proceeds to attract numbers of individuals, they are pressed together . . . they initiate conversation with strangers . . . Through the milling process, the crowd excites itself more and more. Individuals will break off to warn friends, enlist recruits, pass on rumors . . . and generate excitement. As the crowd grows, so do the rumors, and through social facilitation, increasingly dangerous behavior is encouraged . . . by circular influences, stimulation and restimulation of each other, a high state of collective tension and excitement is built up.
>
> As tension mounts, individuals become less and less responsive to stimulation arising outside the group and respond only to influences from within the crowd itself. This process creates among members of the crowd an internal rapport, a kind of collective hypnosis, in which the individual loses his self-control and responds only to the dictates of the crowd as a whole. The individual loses critical self-consciousness . . . for mob anonymity absolves him of individual responsibility . . . As group wrath generates, symbolic behavior becomes incapable of providing a satisfactory outlet for the feeling-states of the individuals involved. Some form of overt, non-symbolic behavior is imperative. Such overt behavior is, of course, always violent and destructive. (pp. 16–17)

Over the past century, a number of both person-oriented and context-oriented theories have been offered in an effort to understand better such collective behavior. As we examine these formulations, I wish to stress a transactional person–environment view, that group aggression will be best understood and moderated when *both* person and contextual forces are jointly taken into account.

THEORIES OF MOB BEHAVIOR

Contagion Theory

In 1895, Gustave Le Bon published his field-observation-based study *The Crowd*, in which he proposed that the central mechanism governing mob formation and behavior was a process of contagion. Speaking of the "mental unity of crowds" and the "crowd mind," Le Bon (who, relevantly, was a physician) noted that specific behaviors and levels of arousal frequently began with a few individuals in the larger collective and spread throughout the crowd, in a manner he saw as analogous to the transmission of an infectious disease. Germ theory was relatively new and of growing popularity in the physical medicine of Le Bon's era, and it was the central theme of his mob-behavior-contagion theory. Interestingly, and equally a reflection of the predominant views of his times, the great interest in the late Nineteenth century in hypnosis and mesmerism was captured in Le Bon's reliance on suggestibility as the primary mechanism underlying mob contagion.

> Via a suggestibility-driven contagious process in the mass, the individual is radically transformed, loses his or her conscious personality, and it is in the grip of the "law of mental unity of crowds," that primitive, irrational elements emerge . . . What emerges is a collective mind that makes people feel, think, and act in a uniform or homogeneous way. (Kruse, 1986, p. 127)

Though group mind and related disembodied notions about collective behavior have largely passed from the contemporary scene, the credit remains to Le Bon for largely initiating and most certainly accelerating this area of inquiry.

Convergence Theory

A second perspective on mob behavior, convergence theory, holds that rather than a more-or-less random group of individuals becoming a collective through a contagious spread of emotion, mobs are formed by the coming together of people sharing conscious or unconscious needs. Forsyth (1983) describes this viewpoint as one suggesting that

> aggregates are not merely haphazard gatherings of dissimilar strangers, but rather represent the convergence of people with compatible needs, desires, motivations, and emotions. By joining in the group the individual makes possible the satisfaction of these needs, and the crowd situation serves as a trigger for the spontaneous release of previously controlled behaviors. (p. 311)

The convergers may share neighborhood grievances, athletic fandom, religious affiliation, or other "surface" concordances, but the theory speaks more to latent rather than to manifest similarities. For example, in one concrete expression of the convergence perspective on collective behavior, Freud (1922) proposed that people join and remain in collectives to satisfy shared repressed unconscious desires—sexual, aggressive, or otherwise.

Emergent-Norm Theory

Turner, R. C., and Killian (1972) have proposed a third perspective on mob behavior, responsive to their beliefs about the weaknesses of both the contagion and convergence approaches. Regarding contagion, a comprehensive theory needs also to explain the substantial portion of crowd members and bystanders who do not "catch the germ" of intensified emotion. A far as convergence is concerned, R. C. Turner and Killian (1972) hold that for most crowds the degree of attitudinal, emotional, or motivational homogeneity is appreciably lower than convergence theory proposes. Instead, in emergent-norm theory, newly developing guides to belief and behavior come into effect and are enacted by members of the emerging collective. As Horowitz (2001) describes this viewpoint:

> The initial decision to participate entails no necessary intention to engage in violent behavior. For that reason, the meeting can attract a heterogeneous group of participants, only a few of whom need be favorable to violence. Once assembled, the gathering becomes susceptible to malevolent interpretations of chance events or to the spread of rumors of aggressive behavior by opposing groups, which then serve to incite violent behavior on the part of people who joined the crowd out of quite different motives. (p. 287)

A variant of this perspective, Rabbie's (1982) norm-enhancement theory, proposes that rather than the development of new norms in a group context, there is an increase in the perceived legitimacy and salience of normative beliefs and attitudes previously held by the individuals constituting the collective and brought with them to the collective's assemblage.

Mob aggression is complexly determined behavior. The three theories we have briefly sketched should be viewed as complementary perspectives, all of which may be operating concurrently in any given mob-aggression event:

> The three perspectives on collective behavior—convergence, contagion, and emergent-norm theory—are in no sense incompatible with one another...For example, consider the behavior of baiting crowds—groups of people who urge on a person threatening to jump from a building, bridge or tower...Applying the three theories, the convergence approach suggests that only a certain type of person would be likely to bait the victim to leap to his or her death. Those shouts could then spread to other bystanders through a process of contagion until the onlookers were infected by a norm of callousness and cynicism. (Forsyth, 1983, p. 315)

Other psychological perspectives on mob behavior have emerged, and they too should be viewed as additive, not conflicting, in the difficult task of seeking to understand such complex collective behavior. Allport (1924), for example, was particularly interested in debunking such notions as group mind or other like constructs that suggested that the group, mob, or crowd was somehow greater than the sum of its individual members. For him, mob action was straightforwardly a process of the interstimulation, intensification, and social facilitation of the actions of individuals through the presence and actions of the others in the collective: "The individual in the crowd behaves just as he would behave alone, only more so" (Allport, 1924, p. 295).

Sociocultural Theories

Mobs consist of individuals, each of whom has his or her own (even if shared) histories, perceptions, emotions, and motivations. To the degree that these individual characteristics are brought to bear in a collective context, and both shape and are shaped in that context, the mob is a *person* phenomenon, and the three psychological theories we have examined are both relevant and useful. However, as concepts such as contagion, convergence, and emergent norms make clear, these person phenomena unfold in a social and cultural context, a context consisting of forces both within and outside the group. Yes, mob behavior is a psychological phenomenon, but it is also simultaneously very much a sociocultural phenomenon. Stated otherwise, mob aggression is very much a person–environment event. Thus, it is necessary that an accurate and comprehensive view of such behavior fully incorporate an ecological perspective.

The work of Erwin Staub is most useful in this regard. In Staub's (1993) view, the ecological context for mob violence consists of three types of instigating circumstances: non-specific instigators, specific instigators and immediate instigators.

Non-specific instigators, providing broad background facilitation, as it were, include such phenomena as crowding and high ambient temperatures. Indeed, the United States Riot commission (1968) pointed to the consistent presence of large proximate populations, in a real sense a pool of potential rioters, located at the eventual riot scene prior to the riots it studied. It also noted that for 9 of the 18 riots examined, the ambient temperature the day the riot began was 90 °F or higher, and in the high 80s for the remainder. Both crowding and high ambient temperature have also been implicated as nonspecific instigators in prison rioting (Barak-Glantz, 1985).

Specific instigators, in Staub's (1993) view, include in particular such background features of the environmental context as its sociocultural climate and its relative economic vitality. He cites the urban riots of the 1960s as but one of many possible examples of a sociocultural context whose characteristics were conducive to generating riotous behavior:

> The urban riots of the 1960s occurred in a social climate created by the desegregation of the Supreme Court and the civil rights movement. There was an increased awareness of discrimination and injustice, and increased expectation by Black people of improvement in their social and economic conditions. There was also a less punitive climate for intense expressions of Black frustration. (p. 12)

Economic considerations are especially salient background facilitators of subsequent mob violence, but most investigators agree that it is relative, rather than absolute, economic deprivation which is particularly significant (Davies, 1969; Gurr, 1970; Runciman, 1966; Stouffer et al., 1949). While straightforward frustration–aggression thinking would predict collective violence from the absolute deprivations associated with slum living, high unemployment, and similar conditions, a variety of evidence suggests that, rather than such direct effects, riots much more frequently grow from a sense of *relative* deprivation. Relative deprivation is the belief that others are climbing up the economic ladder while oneself is not, or the belief that one's own earlier economic gains are being lost. This sense of blocked opportunity and unjust exclusion from economic gain has been an especially potent specific instigator of riot and rebellion in American history (A. P. Goldstein & Segall, 1983; Gurr, 1989). It is a perspective formalized by Davies (1969) and elaborated on by Perry and Pugh (1978), who observe:

> The J-curve of rising expectations . . . is an attempt to explain why riots and revolutions occur *not* when social deprivation is extreme, but rather in periods of improving social conditions. When social conditions are generally improving, people supposedly expect further improvements in the future. A rising standard of living promotes a sense of optimism and the belief that "tomorrow will

bring better things than today." Unfortunately, the rising expectations of many deprived groups may outstrip their capacity for achievement just when some ultimate goal appears to be close at hand. Desired improvements can rarely be achieved quickly enough to avoid an "intolerable gap" between what people want and what they can actually get. According to Davies (1969), the development of an intolerable gap is a direct cause of collective violence. (p. 151)

Given an ecological context in which non-specific and/or specific background conditions instigative of collective violence exist, a number of *immediate instigators* have been suggested by Staub (1993) as being the events which actually light the fuse. In United States history, such flashpoints or precipitating events have included: the assassination of a respected leader (e.g., Martin Luther King); a judicial decision deemed to be unjust by one or more groups (e.g., the verdict in the criminal trial of the police officers who arrested Rodney King); alleged violations of important community mores (e.g., the purported rapes of white women by black males resulting in lynch mobs); local, state, or federal government decisions or policy enactments (e.g., the commitment to armed-forces expansion in Vietnam and the consequent antiwar riots); the taking away of a previously granted privilege [e.g., as has occurred preceding a number of prison riots (Colvin, 1982)]; and the defeat of one's team, an official refereeing decision, or provocation by opposing fans, at an athletic contest [e.g., as Buford (1991) has described as preceding several European soccer riots].

Staub's (1993) summary view of the contribution of these several ecological characteristics as preconditions and instigators of mob violence is of interest:

> Difficult life conditions can affect a whole society, or a specific group of people. They can take the form of economic problems or decline, political upheaval, or great social changes that create the experience of disorganization and chaos with loss of guiding values and a sense of community. Relative deprivation, the perception of unfair treatment and injustice, and powerlessness in improving one's fate or affecting change also function as background instigators. The easing of repression, discrimination or economic problems can give rise to mob violence by decreasing fear, empowering people and increasing hope which remains essentially unfulfilled. The changes involved in such improvements can themselves contribute to social disorganization. Devaluation or antagonism between groups can create persistent cultural potential for mob violence.
>
> The motivations that arise can vary as a function of instigating conditions and cultural characteristics. The reasons for participation in mob violence can include frustration, hostility, exploding anger and the desire to hurt, the desire for institutional and social change motivated partly by self interest and partly by response to perceived injustice, feelings of connection to and unity with others, feelings of control, power and even intense excitement and peak experience that arise from group processes, or the desire for personal gain. (pp. 17–18)

Staub's (1993) description of mob violence as a dynamic process unfolding through a sequence of non-specific (broad background) specific (environmental context) and immediate (triggering) instigators exemplifies in its sequential structure a manner of conceptualizing such behavior common to several approaches to understanding its sources, nature, and course. Unlike contagion, convergence, and emergent norms, and such phenomena as deindividuation, social facilitation, group polarization, risky shift, and rumor—all of which largely seek to explain group aggression *once its actors are on the scene*—Staub's (1993) view, and other sequential perspectives, speak to sociocultural contexts, both broad and local, distal and proximal, which serve as fertile soil for the growth of mob violence, combining with immediate precipitating events, and leading to consequences and outcomes often sustaining the continuance and escalation of such group aggression. Baron, Kerr, and Miller's (1992) proposed sequence, introduced briefly at the conclusion of Chapter 1, speaks in this unfolding process manner to heightened states of arousal derived from contextual sources, combining with aggression-relevant situational cues in the group's immediate context, sparked into action by an often vivid, dramatic, triggering event, leading to its continuance and escalation, often via modeling or imitation of others present.

Proposed broad background and contextual precursors of collective aggression have been many and varied. Among them, in addition to deprivation, both absolute and, especially, relative, are unresponsive (Lieberman & Silverman, 1970) or incompetent (Horowitz, 2001) authorities, media sensationalism (Waddington, Jones & Critcher, 1987), spread of provocative rumors (Gilje, 1996; Perry & Pugh, 1978), perceived threat (Smelser, 1962), a large population of single, unemployed males (Staub & Rosenthal, 1994), level of expectation that rioting will yield hoped-for change (Olzak, 1992), and a host of other societal, demographic, and sociopsychological phenomena. In the specific instance of mob violence in prison riots, McPhail (1971) suggests such contextual precursors as bad food, poorly ventilated cells, overcrowding, boredom, ill-trained staff, and other poor institutional conditions. Equally diverse have been those events and actions pointed to as purported immediate triggers (Staub & Rosenthal, 1994), flashpoints (Waddingon, Jones & Critcher, 1987), threshold (crossing) acts (Buford, 1991), sparking (Perry & Pugh, 1978), and cuing (Rule, 1988) of mob aggression. In addition to those noted above, also included are killings, arrests, assaults on individuals, unwarranted searches, prohibitions, sighting a particular enemy figure, the appearance of an especially tempting target, and, once the violence has begun, awareness of the numbers of persons already involved, seeing friends and allies under attack, the desecration or flourishing of flags, statues, or other sacred symbols, and similar perceived provocations.

Its broad and immediate content propitious, its initiation begun by one or more triggering events, mob aggression may continue and escalate as a consequence of modeling, arousal, conformity, deindividuation, disinhibition, self-stimulation, self-reinforcement, a feeling of connection or belonging, charismatic leadership, a gain in positive social identity, alleviation of the triggering event stresses, victims' expression of pain and injury, tangible rewards, the vicarious rewards of benefits to one's compatriots, and via an "aggression feeds on aggression" positive feedback loop described by Marsh, Rosser, and Harre (1978) as a component of their deviancy amplification theory (Bandura, 1973; Bohstedt, 1994; Goldstein & Segall, 1983; Rule, 1988)

As in the adjourning stage of any group's life (Tuckman, 1965), riots end. They often end because police or other authority extinguishes the mob violence, re-individuates the rioters, distracts them, disperses them, or isolates their leaders, the participants come to believe they have succeeded in their goals, or simply because they become tired, hurt, disillusioned, or distracted.

The dynamic, unfolding nature of collective aggression is similarly well described by Horowitz (2001), in his sequential depiction of ethnic rioting through stages of background then proximal influences, followed by triggering precipitant events, and then escalating or diminishing once it has begun as a function of yet further identifiable sources. The distal fertile context for ethnic violence, he proposes, frequently consists of such phenomena among the initiating collective as economic decline, substantial in-migration of other ethnic groups, past traditions of the use of aggression, decay in respect for authority, disbelief in the impartiality or efficiency of the police, much to gain by opportunities for looting, and some degree of prior organization for perpetrating violence. Aggression, whether individual or group, is properly construed as a perpetrator–victim duet (Goldstein, 1994). Hence, a central component of the distal background of ethnic rioting is target group qualities, and perpetrator–victim transactional characteristics. Horowitz (2001) comments:

> Violence emerges out of an ongoing relationship between groups and target-group characteristics constitute the irritant in the relationship...If a group has a reputation for being aggressive, if it is regarded as a long-standing enemy, if it has been a recent opponent in warfare, if it presents a political threat, if it possesses external connections that augment its internal strength, or if it is thought to exhibit certain characterological traits, it is more likely to be targeted in violence than if it lacks these characteristics. (p. 151)

Proximal variables that next set the stage for triggering, riot-commencing events are conditions promoting uncertainty, impunity, and justification. As Horowitz (2001) notes, "That vast majority of riots occur when aggressors conclude that ethnic politics are dangerously in flux, that they are likely to be able to use violence without adverse consequences to themselves, and that they are thoroughly warranted in their action" (p. 326). Add available targets, social support from fellow ethnics and a "wink" by government officials, and the stage is fully set. All that is needed for the riot to commence is one or more precipitating, triggering events.

This may take concrete form as rumor. Its contents will be grave, threatening, anxiety-arousing, aggressive and/or sexual, and largely unverifiable. "They" have perpetrated a killing, a rape, a desecration, are on the march, have poisoned our water supply, or some other outrage. At times a smaller, impunity-testing riot may serve as the springboard for a larger, more encompassing such event. The precipitating event may be earlier precipitating events, in a "crisis slide" (Horowitz, 2001) in which a destructive spiral of attack–precipitant–further attack–further precipitant unfolds. Among the most common triggers—each serving to confirm the threatening nature of the target group, mobilize ordinary citizens, and justify the violence they are about to perpetrate—are ethnic processions, demonstrations, and mass meetings, official or unofficial changes in the relative status of the two ethnic groups, strikes reflecting ethnic solidarity, and rumored or actual aggression by the target group. The act precipitates because it enables citizens to count on the participation of others, reassures them that these fellow citizens will be similarly motivated to perpetrate violence toward the target group, and that they will do so in unison. Once the precipitating event has occurred, a lull may take place, of hours or days, to process, plan, and mobilize.

Then the violent action begins. Its perpetrators are almost exclusively males, as typically are the majority of its victims. A common progression, observes Horowitz

(2001), is from attacks on property, such as burning homes or shops, to attack on persons. As the riot continues, its initial instigators are joined by fellow ethnics who hold back at first, in what most certainly appears to be a joint outcome of convergence, contagion, and emergent norms. How intense its fury, and how long its duration is an apparent function of the perceived threat posed by the target group, their resistance, their availability, the perpetrating group's organization and leadership, the "success" of their violence, their exhaustion, and the degree to which extant authorities send permissive signals encouraging continuance, or vigorously intervene. Rioting may or may not spread from its precipitating site, and when it does it may be to a contiguous or non-contiguous area. When the latter occurs, suggests Horowitz (2001), it is either because of overt ratification of violence by the duly constituted authorities, communication about the riot in the mass media, or a new precipitating event at the new location(s). It is not uncommon for there to be "recidivist locations" for ethnic riots, the events returning to and reoccurring in the same regions, cities, or sites over and over gain. Sites tend to be urban, mixed ethnic residential, close to the location of the attacker's homes, and not uncommonly— in a manner directly paralleling juvenile youth gang warring—at the borderlines or boundaries at which the factions respective enclaves (turf) meet. To the degree possible, and again underscoring the planfulness of such violence, sites also tend to be opportunistic and risk aversive. As Horowitz (2001) puts it, "The initial choice of locale is shaped by the rioters' desire to avoid target-group defenses and police deployment." (p. 384)

IRRATIONALITY, RATIONALITY, AND CONTAGION REVISITED

Two broad philosophical perspectives have governed research and speculation about mob aggression since it became a topic of focal concern in the writings of Le Bon (1895), Tarde (1898), and Sighele (1898) over 100 years ago. For these early philosopher–social scientists, and largely continuing to mid-Twentieth century, mob aggression was irrational behavior. I earlier noted, for example Le Bon's (1895) emphasis on crowd mind, loss of conscious personality, suggestibility, paralysis of initiative, planlessness, impulsivity, descent down the ladder of civilization into barbarousness, and primitiveness, much of which purportedly transpired via a process of contagion. Freud (1921/1967) similarly viewed such collective behavior as regressive, unconsciously determined, and irrational, as did McDougall (1908), R. E. Park (1950), and later Doob (1952)—who pointedly described mob action as "a device for going crazy together" (p. 292). So, too, those writers describing such behavior as "primordial" (Geertz, 1973) or "primitive" (Staub & Rosenthal, 1994). Moscovici (1985) captures the irrationalist view well:

> Once men have been drawn together and fused into a crowd, they lose most of their critical sense. This is a result of both fear and a desire to conform. Their consciousness gives way to the thrust of illusions . . . Thus, individuals forming a crowd are borne along by limitless waves of imagination and tossed about by emotions which are strong but have no specific object. The only language they understand is one that bypasses reason . . . (p. 31).

And further:

> Individual thought would seem to be critical, that is, logical and making use of conceptual ideas which are mostly abstract in nature. It is also oriented toward reality ... Nothing, in the long run, is accepted if it cannot be shown to be true, and individual thought is therefore objective. Crowd thinking, on the other hand, would seem to be automatic, being determined by stereotyped associations and remembered cliches ... Le Bon went on saying in every possible way that the masses were unable to use abstract reasoning and that it was consequently pointless to address them with an appeal to a faculty that they simply did not possess. (Moscovici, 1985, p. 94)

Other perspectives, quite opposite to that held by this long line of irrationalists, began to emerge in the mid-Twentieth century. They contained such quite explicitly planful notions as rules of disorder (Gilje, 1996), ritualized aggression (Marsh, Rosser, & Harre, 1978), informal blueprint (Staub & Rosenthal, 1994), rational choice (Bell-Fialkoff, 1996), weighing costs, benefits, and expectations for success (Klandersman, 1984), considering economic and social causes as a reflection of a "situationalist" or "circumstantialist" point of view (Forbes, 1997), and commitment to use of abstract principles (Tilly, 1997). Rule (1988) observed:

> By the mid 1960s, the dominance of collective behavior thinking was decidedly on the wane ... Most often these critics found fault with the picture of riotous or rebellious behavior as 'abnormal' or 'disorganized.' Instead, analysts were beginning to see in crowd action evidence of purposeful response to collective interests ... (p. 112).
>
> By the 1960s ... the notions of the irrationalists ... had lost their attraction as a lens for viewing civil violence. Part of the reason for this shift clearly involved matters of fact and evidence. Views of crowd action as purposeless and of participants in such action as socially disconnected simply did not accord well with accounts that were swelling the empirical literatures as these subjects. (p. 116)

In this same spirit, Gilje (1996) quite explicitly held mobs to be rational collectives seeking, with highly charged actions that are neither capricious nor random, to deal with real grievances. Yes, he acknowledge, the "normal rules of society" are put aside, but new rules are formulated—the group's emergent norms—which guide mob behavior. Gilje's (1996) description of mob rioting in America's colonial times, based on a sample of 150 such events, captures well its adherence to rules of disorder:

> ... the crowd would be about fifty to one-hundred strong. The rioters came from a wide social and economic spectrum within the neighborhood, but were almost always male. Maybe members of the mob had disguises, either blackened faces, like some of their English counterparts, or Indian dress. The crowd limited itself to the destruction of property, such as tearing down a house or jail, and would last at most for a couple of hours ... The owners of the property ordinarily acquiesced in the riot. Indeed, it as almost as both sides, those rioting and those against the rioting, knew the prescribed rituals and understood their role in them. (p. 25)

An historically frequent exemplar of mob violence, the ethnic riot, has in its prototypical unfolding sketched above just such a core quality of "rational mayhem" or "planned chaos," i.e., a more or less predictable course, flow, or rhythm, some of whose ingredients *appear* to be random, chaotic, and irrational. Such events are often lethal attacks by the members of one ethnic group upon another, designed to degrade the targeted group, inflict harm or kill them, and thus reduce the ethnic heterogeneity of one's region or state. Horowitz (2001) captures well its rational underpinnings:

> There is a bizarre paradox of rationality in rioting. The riot is often a bestial slaughter, yet it involves elements of prudence and foresight. An orgy of killings is punctuated by interludes of detached planning. Traps maybe laid for victims, who when caught will be butchered with frenzied brutality. Violence of this kind is better described as lucid madness than as blind fury. (p. 124)

Many such implicit and explicit guidelines for rioting emerged early in the collective use of such behavior, and persist in an original or evolved form today, such as selective destruction, the use of disguises, attacks on effigies or symbols of the "other side," mock funeral processions, other marches or parades, use of ritual humiliation, symbolic marking or desecration, and so forth. Rioting at soccer or football matches has been described as unfolding based upon prior explicit or implicit agreements regarding who fights, where, when, and how the fighting occurs, when it starts and stops, how intense and injurious it will be, the respective roles of the fighting group's members, and other parameters of the seemingly unplanned, uncontrolled, spontaneous event (Giulianotti, Bonney, & Hepworth, 1994; Kerr, 1994). In different eras and different riots, the mildness or virulence of the mob's violence has obviously varied, as a shared function of who constituted the mob, its size, weapons at its disposal, its degree of organization, the strength of its target or targets, the presence and strength of restraining forces, and many other variables.

Yet, in spite of the tide of pro-rationalist thinking about mob aggression, perhaps one ought not too fully reject its irrationalist component. Gilje (1996), rationalist as his position may be, adds that it is "important to note that there is always a certain element of the irrational in any given tumult." (p. 7) Rule (1988) urges, and I concur, that the two perspectives need not be viewed as mutually exclusive or so thoroughly incompatible, "and sophisticated analysts ought to be able to find ways of using them complementarily" (p. 118). I would suggest that an examination of the past, and especially recent, history of the concept of contagion provides just such a prototypical opportunity for capturing and blending the best of the irrationalist and rationalist positions.

Contagion of emotions among members of a collective became prominent, as I have noted, in the late Nineteenth century first as a group behavioral metaphor of infectious physical disease. It was a notion lying at the heart of the irrationalist position, whether it was called "contagion" directly, or "milling" (Turner & Killian, 1972), "social unrest" (Park & Burgess, 1921), or "the development of common mood" (Lang & Lang, 1961). Also, as noted above, it largely came into disuse, and even disrepute, as the purported bases for mob behavior became increasingly seen to be a function of planful, rational, and even predictable influences. However, it now seems appropriate to revisit contagion as new research and thinking have appeared regarding its nature, sources, consequences and, especially, reality as a powerful interpersonal influence. Two sources especially valuable for conducting such a re-examination of its proper place in our effort to understand mob behavior are Hatfield, Cacioppo, and Rapson's (1994) book *Emotional contagion* and Lynch's (1996) *Thought contagion: how belief spreads through society*. In broad sweep, the findings, conclusions, and speculations offered by these two books combine assertively to replace contagion as having a significant role in the development and maintenance of mob behavior. I wish below to offer a sample of findings, especially from Hatfield, Cacioppo, and Rapson (1994), in support of this assertion, choosing to emphasize their work because of its emphasis and explicit focus on emotion in a manner that appears particularly relevant to mob aggression. They comment:

> The focus in this text is on rudimentary or primitive emotional contagion—that which is relatively automatic, unintentional, uncontrollable, and largely inaccessible to conversant awareness. This is defined as the tendency automatically to mimic and synchronize facial expressions, vocalizations, postures, and movements with those of another person and, consequently, to converge emotionally. (p. 153–154)

Hatfield, Cacioppo, and Rapson (1994) marshal a particularly substantial number of studies—by themselves and others, on adults and children, with individuals and groups—to test two broad hypotheses. The first is that people tend to mimic and synchronize with the expressions of emotion being displayed by others. The second is that, once having done so, the person then experiences emotions consistent with the other person's emotional expression. Emotions, they suggest, can be "caught" from others by conscious attempts to do so, empathy, modeling, or conditioning. By whatever means, does it happen? The findings reported make clear it most reliably does. Thus, their first hypothesis finds clear support in work on motor mimicry (Bavelas et al., 1987) indicating that people imitate others' expressions of pain, laughter, embarrassment, discomfort, disgust, and more. In speech behavior, people more or less automatically mimic others' accents (Giles & Powesland, 1975), rate of speaking (Street, 1984), vocal intensity (Natale, 1975), vocal frequency (Buder, 1991), latency to respond (Matarazzo & Wiens, 1972), utterance duration (Matarazzo, Weitman, Saslow, & Wiens, 1963), turn durations (Matarazzo & Wiens, 1972), and pauses (Feldstein & Welkowitz, 1978). People also regularly and automatically mimic other persons' muscle activity—both their movements, gestures, and postures (Bernieri, 1988; Kendon, 1970; Tickle-Degnen & Rosenthal, 1987).

Once we are displaying facial expressions, speaking, standing, moving, or gesturing like someone else, do we take on the emotional state he or she is expressing? That is, does contagion happen? Via such processes as facial or musculature feedback (Adelman & Zajonc, 1989; Darwin, 1872/1956) and self-perception (Adelman & Zajonc, 1989), the evidence suggests that we do. With regard to mimicry of facial expression, for example, Hatfield, Cacioppo and Rapson (1994) report:

> In a variety of studies then, we find that people tend to feel emotions consistent with the facial expressions they adopt and, conversely, have trouble feeling emotions inconsistent with those poses. Furthermore, the link between emotion and facial expression appears to be quite specific: When people produced a facial expression of fear, anger, sadness, or disgust, they were more likely to feel the emotion associated not just with any unpleasant emotion but with that specific expression (p. 62)

Speech, movement, and postural mimicry studies reported each yield largely concurring results, namely, once expressions of others' emotions are adopted, the emotions thus expressed are "caught" and experienced. Especially relevant to our concern with group phenomena, Ladd (1962), and Leventhal and Mace (1970) have found such mimicry and emotional adoption effects to be particularly likely among group members. More generally, as Hess and Kerouac (2000) conclude:

> ...social group membership influences the encoding of emotions by predisposing individuals to pay more attention to some events than to others, to evaluate them differently, to conform their displays to the relevant social norms, or to prefer certain behaviors because they confer more advantageous consequences. (p. 371)

Usefully, research conducted by Hatfield, Cacciopo, and Rapson (1994) and others also informs us about persons who are more likely to be effective senders of their emotional state, and those most prone to receive or "catch" the affects sent. Hatfield, Cacciopo, and Rapson (1994) propose that the most powerful senders will feel the emotions in question strongly, be able to express it/them fully (with strength, via several channels), and be unresponsive or insensitive to others experiencing incompatible emotions. They ought be externalizers (Buck, 1980), extraverts (Eysenck, 1967), and fluent, passionate, and multi-channel in their expressiveness (Friedman et al., 1980). Receivers, that is, those most prone to contagion influences, are likely to be sensitizers rather than repressors (Byrne, 1964), to be emotionally reactive, both like and be in relation to the sender (e.g., spouse, employee, child of sending parent), and in a positive rather than negative mood at the time of sending (Hatfield, Cacciopo, & Rapson, 1994). It should be noted, additionally, that some emotional states are more readily "caught" than others (Sullins, 1991) and that susceptibility to "catching" someone elses' emotional state also varies as a function of cultural background and context (Markus & Kitayama, 1991).

Collective aggression in the form of riots, rebellions and related forms of mob action are a hallmark of human history. In addition to its psychological, psychosocial, and group dynamic features, I have in this chapter sought to depict its broadly predictable sequencing, an unfolding which concretizes both its rational underpinnings and irrational ingredients.

Part III

INTERVENTION

Chapter 6

ESTABLISHED AND EMERGING INTERVENTIONS

There exist both established and emerging approaches to the management and reduction of group aggression. The former include, especially, intergroup contact, conflict-reduction techniques, and cooperative learning. In the present chapter, I will describe and examine these three perspectives in depth. In addition, a host of other interpersonally oriented and intergroup-oriented means towards such aggression reduction/resolution ends have been offered, are worth further encouragement, and hence will be considered, at least briefly.

Is it presumptuous to assert, or even aspire to, a strategy purporting that psychology and sociology have something of substance to offer in this context vis a vis "intervention" given the durability, magnitude, and sheer potency of group aggression over the centuries. Forbes (1997) observes:

> Ethnic conflict brings to mind horrible examples...where civilization has collapsed and people again learned what savagery means. Can simple theories about contact and conflict throw any light on such extreme situations?...Conventional social science seems powerless before such bewildering phenomena. (p. 6)

Forbes (1997) is correct in his implications. The task is immense, yet one need not resort to resignation, helplessness, or impotence. Group aggression assumes a very broad range of forms, intensities, and resolution challenges. Social science can do considerably more than nibble around its edges. Some, maybe many, instances of group aggression may be so severe and broadly grounded that, at least as far as the offerings proposed herein are concerned, they are intractable. However, this does not mean that, again quoting Forbes (1997) "The social scientists fiddle while Rome burns." (p. 6). Contact, conflict reduction, and cooperative learning research has indeed demonstrated the utility of these established approaches to group aggression, at least in ranges less severe than its most intense forms. Together, they constitute not only a beginning, but a strong beginning encouraging of further support, evolution, development, testing, and application.

CONTACT

Groups in conflict typically interact with one another in a manner characterized by suspicion, mistrust, tension, competition, stereotyped perceptions and misperceptions, perhaps overt aggression, or they interact not at all. Such destructive contact, or absence of contact, perpetuates, and even exacerbates, the conflict that gave root to such behaviors and attitudes. Early thinking held that individual prejudice was the primary source of intergroup conflict. Such prejudice, it was believed, grew from ignorance about one another, and thus its remediation ought to be largely a matter of education—particularly education provided by interaction and contact exposing the protagonists to the realities of one another. As Pettigrew (1986) observed:

> ... the human relations movement constructed a sanguine theory of intergroup contact. Since it viewed individual prejudice as largely the result of ignorance, it believed that contact between groups could only be advantageous. Once together, all but the most extreme fringe would surely see the common humanity shared by the groups and prejudice would necessarily dissipate. (p. 173)

Such optimistic, information-providing intergroup exposure was concretized in the 1940s by interracial dinners, brotherhood meetings, intergroup summer camps, and similar events and experiences. The early 1950s in America saw this same anti-prejudice spirit reflected in a series of contact-promoting public policy initiatives, especially with regard to employment and housing. These initiatives provided a substantial series of opportunities for social and behavioral scientists to evaluate the real-world consequences of intergroup and interracial contact in such work (Harding & Hogrefe, 1952; Saenger & Gilbert, 1950) and daily living (Deutsch & Collins, 1951; Festinger, Schacter & Back, 1950; Jahoda & West, 1951) contexts. The combined findings revealed the earlier human relations view of the role of contact to be too simplistic. In both the job and housing studies, as well as parallel field research appearing at this time regarding interracial contact in the armed forces (Saenger & Gilbert, 1950; Stouffer et al, 1949), it was clear that the contact–conflict reduction relationship was a complex one. Exposure seemed necessary but not sufficient. A number of conditions in which the contact was embedded either facilitated or inhibited its constructive consequences. When the conditions were met, as in much of the research cited above, intergroup contact often appeared to function to reduce intergroup conflict; when the conditions were not-met as, for example, was true when Sherif et al. (1961) brought their warring camps together in an unstructured manner, out-group hostility actually increased. It fell to Allport (1954) to offer the initial statement of what has come to be known as "the contact hypotheses" which incorporated his then view of its facilitative mediating conditions:

> Prejudice may be reduced by equal status contact between majority and minority groups in the pursuit of common goals. The effect is greatly enhanced if this contact is sanctioned by institutional supports (i.e., by law, custom, or local atmosphere), and provided it is of a sort that leads to the perceptions of common interests and common humanity between members of the two groups. (Allport, 1954, p. 281)

Thus, circa 1954, intergroup contact was held to reduce prejudice and intergroup conflict if the participants in said contact were of equal status, shared common goals, and believed their interaction was supported by relevant social or institutional groups. Enthusiasm for the value of contact grew. The early evaluative studies were a substantial part of the social science statement that accompanied the brief to the US Supreme Court in Brown v. Board of Education, the milestone decision against racial segregation. In both laboratory and field settings, research on the effects of contact, and its facilitators/inhibitors proliferated. In the present chapter we will examine the conditions whose presence promotes and whose absence retards the positive effects of contact, and consider the circumstances that enable such positive consequences to generalize beyond the immediate parties involved in the contact experience to the larger out-groups of which they are a part.

Facilitative and Inhibitory Conditions of Contact

Contact research since the mid-1950s has been both diverse and substantial. Those of the studies conducted in the social psychological laboratory have employed a considerable variety of groups, tasks, measures, and methods—thus adding to the credibility of their collective results. The field studies of intergroup contact, while continuing in employment and housing contexts, have in particular focused upon the effects of contact in America's schools, as the major social experiment of racial desegregation was instituted and implemented in thousands of elementary and secondary educational institutions. What has been learned?

Equal Status

One of the central processes which intergroup contact seeks to influence is individuation. As Wilder and Simon (1998) describe it:

> If deindividuation of target persons lessens our regard for them, then individuation of those persons may enhance our favorability toward them...Individuation of out-group members may mediate a reduction of bias for any of several reasons. First, individuation of the outgroup breaks down the simple perception of the out-group as a homogeneous unit. Second, individuation of out-group members focuses attention on these persons and may enable one to notice points of similarity between oneself and the individuated members of the out-group. Third, if attention is focused on the individuated out-group members, one should be more prone to take their role and, perhaps, empathize with them. (p. 235)

Hence, Wilder and Simon (1998) propose that contact mediated individuation may enhance perceived heterogeneity of the out-group, perceived similarity between in-group and out-group members, and the level of expressed empathy. One of a number of purported means for advancing the process of contact-mediated individuation is for the interacting parties involved to be, or be perceived to be, of equal status. When such perceptions hold, there apparently exists diminished likelihood of categorical responding, and enhanced probability not only of individuated perception, but of positively valenced individuated perception. That is, equal status, as is purportedly true for *all* of the facilitative conditions considered in this chapter "...reduces prejudice because they maximize the probability that shared values and beliefs will be demonstrated and perceived and will therefore provide the basis for interpersonal attraction between in-group and out-group members." (Hewstone & Brown, 1986, p. 6)

Contact research on the role of group member status has, however, questioned whether its positive effects follow from equality of status *within* or *outside* the contact situation itself. Is it that when they actually meet, equality of in-group and out-group members' ability and power are the significant contact effect mediators? Or is it their relative status levels in the groups they each, in effect, represent? Or even of the groups themselves? While debate regarding these alternative views has long continued (Forbes, 1997; Kramer, 1950; Pettigrew, 1971; Norwell & Worchel, 1981), we are in accord with Riordan (1978) who sees merit in each interpretation of "equal status", and views them as interrelated, mutually influencing perceptions. In any event, while acknowledging that seeking to equalize status by reducing or reversing existing status differences may be difficult, and elicit resistance from members of the initially higher status group (Brewer & Miller, 1984), if successful, category distinctions may become less salient and the persons involved in the contact situation may perceive one another more as individuals and less in dichotomous terms.

Casual versus Intimate Contact

Relevant research supports the conclusion that:

> ...casual intergroup contact has little or no effect on basic attitude change. Intimate contact, on the other hand, tends to produce favorable changes. When intimate relations are established, the in-group member no longer perceives the member of the out-group in a stereotyped way but begins to consider him as an individual and thereby discovers many areas of similarity. (Amir, 1969, p. 334)

Miller, Brewer and Edwards (1985) have similarly underscored the opportunity provided by intimate contact for individuating perception. Working in the context of desegregated school settings, they distinguish among three different levels of intergroup interactions: (a) category based, (b) differentiated, and (c) personalized. Category-based contact, at one extreme, is marked by depersonalization and deindividuation of outgroup members. As Miller, Brewer, and Edwards (1985) describe it, "...out-group members are responded to as interchangeable representatives of their social category." (p. 64). Categorical identification and, hence, categorical responding, is much less salient at the other extreme, personalization. Here, more personalized information regarding individual out-group members, information not correlated with category membership, becomes focal. Such enhanced intimacy in intergroup relating, it appears, may not only increase the favorableness of the intergroup contact itself, it may also heighten the likelihood that the positiveness of perception and interaction thus engendered will generalize beyond the parties involved in the contact interaction itself to relations with other members of the out-group.

Multiple Contacts

Toward the same decategorizing, individuating ends, multiple contacts are generally more effective than are single contacts (Forbes, 1997; R. M. Williams, 1964). As S. E. Taylor (1981) aptly describes it:

> ... increasing contact with any category of objects, be it tools, food items, or social groups, enables one to make finer and finer discriminations within the category. For example, although initial contact with a group (e.g., a football team) may lead to trait stereotyping (e.g., big, dumb), eventually contact with the group should facilitate the perception of subtypes (e.g., the playboy; the shy; the arrogant hero type). At some point the diversity and volume of contact with any social group should be substantial enough that abstract trait conceptions of the group would no longer have any descriptive value. (p. 102)

Much the same point is offered by Linville, Salovey and Fischer (1986), in their emphasis on *familiarity* and *exposure* as prime sources of category differentiation. Both Ashmore (1970) and Wilder (1986) add that generalization of such positive consequences of multiple contacts follows from the fact that repeated instances of such experiences are more difficult to dismiss as oddities or exceptions to the rule than are single occurrences. T. L. Rose (1981) also points out that novelty may function as an obstacle to positive contact effects, with multiple exposures functioning to decrease the influence perhaps, as Stephan and Stephan (1989) propose, via the progressive reduction of intergroup anxiety over the course of repeated contacts.

Given the not uncommon, high levels, of intergroup mistrust, hostility, and discrimination that exist in real-world group aggression contexts, it is not surprising that for intergroup contact to have a beneficial effect, multiple exposures appear necessary. It may well be, as Pettigrew (1986) suggests, that single exposures, at best, yield subtle, latent effects that are likely to cumulate and become manifest only after repeated contacts.

Institutional Support

As Allport (1954) concluded, subsequent research has affirmed the view that intergroup contact sanctioned by law, custom, community climate, outside authority, institutional norms favoring intergroup equality, or via other significant social or institutional means, is more likely to yield a reduction in out-group bias and misperception than occurs when such support is weak or lacking. Institutional support, Slavin (1985) suggests, may function in this facilitative manner to the degree that it relieves the in-group member himself or herself from having to make intergroup contact a legitimate activity, and thus may help overcome his or her reluctance to initiate such contact efforts. In addition to legitimization, such support has been shown in school desegregation contexts to lead to an array of pro-contact teacher activities. Epstein (1985), for example, examined teacher attitudes in 94 desegregating elementary schools and found:

> Results suggest that positive attitudes toward integration influence teachers' selection of grouping practices that promote student interaction, such as active learning and equal-status programs. Negative attitudes toward integration, or teachers' beliefs in separate education for Blacks and Whites, promote their use of less flexible, resegregative practices, such as tracking and within-class grouping. (p. 23)

A number of earlier studies, such as those by E. B. Johnson, Gerard and Miller (1975) and the National Opinion Research Center (1973) report similar results, underscoring the central importance of broad, relevant support in order that intergroup contact experiences be more likely to be instituted and to yield positive effects.

Cooperative Contact

Cooperative contact, in contrast to that characterized by competition or independence, appears to foster conflict-reducing, individuating consequences of intergroup contact. Such positive effects are more likely when (a) the cooperative endeavor results in success, rather than failure, (b) when there are multiple, rather than single cooperative contacts, (c) when measures are taken to minimize the negative impact of different levels of task ability, (d) when the in-group and out-group hold similar attitudes, and (e) when the individual personality characteristics of the parties to the interaction are characterized by trust, openmindedness, equalitarianism, and high need for achievement, rather than dogmatism, authoritarianism, suspiciousness, and Machiavellianism (Cook, 1978; Brown & Abrams, 1986; E. Cohen, 1980). Factors that maintain group boundaries despite cooperative encounters will inhibit positive contact effects. According to Worchel (1979), such factors may include distinctive physical or visible differences between in-group and out-group members, the intensity of previous conflict between the groups, and disparities in their relative power.

Examples of desirable outcomes following intergroup cooperative contact, in the form of joint striving to achieve superordinate goals, were examined in detail in Chapter 1, as we presented the Sherif et al. (1961) camp studies. Considerable additional research confirming this general finding has subsequently emerged, largely in the context of cooperative learning in education settings, as examined more fully later in this chapter. Both cross-ethnic interactions in desegregation research (DeVries, Edwards & Slavin, 1978; Slavin, 1977; Slavin & Oickle, 1981) and cross-handicapped interactions in mainstreaming research (Johnson & Johnson, 1975; Martino & Johnson, 1979; Rynders et al., 1980) are significantly enhanced by the shared experience of cooperative learning. Unfortunately, such research findings not withstanding, most classroom intergroup interaction in the United States fails to benefit from this facilitator of contact effects. As Slavin (1983) observes, with the exception of athletics, most school-based contact is anything but cooperative:

> Black, Anglo, Hispanic, and other groups compete for grades, for teacher approval, for places on the student council, or on the cheerleading squad. Interaction between students of different ethnic groups is usually of a superficial nature. In the classroom, the one setting in which students of different races or ethnicities are likely to be at least sitting side by side, traditional instructional methods permit little contact between students that is not superficial. Otherwise, Black, Anglo, and Hispanic students usually ride different buses to different neighborhoods, participate in different kinds of activities, and go to different social functions. Thus, opportunities for positive intergroup interaction are limited. One major exception is sports: sports teams create conditions of cooperation and non-superficial contact among teen members. Correlational research by Slavin and Madden (1979) has shown that students who participate in sports in desegregated high schools are much more likely to have friends

outside of their own race group and to have positive racial attitudes than students who do not participate in integrated sports teams. Sports teams fulfill the requirements of contact theory, in that interaction among teammates tends to be non-superficial, cooperative, and of equal status. (Slavin, 1985, p. 47)

Individual Characteristics

It is clearly not only qualities of the contact experience itself (cooperative versus competitive, single versus multiple, casual versus intimate, etc.) that determine its positive or negative consequences, but also qualities of the participants themselves. One such quality is obvious, and perhaps needs little elaboration, namely the level or intensity of prejudicial belief held toward the out-group. However, there are other, somewhat more subtle or less direct individual member qualities that also apparently influence the degree to which intergroup contact ameliorates or worsens in-group favoritism, out-group bias, and the like. One is the group member's cognitive complexity, his or her ability to integrate information complexly, to make fine and even subtle discriminations.

> An individual with a relatively simple structure is likely to make simplistic black–white categorizations . . . The relatively complex person should be more tolerant of ambiguity, less rigid, and better able to handle exceptions to rules. (Wilder, 1986, pp. 58–59)

Cognitive complexity, in turn, is substantially influenced by the individual's arousal level. As Kahneman and Tversky (1973) have shown, as arousal increases, so too does the restriction of attention to fine discriminations (e.g., among out-group members) as more of the individual's effort is spent monitoring and coping with the arousal. In an intergroup contact situation, if the in-group member anticipates an unpleasant experience, his or her arousal (anxiety) may be particularly high. Stephan and Brigham (1985) suggest in this regard that

> . . . high levels of intergroup anxiety lead to amplified behavioral responses, increased reliance on information-processing biases, intensified self-awareness, and augmented emotional reactions to outgroup members. [This] model helps explain why the absence of the conditions outlined in the contact hypothesis (i.e., unequal status, competition, and lack of support by authority figures) have negative effects on intergroup relations: their absence creates anxiety. A clear implication of the model is that contact situations should be designed to minimize anxiety. (p. 6)

The group member's level of self-esteem is apparently yet one further relevant individual characteristic. Wagner and Schenbach (1984) suggest that low self-esteem may increase the importance of group identification for the individual, as his or her means of establishing a positive social identity. Such persons may be particularly uninfluenced by intergroup contact experiences, as their strongly maintained group identification perpetuates their needed sense of separateness and differentiation.

In addition to cognitive complexity, arousal level, and self-esteem, the degree to which the group member utilizes biased information processing will impact upon the perception and sequelae of the intergroup contact. Wilder (1986) proposes that such biases can be minimized in a number of ways:

1. By making the positive actions of outgroup member(s) as salient as possible, in order to minimize the in-group member's reliance on stereotypes and categorical expectations.
2. By making the behavior of the out-group member(s) consistently positive across a variety of settings, in order to minimize "exception to the rule" discounting of the behavior as an unusual or chance event.
3. By tailoring the positive behaviors of the out-group member(s) so as to increase their appeal to the in-group members, in order to maximize the personalism of the contact experience.
4. By dissociating the positive behaviors of the out-group member(s) from any benefit or gain they could receive from such actions, in order to minimize suspicion of insincerity or attributions of manipulativeness.
5. By providing personal information about or otherwise individuating the out-group member(s) in order to enhance the possibility of an empathic response by members of the in-group.
6. By emphasizing the typicalness of the out-group member(s) contacted to the out-group as a whole, in order to maximize the generalization of perception and behavior by members of the in-group to the full out-group.

I have discussed above the group- and individual-level facilitators of positive contact effects. Stephan and Stephan (1996) further suggest characteristics of the broader societal context that may influence the consequences of contact. These include the society's degree of stratification (e.g., age, gender, religion), the historical relations between the groups in contact, their current relationship, and the groups' socialization practices. With the energy of societal, group, and individual level facilitators working for it, what processes are purported to mediate between the contact(s) taking place and consequent reductions in prejudice, conflict, or other favorable outcomes. Ashmore (1970) proposed that these mediators included stereotype destruction, unlearning assumed dissimilarities, pressures toward consistency among cognitions, and the generalization of positive attitudes from individual group members toward the group as a whole. Other mediators have been suggested. Brislin et al. (1986) offered knowledge of the subjective culture of the other group. In addition: reinforcement of positive attitudes (Forbes, 1997), association of positive affect and extinction of negative affect vis a vis out-group members (Sappington, 1976), and imitation of non-prejudiced attitudes and behavior (R. M. Williams, 1977).

A Case History: Contact Plus Facilitative Conditions

Much of what we have had to say regarding the conditions whose presence are facilitative of constructive consequences as a result of the contact experience is illustrated in the following, brief, case history, drawn from Fox (1970), of a "live in" contact event between police and gang youth in Philadelphia. The apparent success of the experience, as the research we have reviewed would suggest, may well in large part be a result of the structure of the contact involved, namely, equal status (within the experience), multiple exposures, intimate rather than casual contact, and the cooperative nature of both its planning and implementation.

The pre-contact intergroup attitudes of members of both groups, police and gang youth, were singularly negative. Fox (1970) comments:

> A common bond between all the aggressive teenage gang members in Philadelphia is their undisguised and unadulterated hatred of the police. Nowhere was this more pronounced than in the Tioga section of North Philadelphia, where three gangs defended their turf and corners against all comers, including the cops. To them, the policemen were pigs. To the police, the undisciplined and defiant kids were 'fresh punks.' And in between was a mutual disrespect, distrust and actual dislike. (p. 26)

Members of the business, home and school community in which the youth resided, and the police patrolled, believed that an in-depth contact experience between the two groups would foster improved relationships and in-community behavior, and proceeded to secure the funding and other arrangements necessary to carry it out. Contact began with a series of three planning meetings, to which the nine gang youth planners, and the nine "most hated" police officers they nominated, were invited. With initial suspicion and intergroup hostility, a live-in weekend at a retreat estate 20 miles from Philadelphia was agreed upon. The nine officers and 25 gang youth were invited to attend.

At the beginning of the three-day experience, considerable hostility, exchanges of accusations, and intergroup distance largely characterized the police–youth interactions. However, slowly, over the course of a series of structured and unstructured combined group activities, attitudes and behavior began to change. An attitudes-disclosing game was played, in which participants could share their views about drinking, violence, legalizing marijuana, the Black Panthers, abortion, and other salient matters. Police–youth relations were energetically discussed. Meals were shared. Informal football and basketball games emerged; informal rap sessions were held. Some of the youth were given rides on one of the officer's new motorcycles. Three police–youth work groups were formed, and each proceeded to engage in a series of role reversal exercises in which hypothetical police–youth confrontations were structured and the participants had to respond—police as gang youth, gang youth as police. Girlfriends of the youth were bussed in for a Saturday evening dance. On Sunday, further police–youth discussions were held, and an elaborate, formal dinner took place. As part of the ceremony accompanying the dinner

> ...the oldest, biggest and most experienced policeman stood up. Marty Meredith had been hated and ridiculed when he arrived. Now you could sense a glow of respect and a tinge of liking from the boys at the adjoining tables. 'All I got to say is this,' Marty smiled, 'It was better than I thought it would be. I got a chance to know you. You got a chance to know me.' He paused and then continued, 'I'm only one cop, but when I go back to the district I'll tell the others about this. You're only a part of all the kids in Tioga. I hope when you go back to the corner you'll talk to the others, especially the younger ones.' With a sober expression, he ended, 'There's been enough hate, fights and problems between us. Let's try to live together in peace.' (Fox, 1970, p. 235)

Generalization of Contact-Induced Change

As noted earlier, largely as a function of the degree to which the several conditions just considered are present or absent, intergroup contact may be for better or worse. When absent, contact may increase, not decrease intergroup tension. (Mis)perceptions may appear confirmed, dislike may intensify, trust may diminish. Or, with the facilitative-conditions wind in its sails, intergroup contact may augment perceived similarity, demystify the unfamiliar or seemingly strange, diminish tension, increase trust. Out of the laboratory, the real world of intergroup contact is often *not* buttressed by these facilitative conditions, and so it is unfortunately the case that such contact is very often for worse, and is not a conflict-reducing force.

> ... intergroup contact per se has only questionable value for reducing prejudice unless it is accompanied by an equal status between the participants— accompanied, if possible, by cooperative relations and supported by institutional norms. The rub, however, is that prejudice itself is a major obstacle to creating opportunities for equal-status cooperative contact. It leads in-group members to keep out-group members down, to preserve not only distance but also inequality. (Stephen & Brigham, 1985, p. 1)

> The classic prescription for reducing prejudice is intergroup contact, under conditions of equal status, common goals, cooperation, and moderate intimacy. Unfortunately, the in-group/out-group literature indicates that these very conditions are difficult to create as soon as people categorize each other into 'us' and 'them'. Out-groups are perceived as inferior, as adversaries, as competitive, and different from one's own group. (Taylor & Fiske, 1981, p. 166)

In the remainder of this section, we wish to consider those factors that augment or diminish the likelihood that the positive consequences following from intergroup contact will generalize to the out-group as a whole.

As noted above, a substantial amount of research supports the conclusion that the positive consequences of intergroup contact, when they do occur *within* the contact experience, often fail to generalize beyond that contact setting to the larger outgroup. (e.g., Amir, 1976; Wilder & Thompson, 1980; Wilder, 1984). The extent to which generalization occurs may be a function of the manner in which the contact experience is structured. Brewer and Miller (1984) urge that it should be *interpersonally* oriented, that the category or group to which the other belongs should be deemphasized. In this manner, the in-group member will, they believe, be more able perceptually to decategorize the out-group member as it were, see him or her more as an individual and less as one of "them." Brown and Ross (1982), in direct contrast, assert that the out-group member's category should be stressed in the contact situation, in order to decrease the likelihood that the in-group member will, as Allport (1954) put it, "re-fence the group" and perceive the other as "an exception to the rule," as a person whose positive qualities bear little implication for the perception of the outgroup as an entity. Hewstone and Brown (1986) urge, in a manner compatible with this latter view, that effort be made to encourage the outgroup member to be perceived as *typical* of the outgroup. Interestingly, both sets of investigators—Brewer and Miller who wish to minimize the salience of the outgroup members' group membership and Brown and Turner, who wish to maximize it—take their respective positions as a means of promoting generalization of the new, positive, contact-caused, perceptions to the outgroup as a whole. As Ben-Ari and Amir (1986), Pettigrew (1986) and others note, ample theoretical and research support exists for both positions, and it appears to us not unlikely that research may eventually demonstrate that a combination of personalizing and categorical structuring proves optimal for the promotion of generalization.

Other facets of the structure of the intergroup contact experience have also been suggested as being relevant to generalization of its effects. Cook (1978) proposes:

> Attitude change will result from cooperative interracial contact only when such contact is accompanied by a supplementary influence that promotes the process of generalization from favorable contact with individuals to positive attitudes toward [their] group. (p. 103)

Such supplementary influence, Cook suggested, might in particular take the form of support of the new attitude toward the out-group from members of the perceivers' peer (in)group. Peer support offered in this manner, Cook believed, might serve as a generalization-enhancing "cognitive booster." Other such boosters, according to Hewstone & Brown (1986), may include (a) establishing superordinate goals to potentiate the generalization of contact effects by, in effect, creating a new, combined in-group, (b) encouraging cross-cutting group memberships, making sure that such alternative categories do not correspond to the original in-group–out-group division, and (c) manipulation of the generalizability expectancies of the parties to the contact.

Yet generalization of contact-induced gains is not only a function of aspects of the contact experience itself, and is not only influenced by qualities of the out-group whose member(s) were contacted. The macro-context of the intergroup contact also looms large. The seed may be healthy, the rain generous, but the soil infertile. A wider society characterized by Balkanization, polarization, fractiousness, racist norms, and other manifestations of, and support for, us-versus-them structuring, is not likely to be receptive to the growth and spread of contact-induced intergroup harmony. Yet one ought not go too far in assigning potency for intergroup change too singularly to macro-level alteration, as perhaps Reicher (1986) does:

> ... racism will not be overcome through individual acts, which leave the racist structure of British society intact, but only through action to change the nature of that society. It will not change by contact, but by collective action. (p. 167)

We would hold, contrariwise, that a combination of individual action, such as that provided by the contact experience, and collective, structural change—in such domains as employment, housing, politics, the media, immigration—will be most promotive of positive intergroup consequences. The outcomes of desegregation in the United States, reflecting both macro (school, school district) and individual (student contact) alterations are one major positive (if mixed) example (e.g., Higher Education Research Institute, 1980; National Center for Educational Statistics, 1981; Ohio State University Center for Human Resource Research, 1981; Scott & McPartland, 1982; Stephan & Rosenfeld, 1978). We are in accord with Hewstone and Brown (1986) who concluded their book, *Contact and conflict in intergroup encounters*, by urging the combining of micro (contact) and macro (societal) level change:

> The message of this book is that intergroup contact can play a role in improving intergroup relations in society, but that the contact hypothesis as traditionally conceived is too narrow and limited. To create the conditions for truly successful intergroup contact, more radical social changes are a prerequisite. For example ... blacks and other oppressed groups must seek a share of power; members of majority groups secure in *their* identity must learn the value and integrity of *other* groups or cultures ... These changes will not come easily and will have to be fought for on many fronts. (p. 42)

I have considered the role of intergroup contact in promoting intergroup harmony. Early over-enthusiasm for its potency was tempered by research demonstrating that its positive consequences are facilitated or diminished by a number of conditions in which the contact may be embedded. These include the relative status equality of the participants, the intimacy, frequency and cooperativeness of their meetings, relevant social or institutional norms, and a number of individual qualities of the contacting in-group and out-group members. Even when such conditions are present, thus favoring constructive outcomes, whether or not such outcomes will generalize beyond the parties involved in the contact experience itself to the larger groups they in effect represent, is itself a function of several influences. These may be factors characterizing the contact event itself, such as its interpersonal versus intergroup focus.

Forbes (1997) urges that successful prejudice- or conflict-reducing outcomes following upon contact experiences would be much enhanced were "contact" to be more fully and regularly conceptualized as a collective rather than individual phenomenon. In a manner reminiscent of Hogg's (1992) urging (see pp. 100–102) the usefulness of viewing group cohesiveness as not being individual-level intermember attraction but, instead, as group-level attraction to an imagined prototypical group member, Forbes comments:

> ... the variables that determine levels of prejudice and discrimination have little to do with contact among individuals and much to do with relations among groups ... Are the relevant groups divided by important conflicting interests ... or are they united by the pursuit of superordinate goals? Correlations that hold for interpersonal behavior, at the individual level, cannot be simply extrapolated to intergroup behavior, at the aggregate level. (p. 140)

Or generalization may be encouraged or impeded by macro-level forces, particularly the levels of prejudice, racism, polarization or other broad manifestations of us-versus-them belief and behavior operative in the larger society.

Intergroup contact, in sum, is viewed by us not as a panacea, not as *the* cure-all for intergroup disharmony, but as one useful, demonstrably effective part of a broader, multi-faceted strategy for the reduction of in-group–out-group conflict and the promotion of in-group–out-group harmony. The contact hypothesis on which this approach rests, through examined now for over 50 years, still remains a work in progress.

CONFLICT RESOLUTION

In Chapter 1, I considered at length a conflict resolution approach designed around the training of effective communication skills. To help escort warring group members through the storming stage of group life, I offered a catalog of means for preparing for and conducting conflict-reducing skilled communication, and for avoiding an array of pitfalls and obstacles along the way. In that same section in Chapter 1, I briefly defined the processes of mediation, negotiation, and arbitration, and their potential roles as conflict-reducing techniques. In the present section, I wish to elaborate further on what is known about negotiation in particular—the rationale for its use, its diverse forms, its goals, and its apparent outcomes. I choose this emphasis because, in contrast to the alternative routes to conflict resolution, negotiation has the longest history, the firmest research base, and arguably the most promising potential for a favorable outcome.

Wilmot and Hocker (2001) comment:

> Negotiation occurs in conflict resolution when the parties recognize their inter-dependence, have been able to establish their concerns, are willing to work on both incompatible and overlapping goals ... have been able to establish enough power balance so people can 'come to the table,' and when procedures are in place so people can talk to each other in a problem-solving way. Thus, we think of negotiation as the active phase of conflict resolution when people generate many options, brainstorm ideas, give and take, and attempt to get their mutual goals met. (p. 210)

As Wall (1985) observes, negotiation provides the opportunity for the parties in conflict to communicate their positions and preferences, examine each others' views, increase predictability, and work toward solution. In doing so, some will negotiate competitively, others more collaboratively. Competitive negotiators seek to meet *their* goals, either at the expense of (zero-sum) the other party's, or with in-difference toward their outcomes. In brief, they assume an "I win, you lose" stance. To the competitive negotiator, the negotiation's goals target a "fixed pie" to be distributed between the parties. In fact, such negotiation is often termed "distributive bargaining." Competitive negotiators may open with extreme offers, withhold relevant information from each other, concede slowly, exaggerate the value of their own concessions, threaten and confront, manipulate and distort, and in other ways show a strong inclination to coercion, pressure, and persuasion (Murray, 1986; Lax & Sebenius, 1986). Collaborative or cooperative negotiators, strive to reach mu-tually satisfying outcomes. Typically, theirs is a "win–win, let us defeat the problem, not each other" approach to negotiation. Collaborative negotiators, as Wilmot and Hocker (2001) aptly note "assume that creativity can transcend the win/lose as-pect of competitive negotiations." (p. 225) This approach requires and inspires trust, relies on full disclosure of information, values the relationship between the con-tending parties, seeks to meet one's own important goals and also at least some of the other party's. To do so, collaborative negotiators may seek to expand the pie to be distributed, engage in trade off of priority issue settlements, minimize the other's costs for concessions, and invent new options for meeting each other's needs.

Research demonstrates that males are more likely than females to employ com-petitive means; females more likely than males to seek collaboration. However, both males and females are more prone to collaboration than competition when the sec-ond party to the negotiation is female rather than male (Berryman-Fine & Brunner, 1987). Renwick (1977) also found that, in general, accommodating negotiation

Table 6.1 Three approaches to negotiation

The soft negotiator	The hard negotiator	The principled negotiator
Stress that the participants are friends	Stress that the participants are adversaries	Stress that the participants are problem solvers
Make the goal agreement	Make the goal victory	Make the goal a wise outcome reached efficiently and amicably
Make concessions to cultivate the relationship	Demand concessions as a condition of the relationship	Separate the people from the problem
Be soft on the people and the problem	Be hard on the problem and the people	Be soft on the people, hard on the problem
Trust others	Distrust others	Proceed independently of trust
Change your position easily	Dig in to your position	Focus on interests, not on positions
Make offers	Make threats	Explore interests
Disclose your bottom line	Mislead as to your bottom line	Avoid having a bottom line
Accept one-sided losses to reach agreement	Demand one-sided gains as a price of agreement	Invent options for mutual gain
Search for a single answer: the one they will accept	Search for the single answer; the one you will accept	Develop multiple options to choose from; decide later
Insist on agreement	Insist on your agreement	Insist on using objective criteria
Try to avoid a contest of will	Try to win a contest of will	Try to reach a result based on standards independent of will
Yield to pressure	Apply pressure	Reason and be open to reason; yield to principle, not pressure

styles are more common at home, competitive styles at work. Children as young as those in fourth grade can successfully be taught collaborative negotiation behaviors (Clark, O'Dell, & Willingana, 1986), with girls on average being more competent at doing so than boys (Selman & Demarest, 1984).

Fisher and Ury (1981) offer a perspective on negotiations that is somewhat different from the competitive–collaborative dichotomy. Theirs is a three-option view, as depicted in Table 6.1. Their intent, it appears, is to propose a negotiator stance lying somewhere between the competitive-versus-collaborative options presented above.

I include the view of Fisher and Ury (1981) here as a useful exemplar of the notion that negotiation options beyond the competitive–collaborative polarity certainly exist. None the less, it is clearly in the facilitative intergroup spirit of both the guiding thrust of this chapter's other topics and this author's own

Table 6.2   Collaboration checklist

1. *Join with the other*
   Use "we" language
   Seek common interests
   Consult before acting
   Move closer non-verbally
2. *Control the process, not the person*
   Use setting, timing, and other factors creatively
   Either limit or increase the number of people involved
   Encourage the other to expound fully
   Listen actively even when you disagree
3. *Use principles of productive communication*
   Be unconditionally constructive
   Refuse to sabotage the process
   Separate the people from the problem
   Persuade rather than coerce
   Refuse to hate the other
4. *Be firm in your goals and flexible in your means*
   Be provisional—seek alternative means to your goals
   Separate content and relationship issues
   Focus on interests, not positions
5. *Assume that there is a solution*
   Invent options for mutual gain
   Approach issues one at a time
   First tackle issues that you can easily agree upon
   Refuse to be pessimistic

predilections that I emphasize here the demonstrated and potential value of collaborative negotiations in the context of group conflict and group aggression. In that spirit and toward that goal, I close this section with Wilmot and Hocker's (2001) concrete recommendations for facilitating successful collaborative negotiation (Table 6.2).

COOPERATION TRAINING

Cooperation with others, under certain structured conditions, enhances the likelihood of future interindividual and intergroup cooperation, as well as the frequency of several other types of prosocial behavior. In support of this assertion, this section presents two broad approaches designed to increase cooperative behavior. Each approach, in its own way, relies on cooperative activities toward this end. The first are a series of school-based procedures and arrangements termed *cooperative learning*. I will examine its history, rationale, and principles, contrast this approach with alternative learning approaches, describe its specific methods, and discuss research examining its effects upon cooperation and a host of related prosocial behaviors. Cooperative gaming is the second promising route to enhanced cooperation. Games and sports in highly competitive Western societies are typically anything but cooperative. However, cooperative games and cooperative versions of traditional sports do exist, are enjoyed, and appear to help channel behavior in prosocial directions.

Cooperation Defined

Cooperation has been defined in the theoretical and research literature in four different, although related ways. As Slavin (1983) observes:

> It can refer to cooperative behavior, such as working with or helping others. It can refer to a cooperative incentive structure...in which a group of two or more individuals is rewarded based on the performance of all group members. Cooperation often refers to cooperative task structures, in which a group of two or more individuals can or must work together but may or may not receive rewards based on the group's performance. Finally, it can refer to cooperative motives, the predisposition to act cooperatively or altruistically in a situation that allows individuals a choice between cooperative, competitive, or individualistic behavior. (p. 3)

In my own work in this domain (Goldstein, 1999), emphasis is upon cooperative behavior, "defined as working with others for mutual benefit" (Schofield, 1980, p. 161) or, as Sapon-Shevin (1986) illustrates, to acquire such cooperation-defining skills as "listening to one another, coordinating one's movements and energies with those of other children, and engaging in those social behaviors that will facilitate and prolong interacting with other children rather than driving them away" (p. 281). These are but a few of the prosocial behaviors that may define cooperation and its concomitants. Such behaviors exemplify valuable interindividual and intergroup training goals.

I now turn to cooperative learning—its rationale, constituent procedures, operational guidelines, and demonstrated effects.

Cooperative Learning

Cooperative learning is both a philosophy of teaching and a series of different, but related, teaching methods. Across areas of academic content, most of these methods involve a heterogeneous group of youngsters working together on a shared task or project (e.g., a cooperative task structure) and the provision of grades or other rewards to the group as a whole, based either upon the sum of individual improvement scores or on the group's overall task performance (e.g., a cooperative incentive structure). Though the methods of cooperative learning are mostly a phenomenon of the 1970s, like so much that is prosocial in contemporary educational theory and practice, cooperative learning has its spiritual roots in the writings of John Dewey (1916/1952; 1938/1966). Schmuck (1985) describes well this philosophical underpinning:

> Dewey argued that if humans are to learn to live cooperatively, they must experience the living process of cooperation in schools. Life in the classroom should represent the democratic process in microcosm, and the heart of democratic living is cooperation in groups. (p. 2)

Dewey's views, and what eventually came to be seen as the cooperative learning movement, found wide support and implementation in the 1920s (e.g., Kilpatrick,

1925); receded in influence in the face of a strong, procompetition backlash in the 1930s; regained both influence and empirical support via the work of Lewin (1943, 1947), Deutsch (1951, 1957), and their coworkers in the 1940s and the 1950s, and came to fullest operational expression via the cooperative learning methods created in the 1970s. These cooperative learning approaches express principles of cooperative incentive and task structures, task specialization, distributed or shared group leadership, heterogeneous group membership, positive interdependence among this membership, individual accountability, high levels of group autonomy, equal opportunity scoring based on improvement compared to self, not others, and between-group competition. The seven approaches next described are the more frequently used and more thoroughly evaluated of those in existence.

Student teams—achievement divisions

In Slavin's (1978) Student Teams-Achievement Divisions (STAD), four- or five-member learning teams are constituted. Youngsters assigned to each team ideally represent the heterogeneity of the larger class, school, or community (i.e., boys and girls, high-, average-, and low-performing students, students of different ethnic or racial backgrounds). The teacher regularly introduces new material to be learned. In a peer-tutoring format, students study the materials together, take turns quizzing one another, discuss the materials as a group, or use other self-selected means to master the material. The teacher communicates to each team that study of any given material is not complete until all teammates are sure they understand it. Quiz scores are transformed into team scores by the teacher, with each student's contribution to the team score being not the absolute level of his or her performance but, instead, the amount of improvement over that student's past average score. Use of individual improvement scores helps to increase the likelihood that low-performing students will also contribute to the total team score and be fully accepted as group members. In STAD, the team or teams with the highest scores, and the students who exceed their own performance by the greatest amounts, are acknowledged in a weekly one-page class newsletter.

Teams–games–tournaments

The teams–games–tournaments (TGT) approach to cooperative learning, developed by DeVries and Slavin (1978) employs the same team structure, instructional format, and worksheets as STAD. Instead of quizzes, however, students engage in cross-team academic games to demonstrate their individual mastery of the subject matter. These games are played in weekly tournaments in which students compete against members of other teams, comparable in past performance. Slavin (1983) captures the flavor of these games:

> The competitions take place at tournament tables of three students. Thus a high performing student from the "Fantastic Four" might compete with a high performer from the "Pirates" and one from the "Superstars." Another table might have average performing students from the "Pirates," the "Masterminds,"

and the "Chiefs." ... The students are not told which is the highest table, which is next, and so on, but they are told that their competition will always be fair. (p. 26)

To maintain a fair level of competition, students' table assignments are changed every week, with the high scorer at each table being moved to the next higher table and the low scorer at each table being moved to the next lower table. Since any given student's contribution to the total team score is, as in STAD, based on improvement over past performance, this equalizing of tournament competition maximizes all students' potential contributions to the team score. Also, as in STAD, a weekly class newsletter is employed to recognize high-scoring teams and individual tournament winners.

Team assisted individuation

Team assisted individuation (TAI) was developed by Slavin, Leavey, and Madden (1982) for use when the members of a class are too heterogeneous to be taught the same material at the same rate. To date, TAI has been used primarily for the cooperative learning of mathematics. It is the only cooperative learning method to use individual instruction rather than class-paced learning. As in STAD and TGT, heterogeneous groups of four to five students are formed. Diagnostic testing of each student is carried out and, based upon the results of this assessment, a programmed mathematics unit is prescribed for each student. The student works at an individual pace—reading instructions, working on successive skill sheets, taking "checkouts," and being tested. This progression occurs in self-selected teams of two students each. Team members exchange answer sheets and check each other's skill sheets and checkouts. In this cooperative approach, student test scores and the number of tests completed in a given week contribute to a team score if they are in excess of present team performance standards, which results in certificates being awarded to each team member for progress that week.

Jigsaw

In contrast to the individualization feature of TAI, Aronson et al.'s (1978) Jigsaw approach maximizes student interdependence. Interestingly, however, such inter-dependence is reflected in the approach's task structure, not its incentive structure. Students are assigned to heterogeneous six-member teams, and the academic ma-terial to be covered is broken down into five sections. For example, Aronson et al. describe a fifth-grade Jigsaw classroom in which biographies of great Americans were being studied. The teacher created five biographies that respectively described the famous figure's ancestors and arrival in America, childhood and adolescence, early adulthood, education, and employment, middle years and their highlights, and events in society at large during this latter period. Each team member was assigned one of these sections to read and study in order to become expert (six team members for five sections were used to cover absentees). Members of dif-ferent teams who had studied the same section then met as "expert groups" to consider their section. Having thus become experts by study and discussion, students then returned to their own teams and took turns teaching their teammates about their sections. Students were encouraged to listen to, support, and show interest in one another's reports to the team. After the reports were completed, students were individually quizzed across all topics and received individual, not team, grades.

Jigsaw II

As in STAD and TGT, students in Slavin's (1980) Jigsaw II work in heterogeneous teams of four or five members. Unlike Jigsaw, in which team members are responsible for a unique section of the material, Jigsaw II requires all students to read the same chapter or story. Each student is, however, assigned a topic within this context in which to become expert. As in Jigsaw, the students from each group who are assigned the same topic meet in expert groups to discuss the topic and then return to their own teams to teach what they have learned. Individual quizzes are taken, and scores for individual improvement over previous performance are computed and used as the basis for determining an overall team score. As in STAD and TGT, a class newsletter provides public acknowledgment and recognition of high-scoring teams and individuals.

Learning together

Learning together (Johnson & Johnson, 1975) is the most group oriented of the cooperative learning alternatives. Students work on assignment sheets in heterogeneous four- or five-member groups. The group members hand in a single assignment sheet for evaluation. As the method's title indicates, they then receive feedback as a group regarding how well they are "learning together." Reflecting a cooperative incentive structure, grades are based on the average achievement scores of individual members.

Group investigation

Cooperative learning via the group investigation method (Sharon & Sharon, 1976) is a six-stage process initiated and conducted by the participating students themselves. Specifically, the process involves the following steps:

1. Identifying the topic and organizing into self-selected two- to six-member groups.
2. Planning the learning task, in which the members choose subtopics for investigation.
3. Carrying out the investigation (i.e., gathering and evaluating relevant information, drawing conclusions, and so forth).
4. Preparing final report, which requires the coordination and integration of each team member's efforts.

5. Presenting the final report, as a group, to the class. This presentation may be a written document, exhibition, skit, and so on.
6. Evaluating themselves in collaboration with the teacher.

The typical classroom in the United States is far different from what I have described here. Rather than working together for group rewards (i.e., cooperative task and incentive structures), most classes are organized according to an individualistic task structure (e.g., students working alone) or a competitive incentive structure (e.g., curve marking). Slavin (1983) describes the usual classroom situation accurately:

> With regard to task structure, most teachers use some combination of lectures, discussions, individual seatwork, small homogeneous groups working with the teacher, and individual tests. Students are rarely allowed, and even less often encouraged, to help one another with their work; in most schools, peer relationships during school hours are largely restricted to the playground and lunchroom. The almost universal incentive structure used is a grading system, in which students compete for a limited number of good grades. (p. 2)

The interpersonal consequences of the cooperative, competitive, and individualistic orientations can be dramatically different. Johnson and Johnson (1975) offer the schema presented in Table 6.3 to help categorize these consequences.

Table 6.3   Goal structures and interpersonal processes

Cooperative	Competitive	Individualistic
High interaction	Low interaction	No interaction
Mutual liking	Mutual dislike	No interaction
Effective communication	No or misleading communication	No interaction
High trust	Low trust	No interaction
High mutual influence	Low mutual influence	No interaction
High acceptance and support	Low acceptance and support	No interaction
High use of other students' resources	No use of other students' resources	No interaction
High sharing and helping	Attempts to mislead and obstruct	No interaction
High emotional involvement of all	Emotional involvement of winners	No interaction
High coordination of effort	Low coordination of effort	No interaction
Division of labor possible	Division of labor not possible	No interaction
High divergent thinking	Low divergent thinking	No interaction
No self–other comparisons	High self–other comparisons	No interaction

Note: From David W. Johnson/Roger T. Johnson, *Learning Together and Alone*, 1975, p. 27. Reprinted by permission of Prentice Hall.

The typical classroom structure involving individualistic work for competitive rewards may be particularly damaging for low-performing youth. Slavin (1985) comments in this regard that

> For many low-performing students, no amount of effort is likely to put them at the top of the class because they have already missed so much in past years. Thus, the competition for top score in the classroom is poorly matched. Because they have such a small chance of success, low performers may give up or try to disrupt the activity. They can hardly be expected to do otherwise . . . low performing students . . . may turn to delinquency or withdrawal as a means of maintaining self-esteem in the face of what they perceive as a hostile school environment. (p. 6)

A portion of low-performing students are also members of minority groups, and a number of studies demonstrate that African-American and Chicano students appear to respond particularly well to cooperative learning experiences, perhaps because of compatible cultural group-oriented experiences (Beady & Slavin, 1981; Lucker et al., 1976; Slavin, 1977; Slavin & Oickle, 1981).

Thus, cooperative learning does have considerable value, especially for low-performing youth. Decisions about its use, however, must be based primarily on empirical evidence as to whether cooperative learning increases cooperative behavior and other prosocial behaviors.

Research Evaluation

I began this section with the assertion that participation in cooperative learning activities enhances participants' level of cooperative behavior. This assertion is supported solidly by empirical evidence. Hertz-Lazarowitz, Sharan, and Steinberg (1980) found both acquisition and transfer of cooperative effects in a study of elementary school children taking part in a group-investigation cooperative learning program. Participating youngsters, when compared to appropriate control-group children, were more cooperative and altruistic in their behavior both during the training experience and when assigned to new groups. Sharan, Raviv, and Russell (1982) successfully replicated these transfer findings. In a third investigation, Hertz-Lazarowitz, Sapir, and Sharan (1981) found significantly less competitiveness in children participating in group investigation than in control-group youths. D. W. Johnson et al. (1976), using their learning together approach, similarly reported substantial increases in participants' cooperative behavior in comparison to that of youth learning competitively or individually.

Jigsaw has yielded similarly enhanced levels of cooperation, not only in terms of overt cooperative behavior (Aronson et al., 1978), but also with regard to motivation for future cooperativeness (Blaney et al., 1977). In their investigations, Kagan et al. (1985) report similarly enhanced levels of cooperative behavior compared with behavior in traditional classroom structures. However, at both the elementary and high school levels, their research showed that the effect held for minority students (African American, Mexican-American) but not for majority students (Caucasian).

In all, the evidence is clear, substantial, and almost uniformly positive that participation in cooperative learning programs enhances subsequent cooperative behavior. Apparently, it does much more. Such participation has also been demonstrated to increase a host of other personal, prosocial, and cognitive characteristics. Vermette (1998), summarizing the findings of over 300 evaluations of diverse cooperative learning approaches, notes that:

> Overall, the research says that cooperative learning tends to produce more desirable outcomes on motivational, self-esteem, and achievement measures when compared to traditional instructional strategies and competitive or individualistic ones. This generalization is supported by studies across 13 years of schooling and is true for students of both genders, all ethnicities, and across various disabilities. (p. 60)

Resistance to Using Cooperative Learning

Cooperative learning approaches have a remarkably positive research database, but the attitude towards its use expressed in schools is often ambivalent and its employment is minimal. This discrepancy between evaluation outcomes on the one hand and attitudes and use on the other is both remarkable and puzzling. Kohn (1992), Male (1989), and Vermette (1998) have drawn similar conclusions and expressed similar wonderment. Kohn asserts that the resistance to cooperative learning on the part of teachers grows from the manner in which its use (a) reduces teacher control and predictability, (b) demands attention to social, rather than traditional, academic goals, (c) challenges our commitment to individualism and our frequent aversion to collective efforts, and (d) challenges our commitment to the value of competition. Vermette suggests other common teacher concerns: Can students be trusted actually to "work" when left alone with peers? Is the time used in employing cooperative learning procedures wasting the time of brighter students, whose progress may be retarded by the less competent input of others of their teams? Is cooperative learning unsuitable for use by teachers who are more introverted or less interactive in their styles or personalities?

Parents, too, have often voiced objections. Cooperative learning, some assert, is a waste of time, another educational fad, busywork, not "real" teaching, and certainly not what taxes should be used for. In other words, "We pay teachers to teach, not . . ."

The demands on teachers today are substantial and seemingly everexpanding, especially in this era of the "full-service school" (Dryfoos, 1994). And older, accustomed ways of teaching are comfortable and often reasonably effective. Yet the evidence in support of the prosocial outcomes for cooperative learning is remarkable. We strongly urge teachers to be learners, experimenters, and, we hope eventually, sustained users of cooperative learning.

To reduce parents' resistance, we propose two strategies. The first is early and complete orientation to cooperative learning—its rationale, methods, and expected outcomes. The letter to parents presented in Figure 6.1, pertaining to social studies instruction, is a fine start in this direction. A second strategy involves teacher efforts to enhance the likelihood that the cooperative approach yields discernable student academic and/or social progress, especially early in the approach's use. The letter home is the resistance-reducing promise; demonstrable student progress is the resistance-reducing result.

Dear Parent or Guardian,

This year, we will be using a rather interesting and innovative approach in our social studies class: It is called "cooperative learning" and its central theme is that each student benefits from working in teams during class time. As you well know, many of the students here in school have participated in sports teams and after-school clubs where they learned to appreciate the values of unity, loyalty, challenge, and cooperation built into working with others. In many cases, involvement in these "team" activities/settings not only helps the individuals learn more about the sport or club, they also enjoy it more and work harder at it. I wish to use classroom teams to help my students realize these advantages on a regular basis and in my regular classroom.

By the way, cooperative learning has been used successfully in many subjects and at many grade levels, but I feel that it is especially crucial in the social studies. In social studies I wish for learners to understand their own country's heritage, their own individual lives, and the problems and patterns of civilizations. They also need to lean to think critically and responsibly, and they must develop democratic skills and attitudes and learn to appreciate diversity from an individual approach to a cooperative team learning system.

1. *Construction of the Teams.* Approximately once a month, students will be assigned to stable three- or four-member teams. They will not pick their own teams, for in adult life we are expected to work effectively with all different types of people. Here at school I did not pick my colleagues or my students and their parents, yet I must work with them effectively. I am sure that this is true for you in your daily lives as well. We seldom pick our neighbors, our extended families, our workmates; however, we are expected to interact with them in a productive manner.

   Moreover, the point of teamwork on a daily basis is not to have students make friends out of all their classmates. Thankfully, this outcome does often happen, but friendship is not as important a goal as the development of the ability to work with people of different beliefs and backgrounds. Students learn to accept each other and help each other now to prepare themselves for similar roles as future citizens.

2. *Daily Activities.* Every day in class, at least some time will be spent in teamwork. On some occasions, groups will be completing worksheets, creating interpretive projects, rehearsing (quizzing) each other, or doing practice tests.

   While these activities could be done individually, they will be more productive when done by groups. Moreover, there are some new and exciting activities that can only be done by teams. In these lessons, students take responsibility for mastering the material, teaching it to each other, and/or meeting each other in tournament-type play. (Two of these plans are called Jigsaw and Teams–Games–Tournaments.)

   Since social studies also involves the discussion and analysis of issues, problems, and current events, each student is expected to contribute ideas and opinions from his or her perspective. The skill of solving problems in groups is one that modern business also requires of its workers; we will also be doing this as we prepare the students for the demands they will face as adults.

   As you can see, we are planning many different types of activities, some short and some long, some typical of school, and some not. We intend to utilize the many different types of skills and talents that team members possess so that each student will learn some new skills from teammates and broaden his or her understanding of human intelligence and abilities. In this way, every single student will gain knowledge and an appreciation of others' talents.

3. *Grading.* Students do not receive team grades or take team tests on all assignments. Just as some adults bargain for their own wages, and some have groups (e.g., unions) do it for them, we will use diverse types of grading structures. I want the students to understand different reward systems and have them evaluate each.

Figure 6.1   Letter to parents concerning cooperative learning. From MAKING COOPERA-TIVE LEARNING WORK by Vermette 1998. Reprinted by permission of Prentice Hall, Inc., Upper Saddle River, NJ.

There will be group-graded projects, but most of the work will be done here in school so that we can monitor progress. I want to make sure that every student is encouraged to contribute and takes his or her share of the responsibilities. Doing the work here in school also helps to make all groups more equal; it would not be fair to all students if only some teams get together regularly outside of school time or if one person in a team were saddled with all the work. Democratic systems seem to flourish when all citizens take their responsibilities seriously.

4 *Rules for Teamwork*. Since so much time will be spent in group work, students will be asked to help formulate the rules they will follow when working together. This practice, too, is consistent with the democratic principle called "consent of the governed."

Of course the teachers and the parents have a say in this self-governing exercise as well. This is similar to the system of "checks and balances." We will be sending home the list of student-generated rules soon and ask that you discuss them with your youngster. This investigation into laws, governance, and opinions will help the students to understand and appreciate these aspects of their democratic heritage.

In conclusion, I would like to add that we are very excited about this new approach and look forward to your discussion of this letter with your youngster. We have every hope of seeing it work as well here as it has in many other places. Students have learned more, learned to get along better with each other, and felt better about themselves under this system. The demands on future citizens to be knowledgeable, dependable, flexible, tolerant, and cooperative are clearly stated and widely acknowledged; with this new system, students will learn these traits in the classroom as well as on the athletic field and in after-school activities.

Cordially,

cc: Administrators/Students

Figure 6.1   (*continued*)

Cooperative Gaming

My own involvement in the use and recommendation of cooperative gaming began in 1988 as a component of a psychoeducational intervention I developed called the prepare curriculum (Goldstein, 1988). Since program inception, low-achieving youth, acting-out youth, withdrawn youth, delinquent youth, chronically aggressive youth, and those otherwise deficient in prosocial behaviors, have often been the students targeted for its delivery. A central question in the offering of any curriculum concerns its prescriptive appropriateness for the students targeted. Do the contents, format, and manner of delivery of a given curriculum fit the target youths' "channels of accessibility" (Hunt, 1971)?

Many of the youth just identified above may accurately be described, in terms of their optimal channels of accessibility, as action-oriented and relatively non-verbal (Goldstein, 1971, 1973). They are no less expressive than other youth, but they often prefer motor behavior as a means of communication. The use of athletic activities and games furthers our goal of teaching cooperative behavior by responding to these channels of accessibility. Hence, in addition to the cooperative learning approaches described earlier, I wish to examine the use of cooperative sports and games as a promising route for enhancing cooperative behavior in youth displaying chronic prosocial deficiencies.

Cooperative sports and games are activities in which the format, rules, and materials employed explicitly avoid competitive strategies and instead reflect a

Table 6.4   Cooperative gaming

1. Everyone who wishes to play can.
2. Player eliminations are avoided.
3. Everyone plays an equal amount of time via use of simultaneous games and frequent substitutions.
4. Everyone has an equal opportunity to play each position.
5. Players compete against their own past performance, not each other.
6. Skill emphasis is on self-improvement.
7. No goals are counted, no points awarded, no scores kept. If scores are kept, they are kept collectively across all players.
8. Extrinsic rewards (trophies, awards) are deemphasized.
9. Helping one another toward activity goals is actively encouraged.
10. Cooperative skills (e.g., all must touch the ball before a shot can be taken) are promoted.
11. Multiball, multigoal games are employed.
12. Team captains are changed for each game.
13. Individual penalties are not announced, to minimize reinforcer of attention.
14. Expulsion from the game is the consequence for deliberate attempts to injure another player.

cooperative interactional philosophy (i.e., working with others for mutual benefit). The practices listed in Table 6.4 are among the ways this philosophy may be operationalized.

Terry Orlick (1978), who is perhaps the father of the cooperative sports and games movement, communicates its spirit and aspiration:

> the main difference [from competitive games] is that in cooperative games everybody cooperates . . . everybody wins . . . and nobody loses. Children play with one another rather than against one another. These games eliminate the fear of failure and the feeling of failure. They also reaffirm a child's confidence in himself or herself as an acceptable and worthy person. In most games . . . this reaffirmation is left to chance or awarded to just one winner. In cooperative games it is designed into the games themselves. (p. 304)

But Orlick also cautions that

> patience may be needed to learn this "new" form of play, particularly if the participants have never before played cooperatively. However, with appropriate challenges, enlightened supervision, repeated exposure, and players' constructive input on cooperative changes, the games will begin to take off on a positive note. (p. 4)

Orlick stresses the manner in which cooperative play increases the likelihood of future cooperative behavior:

> Cooperation is directly related to communication, cohesiveness, trust, and the development of positive socialinteraction skills. Through cooperative ventures, children learn to share, to empathize with others, to be concerned with others' feelings, and to work to get along better. (pp. 6–7)

Substantial empirical evidence supports Orlick's (1978) assertion. Cooperative play indeed enhances cooperation and a number of its prosocial concomitants.

Bryant and Crockenberg (1974) and Jacovino (1980), have each demonstrated the potency of cooperative games for enhancing such components of cooperation as mutual concern, attentiveness to and feelings of obligation for other students, and mutual liking. DeVries, Muse, and Wells (1971), have successfully used cooperative games to produce a peer climate combining academic involvement and peer encouragement. In a study by DeVries, Edwards, and Wells (1974), cooperative games increased divergent thinking, time on task, student preference for cooperative versus competitive activities, and student belief that peers had a substantial interest in one's academic success. Cook (1969) and DeVries and Edwards (1973) also successfully employed cooperative games to increase cooperative behavior between interracial groups.

In all, cooperative gaming, much like cooperative learning, has been shown to yield reliable and substantial cooperation-enhancing and related prosocial effects in both elementary and secondary level students. A lengthy listing and description of such games, activities, and exercises, organized by age group, is provided in Goldstein (1999).

Some non-violent games are cooperative versions of traditionally competitive ones; some are brand new games and sports. Hundreds of them exist. Here is a small sample. For three- to seven-year olds:

- Cooperative hide and seek. Instead of having one player search for everyone else, everyone else seeks out one player. All players but one count to 100 with their eyes closed, while the single player finds a hiding place big enough to hold everybody. Everyone then searches for the hider. Each one who finds the hider hides there too, until everyone is squashed into the hiding place.
- Non-elimination Simon Says. Two games begin simultaneously, each with their own leader. If a player follows the leader after a "do this" with no "Simon says," that player transfers to the second game and joins in. There is no elimination from play, only movement between two parallel games.

For eight- to twelve-year olds:

- Tug of peace. People sit in a circle with a thick rope inside the circle at their feet. The ends of the rope are tied together. Everyone pulls at the same time so that the entire group can stand up together.
- Long, long, long jump. One child jumps, and a second child uses the place where the first landed as a jump-off place. Players, competing against themselves as they cooperate with each other, can attempt to better their total collective distance on successive tries.

For thirteen- to seventeen-year olds:

- Blindfolded soccer. Players on each team pair up. One of each pair is blindfolded and is the only one who can touch the ball. The other gives verbal instructions but cannot contact the ball. There are no goalies, and two balls are used. After a few goals, the members of each pair change roles.

- Boss, I can't come to work today. This is a mutual storytelling activity in which players first pair up. Pair number one starts a sentence, such as "Boss, I can't come to work today" and then each player in turn expands the story by adding one or more words or phrases to the original sentence.

Our experience, and that of others, playing such games with children of all ages is that, first, they think it (as we also may) quite strange. Their set is to compete, not cooperate when playing. However, almost without exception, when you can ease them into trying the game they indeed enjoy it very much. Competition often breeds aggression. Cooperation often breeds cooperation. I very strongly recommend non-violent cooperative games.

In contrast to contact, conflict resolution, and cooperative learning—each a long-standing and well-established approach to altering the underpinnings of group conflict and aggression—the remainder of this chapter is devoted to description of intervention approaches that for their group aggression modification potential are appropriately considered emergent techniques and procedures.

EMPATHY TRAINING

Throughout this book, repeated reference is made to an array of related psychological processes that enable one group both to view another group as set apart and then to act toward that out-group in a discriminatory, hostile, and even physically harmful manner. The processes thus involved have been variously labeled differentiation, compartmentalization, categorization, diminishment, scapegoating, devaluation, depersonalization, enmification, and, in extremis, dehumanization. In each instance, the in-group perceivers views the out-group target as increasingly separate, increasingly different, increasingly undesirable and, as the process unfolds, increasingly less than human. D. L. Horowitz (2001) describes this phenomenon as accompanied by a pseudospeciation process, in which " . . . while man is obviously one species, he . . . split(s) up into groups (from tribes to nations, from castes to classes, from religions to ideologies) which provide their members with a firm sense of unique and superior human identity . . . "

In the present section, I propose that an especially significant source of intergroup conflict is insufficient levels of between-group empathy and, thus, that heightened capacity for and utilization of empathy can help decompartmentalize, decategorize, personalize, and humanize in-group–out-group perceptions and relationships. Others have offered a similar view regarding the centrality of empathy. Allport (1954) held empathy to be "the most important quality required to improve relations among ethnic groups," as did White (1984) who asserted that "empathy is the *great* corrective for all forms of war-promoting misperception." Keefe (1976) has defined empathy as a process consisting of perceptual, reverberatory, cognitive analysis, and communication components. The first phase of the empathic process begins, according to Keefe, as the observer perceives the feeling state and thoughts of the other by means of the overt behavioral cues displayed by the other. In the second phase, the observer's perceptions generate both cognitive and affective responses in himself or herself. Here, the observer seeks to avoid stereotyping, value judgments, the formulation of hypotheses, or other forms of cognitive analysis. Instead, he or she seeks to hold such cognitive processes in abeyance while allowing and encouraging a largely unfettered, "as-if" experiencing of the other's affective world. Next, in the detachment and decoding phase of cognitive analysis, the observer seeks to distinguish among, sort out, and label his or her own feelings and those he or she perceives as being experienced by the other person. In the fourth phase of Keefe's definition of empathy the observer communicates accurate feedback to the other regarding the other's affect.

Why train empathy? Enhanced empathic ability may reduce in-group favoritism and out-group bias (Hoffman, 1977), as well as favorably influencing such other group relevant dispositions and behaviors as altruism and cooperativeness. Empathy also has a consistently negative association with aggressive behavior (Eisenberg & Miller, 1987; Feshbach, 1982; Selman, 1980). The more we tune in to the other person, experience her emotional and/or cognitive world, and take her perspective, the less likely or able are we to inflict harm or injury on the other. As noted earlier, those interested in promoting aggression, whether via interpersonal conflict or military warfare, capitalize on the reciprocal of this finding—that is, the more we can dehumanize others (label them pejoratively, ignore their perspectives)—the better able we are to aggress against them.

The positive relatedness of empathy to prosocial behavior, and its inverse association with aggressive behavior, while certainly not invariant (Eisenberg & Miller, 1987), and stronger for adults than for children (Goldstein & Michaels, 1985), are nevertheless substantial and reliable research findings. They are findings which provide a substantial, empirically based justification for our assertion that the enhancement of empathy can and does serve an ameliorative role in in-group–out-group conflict and, hence, that its training is a worthwhile pursuit.

If as I believe, agreeing with Keefe (1976), that empathy is most accurately conceptualized as a four-stage sequence consisting of perception, affective reverberation, cognitive analysis and communication, such should dictate both the manner and content defining its teaching. I have developed and presented just such an empathy training program (Goldstein, 1999a), adding to this four-stage sequence a preprogram, readiness training stage, and a post-program transfer- and maintenance-enhancement stage, and summarize its constituent procedures in Table 6.5. Note that the procedures listed for each of its six training component goals are to be considered as *alternative* routes to such goals.

The stage-oriented empathy training program presented is admittedly complex, its implementation demanding. Yet I recommend it both because empathy itself is multifaceted and literally requires multifaceted intervention for its enhancement, and because I believe its implementation demandingness is worth the effort in probable prosocial, conflict-reducing payoff.

MORAL EDUCATION

Moral education, broadly defined, consists of didactic and experiential activities and contents designed to enhance the prosocial quality of student thinking and behavior. The explicit educational goals of these activities have variously been

Table 6.5   Empathy training: a components approach

I. *Readiness training*
  1. Acquisition of empathy preparatory skills (Frank, 1977)
     (a) Imagination skills—To increase accurate identification of implied meanings
     (b) Behavioral observation skills—To increase accurate prediction of other's overt behavior
     (c) Flexibility skills—To increase differentiation ability in shifting from (a) to (b)
  2. Elimination of empathy skill acquisition inhibitors
     (a) Programmed self-instruction to understand one's perceptual biases (Bullmer, 1972)
     (b) Interpersonal Process Recall to reduce affect-associated anxiety (Pereira, 1978)
II. *Perceptual training*
  1. Programmed self-instruction (Bullmer, 1972) to increase interpersonal perceptual accuracy and objectivity
  2. Observational sensitivity training (H. C. Smith, 1973) to increase competence in recording sensory impressions, and discriminate them from inferential, interpretive impressions
III. *Affective reverberation training*
  1. Meditation (Goleman, 1977; Lesh, 1970)
  2. Structural integration or Rolfing (Keen, 1970; Rolf, 1977)
  3. Reichian therapy (Lowen & Lowen, 1977; Reich, 1933/1949)
  4. Bioenergetics (Lowen & Lowen, 1977)
  5. Alexander Technique (Alexander, 1969)
  6. Feldenkrais' Awareness Through Movement (Feldenkrais, 1970; 1972)
  7. Dance therapy (Bernstein, 1975; Pesso, 1967)
  8. Sensory awareness training (Brooks, 1974; Gunther, 1968)
  9. Focussing (Gendlin, 1984)
  10. Laban–Bartenieff method (Bartenieff & Lewis, 1980)
IV. *Cognitive analysis training*
  1. Discrimination training (Carkhuff, 1969) in utilizing perceptual (II) and reverberatory (III) information
  2. Exposure (to e.g., facial expressions) plus guided practice and feedback on affective labeling accuracy (Allport, 1924; Davitz, 1964)
V. *Communication training*
  1. Didactic-experiential training (Carkhuff, 1969)
  2. Interpersonal living laboratory (Egan, 1976)
  3. Relationship enhancement (Guerney, 1964)
  4. Microtraining: enriching intimacy program (Ivey & Authier, 1971)
  5. Structured learning training (Goldstein, 1981)
VI. *Transfer and maintenance training*
  1. Provision of general principles (Duncan, 1959; Judd, 1902)
  2. Maximizing identical elements (Osgood, 1953; Thorndike & Woodworth, 1901)
  3. Maximizing response availability (Mandler, 1954; Underwood & Schulz, 1960)
  4. Maximizing stimulus variability (Callantine & Warren, 1955; Shore & Sechrest, 1961)
  5. Programmed, real-world reinforcement (Goldstein, 2000)

termed values, humanism, character, morality, emotionality and social awareness, and social problem solving. The particular programs existing toward these ends are both many and varied. In addition to the three we will look at in a bit more detail—character education (American Institute for Character Education, 1974), values clarification (Raths, Harmon, & Simon, 1966), and moral education (Kohlberg, 1969, 1971, 1976)—there exist ultimate life goals (Beck, 1971), the learning to care program (McPhail, Ungoed-Thomas, & Chapman, 1975), Shaver's public issues program (Newman & Oliver, 1970), moral components (J. Wilson, 1972), the classroom meeting (Glasser, 1969), identity education (Weinstein & Fantini, 1970), affective education (J. P. Miller, 1976), confluent education (Castillo, 1974), and human relations training in school contexts (Bradford, Gibb, & Benne, 1964).

Character Education, in its several forms—*The good American program* (Mayer, 1964); *Freedom's code* (Hill, 1965); *The American heritage: Design for national character* (Trevitt, 1964) and, especially the *Living with me and others* (American Institute for Character Education, 1974)—typically is used with lower, elementary grade children and employs a variety of didactic and participatory techniques—e.g., lecture, readings, group discussion, role play—to teach explicitly an array of character traits and standards of ethical conduct, such as generosity, honesty, courage, fairness, responsibility, and tolerance. Advocates of this approach to morality provide impressionistic evidence of its effectiveness, while educators and others opposed to its utilization in public schools object in particular to the manner in which character education programs appear to constitute an indoctrinational orientation to the teaching of specific values.

The values clarification (Raths, Harmon, & Simon, 1966) approach to teaching morality became popular in the United States in the mid-1960s, in part in response to this antiindoctrination viewpoint. Values, they held, are not fixed, immutable, universal, nor is inculcation the appropriate means to their acquisition. Instead, in their view, values are relative to subgroups within society, to time, place, and circumstances, often conflict with one another, and, in any event, are a matter of personal discovery and choice, not external inculcation. Thus, rather than teaching a specific set of prosocial values, the values-clarification approach seeks to teach youngsters how to develop and clarify their own values, i.e., the process of valuing. Specifically, teaching goals include how to choose values freely, how to choose from among alternatives, how to weigh and consider alternative values carefully, how to act upon one's value choices, and related valuing processes.

Values clarification, therefore, proceeds not by (as in character education) teacher moralizing, sermonizing, advice-giving, or evaluating, but by what Raths, Harman, and Simon (1966) call the value-clarifying response. Using an array of exercises, didactic and other discussion-generating activities and materials (see, for example, Simon, Howe, & Kirschenbaum, 1972), the teacher employing values clarification responds to students in ways that raise value questions in the student's mind, encourage him/her to examine value-relevant beliefs and actions, stimulate him/her to consider alternative values and their bases, and thus clarify his/her own values.

The values clarification approach has become a part of curricular activities in many elementary and secondary schools in the United States, and, it appears, will continue to have a substantial prosocial impact in the years ahead. Much the same hopeful conclusion may be drawn regarding the final approach to teaching aggression alternatives in public education that we wish to consider, moral education.

Though the moral education perspective has a number of proponents in America, Lawrence Kohlberg has been its most active theoretician and developer (e.g.,

Kohlberg, 1969, 1971, 1976). While concurring with the values-clarification view that the teaching of particular values, as in character education, is indoctrination and to be avoided, Kohlberg also feels that major aspects of the values clarification stance favoring value relatively are erroneous. Instead, he holds, there is a basic consistency across people and across cultures in the stages through which people pass in their development of personal and social values, and, further, that certain of these stages of moral reasoning are better or more adequate than others. In his Piaget-like, cognitive-developmental stage theory of moral development, Kohlberg holds that the highest stage is the ideal end-point of moral development, that movement across stages occurs in an invariant sequence, that each successive stage reflects an increasingly more integrated and effective mode of moral reasoning, and that the motivation for stage transition is cognitive conflict. The educational implication of this perspective is that moral education should take place by means of stimulating the development of increasingly more integrated and effective moral reasoning, i.e., facilitation through an invariant sequence toward the highest stage of moral development of which that individual is capable.

The specific stages of moral development in this view are:

1. *Preconventional level*. The focus at this level is on the physical impact of behavior (punishment, reward) and the power of those who enunciate society's rules and regulations.
2. *Conventional level*. Maintaining the expectations of the individual's family, group, or nation is perceived as valuable in its own right, regardless of the immediate or obvious consequences of such behavior.
3. *Postconventional level*. Morality is sought in values and principles that have validity apart from authority of those holding such values.

I noted Kohlberg's belief that motivation for stage transition is cognitive conflict. Consistent with this belief, the primary means utilized in the moral education approach for stimulating transition or movement as far along the six-stage sequence as the person is capable of moving is by the use of moral dilemmas. The presentation of a range of such dilemmas to groups of students whose members collectively show at least a one- to two-stage spread in their levels of moral development, and a free and open discussion of the dilemma, its alternative solutions, and the rationale for such alternatives can engender precisely the intensity of cognitive conflict necessary to stimulate stage transition.

Lest the relevance of moral education and the enhanced levels of moral development it can promote be obscure as a prosocial alternative to aggression, it should be noted that, in the United States, according to Kohlberg (1976) and others (Fodor, 1972; Hudgins and Prentice, 1973), preconventional moral reasoning is characteristic of children under age 10, some adolescents, and the vast majority of juvenile delinquents and adult criminals. Further, it should be noted that conventional moral reasoning is characteristic of the large majority of American adults and adolescents. Yet it is postconventional moral reasoning which correlates most highly with such prosocial behaviors as non-violence, altruism, resistance to cheating, and the like. It is clear, therefore, that moral education's already substantial inroad into American public education is to be greatly encouraged.

CROSS-CULTURAL TRAINING

> Cross-cultural training programs (also called intercultural communications training programs) are short term efforts to prepare people to live and work effectively with people from other cultural backgrounds. Training can also prepare people for emotional experiences stemming from intercultural contact, such as culture shock, confrontations with their prejudices, and challenges to their existing stereotypes. (Brislin & Horvath, 1997, p. 332)

The goals of such training programs are several and complementary. One is to change people's *thinking*, by providing knowledge about cultural differences and likely issues to be faced when in contact. Primary here is aiding trainees to think more complexly and take multiple viewpoints. A second goal of the several cross-cultural training methods targets trainees' *emotional* response to new cultural experiences, and aims at reducing the stress and feelings of confusion and ineffectiveness that characterize culture shock. Such training also targets *behavior*, offering those involved opportunities to practice in advance the unfamiliar behaviors that are likely to be adaptive in other cultures.

Specific cross-cultural training approaches may be cognitive, attributional, experiential, focused on self-awareness or, optimally, a combination of such methods. Cognitive methods provide facts and information about specific cultures and about the general challenges of cross-cultural interaction. Attributional means emphasize cultural relativity, and the manner in which critical events may be interpreted quite differently from culture to culture. Experiential techniques seek to give a more direct "feel" for cross-cultural contact by means of role plays, simulations, field trips, and case studies. Finally, self-awareness training seeks to help trainees become more aware of their own culture, and the impacts on oneself when persons from other cultures challenge our own cultural assumptions.

INTERGROUP WORKSHOP

This approach to aiding in the reduction of intergroup conflict, pioneered by Kelman (1998), might alternatively be termed "negotiation-readiness training." Trainers comprise of a panel of social scientists possessing, among them, group process and intergroup conflict expertise, as well as familiarity with the groups in conflict. Kelman (1998) comments:

> The role of the third party in our model differs from that of the traditional mediator. Unlike many mediators, we do not propose (and certainly, unlike arbitrators, we do not impose) solutions. Rather, we try to facilitate a process. The task of the third party is to provide the setting, create the atmosphere, establish the norms, and offer occasional interventions that make it possible for such a process to evolve. (p. 310)

Emphasis in the intergroup workshop is on identifying and ameliorating barriers to the initiation of meaningful negotiation. It is, in brief, an intergroup "prepping" approach. Through their facilitated interaction, the parties in conflict are helped to generate means for collaboratively coming to the negotiating table. To do so, respective views and positions of the parties present and the groups they represent are discussed, as are obstacles to solution, fears, goals, and other central features of the conflict-resolution process. Kelman (1998) observes:

> ...the participants are asked to explore the overall shape of a solution that would meet the needs and calm the fears of both sides. Each is expected to think actively about solutions that would be satisfactory to the other, not only to themselves. Next, the participants are asked to discover the political and psychological constraints that make it difficult to implement such solutions. Finally, the discussion turns to the question of how these constraints can best be overcome and how the two sides can support each other in such an effort. (p. 314)

Kelman's (1991, 1998) extended use of such workshopping with politically active Israeli and Palestinian citizens, led him to conclude that participants learn that there is someone on the other side to talk to and something worthwhile to talk about. They gain, he claims, insight into each others' perspectives, awareness of both obstacles to change and possibilities for its occurrence, and ways of promoting such change through one's own actions.

NON-VIOLENT ACTION

Non-violent action is, first of all, *action*. It is neither inaction, passivity, nor surrender. Quite the contrary. Its techniques, as G. Sharp (1998) describes, use "non-military weapons: psychological, political, social, and economic ones." (p. 375) In broad terms, non-violent action involves its users either refusing to do things they are expect or required to do, or insisting on doing things they normally do not do or that are forbidden. Sharp (1998) comments:

> Non-violent struggle operates by mobilizing the power potential of people and institutions to enable them to wield power themselves and to restrict or sever the sources of power of their opponents ... This capacity to wield power themselves and to undermine the power of opponents is important because the power of all oppressive groups, of all dictators and aggressors, depends upon the support they receive. This support refers to acceptance of their authority and the duty to obey, the operation of the economic system and the continued functioning of the civil service and the bureaucracy, the loyalty of the army and the reliability of the police, the blessing of the rulers by religious bodies, and the cooperation of workers and managers. Non-violent struggle is a type of action uniquely suited to undermining and withdrawing these "pillars of support" that uphold an oppressive system. (p. 375)

Non-violent action may be effective in one or more of four ways: conversion, accommodation, coercion, and disintegration. In conversion, the target of the non-violent action "comes over" in its beliefs and behaviors to the non-violent group's position. In accommodation, they partially do so, perhaps in the form of compromise. Non-violent coercion occurs when the opponent group yields to the demands being made, and disintegration occurs when "the non-cooperation and defiance have so severed the opponent group's sources of power that the system or regime completely falls apart." (p. 376)

What are these methods? Sharp (1998) notes three types. *Non-violent protest and persuasion* is exemplified by such symbolic acts as vigils, marches, flag displays. *Non-cooperation* includes boycotts, labor strikes, political non-cooperation. *Non-violent intervention* takes form in sit-ins, hunger strikes, establishing parallel governments. As can be seen, its methods are varied, differing in mode, target, and intensity—but each employs non-violent means to impact, often successfully, on forces whose opinions, beliefs, behaviors the acting group seeks to change.

ECOLOGICAL MODIFICATION

Every act of aggression, whether perpetrated by individuals or groups, is a person–environment event. I have elsewhere termed the interaction of person characteristics and qualities of the physical and social context in which the aggression takes place a "person–environment duet." (Goldstein, 1994). This view is consistent with the emphasis in contemporary personality theory in viewing all forms of behavior as a resultant of the interaction of person and environment. Altman et al. (1992) represent this interactionist perspective well:

> People and psychological processes are embedded in and inseparable from their physical and social contexts...There are no separate actors in an event; the actions of one person are understood in relation to the actions of other people, and in relation to spatial, situational, and temporal circumstances in which the actors are embedded. (p. 195)

All of the intervention approaches I have examined in this chapter have been person-oriented in their targetting, seeking to alter the actions of either potential perpetrators of group aggression or the "other side's" persons with whom they are interacting. In the present section, I wish to urge similarly that group aggression may be made less likely if one is able creatively to alter the nature, locale, or contents of the protagonists' physical environments. Step one in doing so would appear to be identifying the locations in which such events are likely. Earlier, I wrote of borderline and boundary areas between ethnic gangs or ethnic enclaves. Forbes (1997) provides evidence that particular cities and regions, in contrast to parallel other venues, have been the sites of rioting over and over again. A number of features of neighborhood ecology, particularly its level of incivilities (e.g., litter, graffiti, abandoned homes and stores, broken windows, and similar expressions of decline) and its density (amount of space in relation to number of people) have both been shown to be precursors to aggressive behavior (Skogan, 1990; Stokols, 1978). Within certain physical structures, such as sports stadia or rock concert halls, hard experience has provided riot-proneness information of value in this context.

To the extent that group aggression-friendly venues, whether micro-sites such as particular buildings or macro-sites such as particular cities, can be identified as aggression-probable locations, to that extent a strategy of ecological modification becomes possible. To date, that strategy has taken its most prominent concrete form in an array of steps directly contrary to both the spirit and methods of intergroup contact. What has been recommended, in fact, is a no-contact policy. In sports venues, especially in response to rioting by fans of contending soccer teams, one finds recommendations for separating such groups by use of fences or dry moats, increased presence of police and other control agents, and arranging that not all fans leave at the same time, for example, by having postgame concerts or several games in succession.

In the same preventive spirit, but on a much larger scale, Bell-Fialkoff (1996) comments with regard to intractable ethnic rioting:

> Thus the question, ultimately, boils down to this: what to do with recalcitrant minorities when every solution, every compromise has been tried and failed? In such cases, the only workable solution is population transfer and resettlement. It goes without saying that the transfer has to be conducted in a humane, well-organized manner... Although painful to the evicted populations, historically such forced migrations have played a positive role: they have helped to separate the combatants, stabilize the situation, prevent future outbreaks of violence, and promote regional peace. (p. 220)

Toward the same goal of physical separation, and in particular targeted to minimizing the spread as diffusion of group aggression from one locale to another, Weller and Quarantelli (1973) urges steps leading to "isolation" and Horowitz (2001) does similarly toward "quarantining" the aggression. Group aggression in its diverse forms is quite typically multiply determined, and thus requires an array of alternative means for its control and reduction. I suggest that ecological modification is a worthy strategy to be included in such an intervention array.

My intervention recommendations in the context of group aggression are decisions based on variable proportions of data, experience, and opinion. On such a less than perfect basis, I have highlighted a series of what I have classified as established and emerging such approaches. It is these several means, in particular, that I wish to urge for further use, development, and evaluation of efficacy. However, there are of course a large number of additional interventions in past, present, or potential use for reducing collective conflict, aggression, and violence, and they ought at least be enumerated here. These include integrative bargaining (Sandole & Sandole-Staroste, 1987), coexistence training (White, 1977), antibias education (Derman-Sparks, 1998), intergroup interaction skills training (Goldstein, 1999), anger control training (Feindler & Ecton, 1986), unilateral de-escalation (Osgood, 1953), facilitated problem solving (Pruitt & Rubin, 1986), concession-making (Christie, Wagner, & Winter, 2001), town meetings (Volpe, 1998), mobilizing regional and international organizations (Chayes & Chayes, 1998) and, appropriately lastly, use of deterrence and threat (Jervis, 1986)—all of which are strongly recommendable alternatives to the choice too frequently made: the use of deadly force.

REFERENCES

Abadinsky, H. (1979). *Social service in criminal justice.* Englewood Cliffs, NJ: Prentice-Hall.

Abrahams, R. D. (1962). Playing the dozens. *Journal of American Folklore,* **75**, 209–220.

Adelmann, P. K., & Zajonc, R. (1989). Facial efference and the experience of emotion. *Annual Review of Psychology,* **40**, 249–280.

Adorno, T. W., Frenkel-Brunswik, E., Levinson, D. J., & Sanford, R. M. (1950). *The authoritarian personality.* New York: Harper.

Ahmed, Y., & Smith, P. (1994). Bullying in schools and the issue of sex differences. In J. Archer (Ed.), *Male violence.* London: Routledge.

Alberts, J. K., Kellar-Guenther, Y., & Corman, S. R. (1996). That's not funny: Understanding recipients' responses to teasing. *Western Journal of Communication,* **60**, 337–357.

Aldag, R. J., & Fuller, S. R. (1993). A reappraisal of the groupthink phenomenon and new model of group decision processes. *Psychological Bulletin,* **13**, 533–552.

Alexander, F. M. (1969). *The resurrection of the body.* New York: Dell.

Allport, F. H. (1924). *Social psychology.* New York, Boston: Houghton Mifflin.

Allport, G. W. (1954). *The nature of prejudice.* Cambridge/Reading, MA: Addison-Wesley.

Allport, G. W., & Postman, L. (1947). *The psychology of rumor.* New York: Holt, Rinehart & Winston.

Altman, I., Brown, B. B., Staples, B., & Werner, C. M. (1992). A transactional approach to close relationships. In W. B. Walsh, K. H. Craik & R. H. Price (Eds.), *Person-environment psychology: Models and perspectives.* Hillsdale, NJ: Erlbaum.

American Association of University Women (1993). *Sexual harassment at school: A national survey.* Washington, DC.

American Institute for Character Education (1974). *Living with me and others.* San Antonio, TX.

Amir, Y. (1969). Contact hypothesis in ethnic relations. *Psychological Bulletin,* **71**, 319–342.

Amir, Y. (1976). The role of intergroup contact in change of prejudice and race relations. In P. Katz & D. A. Taylor (Eds.), *Towards the elimination of racism.* New York: Pergamon.

Aronson, E. (1961). The effect of effort on the attractiveness of rewarded and unrewarded stimuli. *Journal of Abnormal and Social Psychology,* **63**, 375–380.

Aronson, E., & Mills, J. (1959). The effects of severity of initiation on liking for a group. *Journal of Abnormal and Social Psychology,* **59**, 177–181.

Aronson, E., Blaney, N., Stephan, C., Sikes, J., & Snapp, M. (1978). *The jigsaw classroom.* Beverly Hills, CA: Sage.

Arora, C. M. J. (1994). Is there any point in trying to reduce bulllying in secondary schools? *Educational Psychology in Practice,* **10**, 155–162.

Arrow, H., & McGrath, J. E. (1995). Membership dynamics in groups at work: A theoretical framework. *Research in Organizational Behavior,* **17**, 373–411.

Asbury, H. (1971). *The gangs of New York.* New York: Capricorn. (original work published 1927)

Asher, S. R., & Coie, J. D. (Eds.), (1990). *Peer rejection in childhood.* New York: Cambridge University Press.

Ashmore, R. D. (1970). Solving the problem of prejudice. In B. E. Collins (Ed.), *Social psychology.* Reading, MA: Addison-Wesley.

Bailey, L. A., & Timm, L. A. (1996). More on women's—and men's—expletives. *Anthropological Linguistics*, **8**, 438–449.

Baier, J. L., & Williams, P. (1983). Fraternity hazing revisited: Attitudes towards hazing. *Journal of College Student Personnel*, **24**, 301.

Bandura, A. (1973). *Aggression: A social learning analysis*. Englewood Cliffs, NJ: Prentice-Hall.

Barak-Glantz, F. L. (1985). The anatomy of another prison riot. In M. Braswell, S. Dillingham, & R. Montgomery (Eds.), *Prison violence in America*. Cincinnati, OH: Anderson.

Barash, D. P. (1991). *Beloved enemies: Our need for opponents*. New York: Prometheus Books.

Barner-Barry, C. (1986). Rob: Children's tacit use of peer ostracism to control aggressive behavior. *Ethology and Sociobiology*, **7**, 281–293.

Baron, R. A., & Richardson, D. R. (1994). *Human aggression*. New York: Plenum Press.

Baron, R. S., Kerr, N. L., & Miller, N. (1992). *Group process, group decision, group action*. Pacific Grove, CA: Brooks/Cole.

Bar-Tal, D. (1990). Group beliefs and group changes. In D. Bar-Tal (Ed.), *Group beliefs*. New York: Springer-Verlag.

Bartenieff, I., & Lewis, D. (1980). *Body movement: Coping with the environment*. New York: Gordon & Breach.

Bass, B. M., & Dunteman, G. (1963). Biases in the evaluation of one's own group, its allies and opponents. *Journal of Conflict Resolution*, **7**, 16–20.

Bass, M. (1981). *Stogdill's handbook of leadership*. New York: Free Press.

Batsche, G., & Knoff, H. M. (1994). Bullies and their victims: Understanding a pervasive problem in the schools. *School Psychology Review*, **23**, 165–174.

Bavelas, J. B., Black, A., Lemery, C. R., & Mullett, J. (1987). Motor mimicry as primitive empathy. In N. Eisenberg & J. Strayer (Eds.), *Empathy and its development* (pp. 317–338). New York: Cambridge University Press.

Beady, C., & Slavin, R. E. (1981). Making success available to all students in desegregated schools. *Integrated Education*, **18**, 28–31.

Beck, C. (1971). *Moral education in the schools: Some practical suggestions*. Toronto: Ontario Institute for Studies in Education.

Becker, H. S. (1963). *Outsiders: Studies in the sociology of deviance*. Glencoe, IL: Free Press.

Beene, K. D., & Sheats, P. (1948). Functional roles of group members. *Journal of Social Issues*, **4**, 41–49.

Bell-Fialkoff, A. (1996). *Ethnic cleansing*. New York: St. Martin's Press.

Ben-Ari, R., & Amir, Y. (1986). Contact between Arab and Jewish youth in Israel: Reality and potential. In M. Hewstone & R. Brown (Eds.), *Contact and conflict in intergroup encounters* (pp. 45–58). London: Basil Blackwell.

Bentley, K. M., & Li, A. K. (1994). Bully and victim problems in elementary schools and students' beliefs about aggression. *Canadian Journal of School Psychology*, **11**, 153–165.

Berkowitz, L. (n.d.). *When the trigger pulls the finger*. Washington, DC: American Psychological Association.

Berkowitz, L., & LePage, A. (1967). Weapons as aggression-eliciting stimuli. *Journal of Personality and Social Psychology*, **7**, 202–207.

Berkowitz, L., Lepinski, J. P., & Angulo, E. J. (1969). Awareness of own anger level and subsequent aggression. *Journal of Personality and Social Psychology*, **11**, 293–300.

Bernieri, F. J. (1988). Coordinated movement and rapport in teacher–student interactions. *Journal of Nonverbal Behavior*, **12**, 120–138.

Bernstein, J. Y., & Watson, M. W. (1997). Children who are targets of bullying: A victim pattern. *Journal of Interpersonal Violence*, **12**, 483–498.

Bernstein, P. (1975). *Theory and methods in dance-movement therapy*. Dubuque, IA: Kendall/Hunt.

Berryman-Fine, C., & Brunner, C. C. (1987). The effects of sex of source and target on interpersonal conflict management styles. *Southern Speech Communication Journal*, **53**, 38–48.

Besag, V. (1997). The playground. In M. Elliott (Ed.), *Bullying: A practical guide to coping with schools*. London: Pitman Publishing.

Billig, M. G. (1973). *Social psychology and intergroup relations*. London: Academic Press.

Billig, M. G., & Tajfel, H. (1973). Social categorization and similarity in intergroup behaviour. *European Journal of Social Psychology*, **3**, 27–52.

Bjerregeard, B., & Lizotte, A. J. (1990). Gun ownership and gang membership. *Journal of Criminal Law and Criminology*, **81**, 501–511.

Bjorkqvist, K. L., Lagerspetz, K. M. J., & Kaukiainen, A. (1992). Do girls manipulate and boys fight? *Aggressive Behavior*, **18**, 117–127.

Blake, R. R., & Mouton, J. S. (1961). Reactions to intergroup competition under win–lose conditions. *Management Science*, **7**, 420–435.

Blake, R. R., & Mouton, J. S. (1986). From theory to practice in intergroup problem solving. In S. Worchel & W. G. Austin (Eds.), *Psychology of intergroup relations*. Chicago: Nelson-Hall.

Blaney, N. T., Stephen, S., Rosenfield, D., Aronson, E., & Sikes, J. (1977). Interdependence in the classroom: A field study. *Journal of Educational Psychology*, **69**, 121–128.

Block, C. R. (1985). Lethal violence in Chicago over seventeen years: Homicides known to the police, 1965–1981. Report to the Illinois Criminal Justice Information Authority.

Block, C. R., Christakos, A., Jacob, A., & Przybylski, R. (1996). *Street gangs and crime: Patterns and trends in Chicago.* Chicago, IL: Illinois Criminal Justice Information Authority.

Blumer, H. (1958). Race prejudice as a sense of group position. *Pacific Sociological Review*, **1**, 3–7.

Blumer, H. (1960). Race prejudice as a sense of group position. *Pacific Sociological Review*, **1**, 3–5.

Bodenhausen, G. V. (1985). Stereotypic biases in social decision making and memory: Testing process models of stereotype use. *Journal of Personality and Social Psychology*, **55**, 726–737.

Bogardus, E. S. (1943). Gangs of Mexican-American youth. *Sociology and Social Research*, **28**, 55–66.

Bohstedt, J. (1994). The dynamics of riots: Escalation and diffusion/contagion. In M. Potegal & J. F. Knutson (Eds.), *The dynamics of aggression*. Hillsdale, NJ: Erlbaum.

Boldizar, J., Perry, D. G., & Perry, L. C. (1989). Outcome values and aggression. *Child Development*, **60**, 571–579.

Bond, M. H., & Venus, C. K. (1991). Resistance to group or personal insults in an ingroup or outgroup context. *International Journal of Psychology*, **26**, 83–94.

Borden, R. J. (1975). Witnessed aggression: Influence of an observer's sex and values on aggressive responding. *Journal of Personality and Social Psychology*, **31**, 567–573.

Boulton, M. J., & Smith, P. K. (1994). Bully/victim problems in middle school children: Stability, self-perceived competence, peer perceptions, and peer acceptance. *British Journal of Developmental Psychology*, **12**, 315–329.

Boulton, M. J., & Underwood, K. (1992). Bully/victim problems among middle school children. *British Journal of Educational Psychology*, **62**, 73–87.

Bradford, L. P., Gibb, J. R., & Benne, K. R. (1964). *T-group theory and laboratory method*. New York: Wiley.

Brewer, M. B. (1979). In-group bias in the minimal intergroup situation: A cognitive-motivational analysis. *Psychological Bulletin*, **86**, 307–324.

Brewer, M. B., & Brown, R. J. (1998). Intergroup relations. In D. T. Gilbert, S. T. Fiske, & G. Lindzey (Eds.). *The handbook of social psychology*, New York: McGraw-Hill.

Brewer, M. B., & Miller, N. (1984). Beyond the contact hypothesis: Theoretical perspectives on desegregation. In N. Miller & M. B. Brewer (Eds.), *Groups in contact: The psychology of desegregation*. New York: Academic Press.

Brewer, M. B., & Miller, N. (1996). *Intergroup relations*. Pacific Grove, CA: Brooks/Cole.

Brislin, R. W., & Horvath, A. (1997). Cross-cultural training and multicultural education. In J. W. Berry, M. H. Segall, & C. Kagitcibasi (Eds.), *Handbook of cross-cultural psychology*. Needham, MA: Allyn & Bacon.

Brislin, R. W., Cushner, K., Cherrie, C., & Yong, M. (1986). *Intercultural interactions: A practical guide*. Beverly Hills, CA: Sage.

Brooks, C. V. W. (1974). *Sensory awareness: The rediscovery of experiencing.* New York: Viking.

Brown, R. J., & Abrams, D. (1986). The effects of intergroup similarity and goal interdependence on intergroup attitudes and task performance. *Journal of Experimental Social Psychology*, **22**, 78–92.

Brown, R. J. & Ross, G. F. (1982). Interpersonal and intergroup behaviour. In J. Turner & H. Giles (Eds.), *Intergroup behaviour*. Oxford: Basil Blackwell.

Brown, R. M. (1989). Historical patterns of violence. In T. R. Gurr (Ed.), *Violence in America*. Newbury Park, CA: Sage.

Bruner, J. S. (1957). On perceptual readiness. *Psychological Review*, **64**, 123–151.

Bryan, W. A. (1987). Contemporary fraternity and sorority issues. In R. B. Winston, Jr., W. R. Nettles, III, & J. H. Opper, Jr. (Eds.), *Fraternities and sororities on the contemporary college campus*. San Francisco: Jossey-Bass.

Bryant, B. K., & Crockenberg, S. B. (1974). Cooperative and competitive environments. *Catalogue of Selected Documents in Psychology*, **4**, 53.

Buchanan, E. T., Shanley, M., Correnti, R., & Hammond, E. (1982). Hazing: Collective stupidity, insensitivity and irresponsibility. *NASPA Journal*, **20**, 56–68.

Buck, R. (1980). Nonverbal behavior and the theory of emotion: The facial feedback hypothesis. *Journal of Personality and Social Psychology*, **38**, 811–824.

Buder, E. (1991). *Vocal synchrony in conversations: Spectral analysis of fundamental voice frequency*. Unpublished doctoral dissertation, Department of Communication Arts, University of Wisconsin-Madison.

Buford, B. (1991). *Among the thugs: The experience, and the seduction of crowd violence*. New York: W. W. Norton.

Bukowski, W. M., & Sippola, L. K. (2001). Groups, individuals, and victimization. In J. Juvonen & S. Graham (Eds.), *Peer harassment in school*. New York: Guilford Press.

Bullmer, K. (1972). Improving accuracy of interpersonal perception through a direct teaching method. *Journal of Counseling Psychology*, **19**, 37–41.

Buss, D. M., Gomes, M., Higgins, D. S., & Lauterbach, K. (1987). Tactics of manipulation. *Journal of Personality and Social Psychology*, **52**, 1219–1229.

Byrne, D. (1964). Repression-sensitization as a dimension of personality. In B. A. Maher (Ed.), *Progress in experimental personality research* (pp. 169–220). New York: Academic Press.

Cairns, R. B., & Cairns, B. D. (1991). Social cognition and social networks: A developmental perspective. In D. J. Pepler & K. H. Rubin (Eds.), *The development and treatment of childhood aggression*. Hillsdale, NJ: Erlbaum.

Callantine, M. F., & Warren, J. M. (1955). Learning sets in human concept formation. *Psychological Reports*, **1**, 363–367.

Cameron, P. (1969). Frequency and kinds of words in various social settings, or what the hell is going on? *Pacific Sociological Review*, **12**, 101–104.

Campbell, D. T. (1958). Common fate, similarity and other indices of the status of aggregates of persons as social entities. *Behavioural Science*, **3**, 14–25.

Campbell, D. T. (1965). Ethnocentric and other altruistic motives. In D. Levine (Ed.), *Nebraska symposium on motivation* (Vol. 13). Lincoln: University of Nebraska Press.

Capozza, D., & Brown, R. (2000). Social identity theory in retrospect and prospect. In D. Capozza & R. Brown (Eds.), *Social identity processes: Trends in theory and research*. Thousand Oaks, CA: Sage.

Carkhuff, R. (1969). *Helping and human relations*, 2 Vols. New York: Holt, Rinehart and Winston.

Carlson, M., Marcus-Newhall, A., & Miller, N. (1990). Effects of situational aggression cues: A quantitative review. *Journal of Personality and Social Psychology*, **58**, 622–633.

Carron, A. V. (1980). *Social psychology of sport*. Ithaca, NY: Mouvement.

Carter, S. F. (1998). *Civility: manners, morals, and the etiquette of democracy*. New York: Basic Books.

Cartwright, D. S. (1975). The nature of gangs. In D. S. Cartwright, B. Tomson, & H. Schwartz (Eds.), *Gang delinquency*. Pacific Grove, CA: Brooks/Cole.

Cartwright, D. S., Howard, K., & Reuterman, N. A. (1970). Multivariate analysis of gang delinquency: II. Structural and dynamic properties of groups. *Multivariate Behavioral Research*, **5**, 303–324.

Cash, T. F. (1995). Developmental teasing about physical appearance: Retrospective descriptions and relationships with body image. *Social Behavior and Personality*, **23**, 123–130.

Castillo, G. (1974). *Left-handed teaching.* New York: Praeger.

Chaplin, J. P. (1985) *Dictionary of psychology.* New York: Bantam, Doubleday, Day.

Chayes, A. H., & Chayes, A. (1998). Mobilizing international and regional organizations for managing ethnic conflict. In E. Weiner (Ed.), *The handbook of interethnic coexistence.* New York: Continuum.

Chelladurai, P., & Saleh, S. D. (1978). Preferred leadership in sport. *Canadian Journal of Applied Sport Sciences*, **3**, 85–97.

Christie, D. J., Wagner, R. V., & Winter, D. D. (2001). *Peace, conflict, and violence.* Upper Saddle River, NJ: Prentice Hall.

Clark, R. A., O'Dell, L. L., & Willingana, S. C. (1986). The development of compromising as an alternative to persuasion. *Central States Speech Journal*, **37**, No. 4, 220–224.

Clarke, R. V. G. (1977). Psychology and crime. *Bulletin of the British Psychological Society*, **30**, 280–283.

Cleckley, H. (1964). *The mask of sanity.* St. Louis: Mosby.

Cloward, R. A., & Ohlin, L. E. (1960). *Delinquency and opportunity: A theory of delinquent gangs.* New York: Free Press.

Cohen, A. K. (1966). The delinquency subculture. In R. Giallombardo (Ed.), *Juvenile delinquency.* New York: Wiley.

Cohen, A. K. (1955). *Delinquent boys: The culture of the gang.* New York: Free Press.

Cohen, E. (1980). Design and redesign of the segregated school: Problems of status, power, and conflict. In W. G. Stephan & J. Feagin (Eds.). *School desegregation.* New York: Plenum.

Coie, J. D., & Dodge, K. A. (1983). Continuities and changes in children's sociometric status: A five-year longitudinal study. *Merrill-Palmer Quarterly*, **29**, 261–282.

Coie, J. D., Dodge, K. A., Terry, R., & Wright, V. (1991). The role of aggression in peer relations: An analysis of aggressive episodes in boy's play groups. *Child Development*, **62**, 812–826.

Colvin, M. (1982). The 1980 New Mexico prison riot. *Social Problems*, **29**, 119–153.

Cook, S. W. (1969). Motives in conceptual analysis of attitude-related behavior. In W. J. Arnold & D. Levine (Eds.), *1969 Nebraska Symposium on Motivation.* Lincoln, NE: University of Nebraska Press.

Cook, S. W. (1978). Interpersonal and attitudinal outcomes in cooperating interracial groups. *Journal of Research and Development in Education*, **12**, 97–113.

Cooper, J., & Fazio, R. H. (1979). The formation and persistence of attitudes that support intergroup conflict. In W. G. Austin & S. Worchel (Eds.), *The social psychology of intergroup relations.* Pacific Grove, CA: Brooks/Cole.

Coser, L. A. (1956). *The functions of social conflict.* Glencoe, IL: Free Press.

Cowie, H., & Sharp, S. (1996). *Peer counselling in schools: A time to listen.* London: David Futton.

Craig, W., & Pepler, D. (1995). Peer processes in bullying and victimization: An observational study. *Exceptional Education in Canada*, **5**, 81–95.

Craighead, W. E., Kimball, W. H., & Rehak, P. J. (1979). Mood changes, physiological responses, and self-statements during social rejection imagery. *Journal of Consulting and Clinical Psychology*, **47**, 385–396.

Cratty, B. J. (1981). *Social psychology in athletics.* Englewood Cliffs, NJ: Prentice-Hall.

Cullen, F. T., Clark, G. A., & Polanzi, C. (1982). The seriousness of crime revisited. *Criminology*, **2**, 83–102.

Curry, G. D., & Spergel, I. A. (1992). Gang involvement and delinquency among Hispanic and African-American adolescent males. *Journal of Research in Crime and Delinquency*, **29**, 273–291.

Dansky, B. S., & Kilpatrick, D. G. (1997). Effects of sexual harassment. In W. O'Donohue (Ed.), *Sexual harassment: Theory, research, and treatment.* Boston, MA: Allyn & Bacon.

Darwin, C. (1872/1956). *The expression of the emotions in man and animals*. Chicago: University of Chicago Press.

Davies, J. L. (1969). The J-curve of rising and declining satisfactions as a cause of some great revolutions and a contained rebellion. In H. D. Graham & T. R. Gurr (Eds.), *Violence in America*. New York: Bantam Books.

Davis, L. A. (1997). Hazing in the workplace. Unpublished doctoral dissertation. The Union Institute.

Davis, M. H. (1994). *Empathy: A social psychological approach*. Boulder, CO: Westview Press.

Davitz, D. (1964). *The communication of emotional meaning*. New York: McGraw-Hill.

Dawkins, R. (1989). *The selfish gene*. Oxford: Oxford University Press.

De Angelis, T. (1998). Ostracism. *American Psychological Association Monitor*, **29**. 17–18.

Deal, T. E., & Kennedy, A. A. (1982). *Corporate cultures—The rites and rituals of corporate life*. Reading, MA: Addison-Wesley.

Deaux, K. (2000). Models, meanings, and motivations. In K. Deaux, D. Capozza, & R. Brown (Eds.), *Social identity processes*. Thousand Oaks, CA: Sage.

DeKlerk, V. (1991). Expletives: Men only? *Communication Monographs*, **58**, 156–169.

Delisle, J. R. (1994). Reach out, but don't touch. *Education Week,* September 21, p. 33.

Derman-Sparks, L. (1998). Antibias education: Toward a world of justice and peace. In E. Weiner (Ed.), *The handbook of intercultural coexistence*. New York: Continuum.

Deschenes, E. P., & Esbensen, F. (1999). Violence in gangs: Gender differences in perceptions and behavior. *Journal of Quantitative Criminology*, **15**, 63–96.

Deur, J. L., & Parke, R. D. (1970). The effects of inconsistent punishment on aggression in children. *Developmental Psychology*, **2**, 403–411.

Deutsch, M. (1951). Social relations in the classroom and grading procedures. *Journal of Educational Research*, **45**, 145–152.

Deutsch, M. (1957). *Conditions affecting cooperation: I. Factors related to the initiation of cooperation. II. Trust and cooperation*. Washington, DC: Office of Naval Research.

Deutsch, M. (1973). *The resolution of conflict*. New Haven, CT: Yale University Press.

Deutsch, M., & Collins, M. (1951). *Interracial housing: A psychological evaluation of a social experiment*. Minneapolis: University of Minnesota Press.

Deutsch, M., & Krauss, R. M. (1960). The effect of threat upon interpersonal bargaining. *Journal of Abnormal and Social Psychology*, **61**, 181–189.

DeVries, D. L., & Edwards, K. J. (1973). Learning games and student teams: Their effects on classroom processes. *American Educational Research Journal*, **10**, 307–318.

DeVries, D. L, & Slavin, R. E. (1978). Teams–games–tournaments (TGT): Review of ten classroom experiments. *Journal of Research and Development in Education*, **12,** 28–38.

DeVries, D. L., Edwards, K. J., & Slavin, R. E. (1978). Biracial learning teams and race relations in the classroom. Four field experiments using teams–games–tournament. *Journal of Educational Psychology*, **70,** 356–362.

DeVries, D. L., Edwards, K. J., & Wells, E. H. (1974). *Team competition effects on classroom processes*. Baltimore, MD: Johns Hopkins University, Center for Social Organization of Schools.

DeVries, D. L., Muse. D., & Wells, E. H. (1971). *The effects on students of working in cooperative groups: An exploratory study*. Baltimore: Johns Hopkins University, Center for Social Organization of Schools.

Dewey, J. (1952). *Democracy and education*. New York: Free Press (original work published 1916).

Dewey, J. (1966). *Experience and education*. New York: Collier (original work published 1938).

Diab, L. (1970). A study of intragroup and intergroup relations among experimentally produced small groups. *Genetic Psychology Monographs*, **82**, 49–82.

Dion, K. L. (1973). Cohesiveness as a determinant of ingroup–outgroup bias. *Journal of Personality and Social Psychology*, **28**, 163–171.

Dodge, K. A., & Murphy, R. R. (1984).The assessment of social competence in adolescents. In P. Caroly & J. J. Steffen (Eds.), *Advances in child behavior analysis and therapy*, Vol. 4. New York: Plenum.

Doise, W. (1971). An apparent exception to the extremitization of collective judgements. *European Journal of Social Psychology*, **1**, 511–518.

Doise, W., & Weinberger, M. (1973). Représentations masculines dans différentes situations de rencontres mixtes. *Bulletin de Psychologie*, **26**, 649–657.

Doise, W., Deschamps, J. C., & Meyer, G. (1978). The accentuation of intra-category similarities. In H. Tajfel (Ed.), *Differentiation between social groups*. London: Academic Press.

Doise, W., Csepeli, G., Dann, H. D., Gouge, C., Larsen, K., & Ostell, A. (1972). An experimental investigation into the formation of intergroup representations. *European Journal of Social Psychology*, **2**, 202–204.

Doob, L. (1952). *Social psychology*. New York: Holt.

Dovidio, J. F., Isen, A. M., Guerra, P., Gaertner, S. L., & Rust, M. (1998). Positive affect, cognition, and the reduction of intergroup bias. In C. Sedikides, J. Schopler, & C. A. Insko (Eds.), *Intergroup cognition and intergroup behavior*. Mahwah, NJ: Erlbaum.

Driscoll, J. M. (1981). Aggressiveness and frequency-of-aggressive-use ratings for pejorative epithets by Americans. *Journal of Social Psychology*, **104**, 111–126.

Dryfoos, J. G. (1994). *Full service schools*. San Francisco: Jossey-Bass.

Dumpson, J. R. (1949). An approach to antisocial street gangs. *Federal Probation*, **13**, 22–29.

Duncan, A. (1996). The shared concern method for resolving group bullying in schools. *Educational Psychology in Practice*, **12**, 94–98.

Duncan, C. P. (1959). Recent research on human problem solving. *Psychological Bulletin*, **56**, 397–429.

Edgerton, R. (1988). Foreword. In J. D. Vigil, *Barrio gangs: Street life and identity in Southern California*. Austin: University of Texas Press.

Edman, I. (1919). *Human traits and their social significance*. New York: Houghton Mifflin.

Egan, G. (1976). *Interpersonal living: A skills/contract approach to human-relations training in groups*. Pacific Grove, CA: Brooks/Cole.

Einarsen, S. (2000). Harassment and bullying at work: A review of the Scandinavian approach. *Aggression and Violent Behavior*, **5**, 379–401.

Eisenberg, N., & Miller, P.A. (1987). The relation of empathy to prosocial and related behaviors. *Psychological Bulletin*, **101**, 91–119.

Elliott, D. S. (1994). Serious violent offenders: Onset, developmental course, and termination. *Criminology*, **32**, 1–21.

Elliott, D. S., & Voss, H. L. (1974). *Delinquency and dropout*. Toronto: Lexington.

Elliott, D. S., Ageton, S. S., & Canter, R. J. (1979). An integrated theoretical perspective on juvenile delinquency. *Journal of Research in Crime and Delinquency*, **16**, 3–27.

Elliott, M. (1997a). Bullies and victims. In M. Elliott (Ed.), *Bullying: A practical guide to coping for schools*. London: Pitman Publishing.

Elliott, M. (1997b). Bullying and the under fives. In M. Elliott (Ed.), *Bullying: A practical guide to coping for schools*. London: Pitman Publishing.

Elliott, M., & Kilpatrick, J. (1994). *How to stop bullying: A kidscape training guide*. London: Kidscape.

Emler, N. (1994). Gossip, reputation, and social adaptation. In R. F. Goodman & A. Ben-Ze'ev (Eds.), *Good gossip*. Lawrence, KS: University Press of Kansas.

Epstein, J. L. (1985). After the bus arrives: Resegregation in desegregated schools. *Journal of Social Issues*, **41**, 23–43.

Epstein, M. H., Repp, A. C., & Cullinan, D. (1978). Decreasing "obscene" language of behaviorally disordered children through the use of a DRL schedule. *Psychology in the Schools*, **15**, 419–423.

Eron, L. D., Huesmann, R., Dubow, E., Romanoff, R., & Yarmel, P. W. (1987). Aggression and its correlates over 22 years. In D. H. Crowell, I. M. Evans, & C. P. O'Connell (Eds.), *Childhood aggression and violence*. New York: Plenum.

Esbensen, F., & Huizinga, D. (1993). Gangs, drugs, and delinquency in a survey of urban youth. *Criminology*, **31**, 565–589.

Esbensen, F., & Osgood, D. W. (1997). *National evaluation of GREAT* Washington, DC: US Department of Justice.

Esser, J. K., & Lindoefer, J. S. (1989). Groupthink and the space shuttle Challenger disaster. *Journal of Behavioral Decision Making, 2,* 167–177.

Evans, C., & Eder, D. (1993). "No exit:" Processes of social isolation in the middle school. *Journal of Contemporary Ethnography, 22,* 139–170.

Evans, N. J., & Jarvis, P. A. (1980). Group cohesion: A review and reevaluation. *Small Group Behavior, 11,* 359–370.

Eysenck, H. J. (1967). *The biological basis of personality.* Springfield, IL: Thomas.

Fagan, J. (1990). Social processes of delinquency and drug use among urban gangs. In C. R. Huff (Ed.), *Gangs in America.* Newbury Park, CA: Sage.

Fahlberg, V. (1979). *Attachment and separation: Putting the pieces together* (DSS Publication No. 429). Lansing, MI: Michigan Department of Social Services.

Falbo, T. (1977). The multidimensional scaling of power strategies. *Journal of Personality and Social Psychology, 35,* 537–548.

Farrington, D. P. (1991). Childhood aggression and adult violence: Early precursors and later-life outcomes. In D. J. Pepler, & K. H. Rubin (Eds.), *The development and treatment of childhood aggression.* Hillsdale, NJ: Erlbaum.

Farrington, D. P., Gundry, G., & West, D. J. (1975). The familial transmission of criminality. *Medicine, Science and the Law, 15,* 177–186.

Federal Bureau of Investigation (1998). *Uniform crime report, 1998.* Washington, DC: US Government Printing Office.

Federation on Child Abuse and Neglect (1990). *Fact sheet.* New York: National Committee for Prevention of Child Abuse.

Feindler, E., & Ecton, R. B. (1986). *Adolescent anger control: Cognitive-behavioral techniques.* New York: Pergamon.

Feldenkrais, M. (1970). *Body and mature behavior.* New York: International Universities Press.

Feldenkrais, M. (1972). *Awareness through movement.* New York: Harper & Row.

Feldman, E., & Dodge, K. A. (1987). Social information processing and sociometric status: Sex, age, and situational effects. *Journal of Abnormal Child Psychology, 15,* 211–227.

Feldstein, S., & Welkowitz, J. (1978). A chronography of conversation in defense of an objective approach. In A. W. Siegman & S. Feldstein (Eds.), *Nonverbal behavior and communication* (pp. 435–499). Hillsdale, NJ: Erlbaum.

Ferguson, C. K., & Kelly, H. H. (1964). Significant factors in overevaluation of our group's product. *Journal of Abnormal and Social Psychology, 69,* 223–238.

Feshbach, N. D. (1982). Empathy training and the regulation of aggression in elementary school children. In R. M. Kaplan, V. J. Konecni, R. Novoco (Eds.), *Aggression in children and youth.* Alphen den Rojn, The Netherlands: Sujthoff/Noordhoff Publishers.

Festinger, L. (1954). A theory of social comparison processes. *Human Relations, 7,* 117–140.

Festinger, L., Schacter, S., & Back, K. (1950). *Social pressures in informal groups.* New York: Harper.

Fine, G. A. (1977). Social components of children's gossip. *Journal of Communication, 27,* 181–185.

Fine, G. A., & Rosnow, R. L. (1978). Gossip, gossipers, gossiping. *Personality and Social Psychology Bulletin, 4,* 161–169.

Fisher, R., & Ury, W. (1981). *Getting to yes: Negotiating agreement without giving in.* Boston, MA: Houghton Mifflin.

Fitzgerald, L. F., Gold, Y., & Brock, K. (1990). Responses to victimizaiton: Validation of an objective policy. *Journal of College Student Personnel, 27,* 34–39.

Fitzgerald, L., & Shullman, S. (1993). Sexual harassment: A research analysis and agenda for the 90s. *Journal of Vocational Behavior, 42,* 5–29.

Floyd, N. M. (1985). "Pick on somebody your own size": Controlling victimization. *The Pointer, 29,* 9–17.

Fodor, E. (1972). Delinquency and susceptibility to social influence among adolescents as a function of level of moral development. *Journal of Social Psychology, 86,* 257–260.

Fonzi, A. (1997). *Il bullismo in Italia.* Firenze: Giunti.

Foote, R., & Woodward, J. (1973). A preliminary investigation of obscene language. *Journal of Psychology, 83,* 263–275.

Forbes, H. D. (1997). *Ethnic conflict: Commerce, culture, and the contact hypothesis*. New Haven, CT: Yale University Press.

Forgas, J. P., Brown, L. B., & Menyhart, J. (1980). Dimensions of aggression: The perception of aggressive episodes. *British Journal of Social and Clinical Psychology*, **19**, 215–227.

Forsyth, D. R. (1983). *An introduction to group dynamics*. Pacific Grove, CA: Brooks/Cole.

Forsyth, D. R. (1999). *Group dynamics*. (Third ed.). Belmont, CA: Brooks/Cole.

Fox, H. G. (1970). Gang youth and police. Live-in. *The Police Chief*, **37**, 233–235.

Frank, S. J. (1977). *The facilitation of empathy through training in imagination*. Unpublished doctoral dissertation, Yale University, New Haven, Connecticut.

Freeman, J. (1993). Hardhats: Construction workers, manliness, and the 1970 pro-war demonstrations. *Journal of Social History*, **26**, 725.

Frei, D. (1986). *Perceived images*. Totowa, NJ: Rowman & Allenheld.

French, J. R. P., Jr., & Raven, B. (1959). The bases of social power. In D. Cartwright (Ed.), *Studies in social power*. Ann Arbor, MI: University of Michigan, Institute for Social Research.

Freud, S. (1921/1967). *Group psychology and analysis of the ego*. New York: Livewright Publishing.

Freud, S. (1922). *Group psychology and the analsis of the ego*. London: Hogarth Press.

Friedman, C. J., Mann, F., & Friedman, A. S. (1975). A profile of juvenile street gang members. *Adolescence*, **40**, 563–607.

Friedman, H. S., Prince, L. M., Riggio, K. E., & DiMatteo, M. R. (1980). Understanding and assessing non-verbal expressiveness: The affective communication test. *Journal of Personality and Social Psychology*, **39**, 333–351.

Fry, D. P. (1992). "Respect for the rights of others is peace": Learning aggression versus nonaggression among the Zapotec. *American Anthropologist*, **94**, 621–639.

Furfey, P. H. (1926). *The gang age*. New York: Macmillan.

Gannon, T. M. (1967). Emergence of the "defensive gang." *Federal Probation*, **30**, 44–48.

Gardner, C. B. (1995). *Passing by: Gender and public harassment*. Berkeley, CA: University of California Press.

Gardner, S. (1983). *Street gangs*. New York: Franklin Watts.

Garrity, C., Jens, K., Porter, W., Sager, N., & Short-Camilli, C. (1994). *Bully-proofing your school*. Longmont, CO: Sopris West.

Geertz, C. (1973). *The interpretation of cultures: Selected essays*. New York: Basic Books.

Geller, D. M., Goodstein, L., Silver, M., & Sternberg, W. C. (1974). On being ignored: The effects of violation of implicit rules of social interaction. *Sociometry*, **37**, 541–556.

Gendlin, E. (1984). *Teaching psychological skills*. Monterey, CA: Brooks/Cole.

Gerard, H. B., & Hoyt, M. F. (1974). Distinctiveness of social categorization and attitude toward in-group members. *Journal of Personality and Social Psychology*, **29**, 836–849.

Gibb, J. R. (1961). Defensive level and influence potential in small groups. In L. Petrullo & B. M. Bass (Eds.), *Leadership and interpersonal behavior*. New York: Holt, Rinehart & Winston.

Gibb, J. R. (1973). Defensive communication. In W. G. Bennis, D. E. Berlew, E. H., Schein, & F. I. Steele (Eds.), *Interpersonal dynamics*. Homewood, IL: Dorsey.

Giles, H., & Powesland, P. F. (1975). *Speech style and social evaluation*. London, Academic Press.

Gilje, P. A. (1996). *Rioting in America*. Bloomington, IN: Indiana University Press.

Gilliam, J., Stough, L., & Fad, K. (1991). Interventions for swearing. In G. Stoner, M. R. Shinn, & H. M. Walker (Eds.), *Interventions for achievement and behavior problems*. Silver Spring, MD: National Association of School Psychologists.

Giulianotti, R., Bonney, N., & Hepworth, M. (1994). *Football, violence, and social identity*. London: Routledge.

Glaser, D. (1956). Criminality theories and behavioral images. In D. R. Cressey & D. A. Ward (Eds.), *Delinquency, crime, and social process*. New York: Harper & Row.

Glasser, W. (1969). *Schools without failure*. New York: Harper & Row.

Gleason, J. H., Alexander, A. M., & Somers, C. L. (2000). Later adolescents' reactions to three types of childhood teasing: Relations with self-esteem and body image. *Social Behavior and Personalitiy*, **28**, 471–480.

Gold, M. (1963). *Status forces in delinquent boys*. Ann Arbor: University of Michigan Press.

Goldstein, A. P. (1971). *Psychotherapeutic attraction*. New York: Pergamon.

Goldstein, A. P. (1973). *Structured learning therapy: Toward a psychotherapy for the poor*. New York: Academic.

Goldstein, A. P. (1981). *Psychological skill training*. New York: Pergamon.

Goldstein, A. P. (1989). Aggression reduction strategies: Effective and ineffective. *School Psychology Quarterly*, **14**, 40–58.

Goldstein, A. P. (1991). *Delinquent gangs: A psychological perspective*. Champaign, IL: Research Press.

Goldstein, A. P. (1994). *The ecology of aggression*. New York: Plenum.

Goldstein, A. P. (1996). *Violence in America*. Palo Alto, CA: Davies-Black.

Goldstein, A. P. (1999a). *The prepare curriculum*. Champaign, IL: Research Press.

Goldstein, A. P. (1999b). *Low-level aggression: First steps on the ladder to violence*. Champaign, IL: Research Press.

Goldstein, A. P. (2000). *Lasting change: Methods for enhancing generalization of gain*. Champaign, IL: Research Press.

Goldstein, A. P., & Conoley, J. C. (1997). *School violence intervention: A practical handbook*. New York: Guilford.

Goldstein, A. P., & Keller, H. (1987). *Aggressive behavior: Assessment and intervention*. New York: Pergamon.

Goldstein, A. P., & Michaels, G. Y. (1985). *Empathy: Development, training and consequences*. Hillsdale, NJ: Erlbaum.

Goldstein, A. P., & Segall, M. (1983). *Aggression in global perspective*. Elmsford, NY: Pergamon.

Goldstein, A. P., Heller, K., & Sechrest, L. (1966). *Psychotherapy and the psychology of behavior change*. New York: Wiley.

Goldstein, A. P., Palumbo, J., Striepling, S. H., & Voutsinas, A. M. (1995). *Break it up*. Champaign, IL: Research Press.

Goldstein, J. (1998). *Why we watch: The attractions of violent entertainment*. New York: Oxford University Press.

Goldstein, J. H., Davis, R. W., & Herman, D. (1975). Escalation of aggression: Experimental studies. *Journal of Personality and Social Psychology*, **31**, 162–170.

Goldstein, J. H., Davis, R. W., Kermis, M., & Cohn, E. S. (1981). Retarding the escalation of aggression. *Social Behaviors and Personality*, **9**, 65–70.

Goleman, D. (1977). *The varieties of the meditative experience*. New York: Dutton.

Gott, R. (1989, May). *Juvenile gangs*. Paper presented at the Conference on Juvenile Crime, Eastern Kentucky University, Richmond.

Gough, H. G. (1948). A sociological theory of psychopathy. *American Journal of Sociology*, **53**, 359–366.

Graham, M. (1986). Obscenity and profanity at work. *Employee Relations Law Journal*, **11**, 662–677.

Gray, K. C., & Hutchison, H. C. (1964). The psychopathic personality: A survey of Canadian psychiatrists' opinions. *Canadian Psychiatric Association Journal*, **9**, 452–461.

Greenbaum, S. (1989). *Set straight on bullies*. Malibu, CA: Pepperdine University Press.

Greenbaum, S., Turner, B., & Stephens, R. D. (1989). *Set straight on bullies*. Malibu, CA: National School Safety Center.

Grossman, C. D. (1995). *On killing*. Boston: Little, Brown.

Gruber, J. E. (1992). A typology of personal and environmental sexual harassment: Research and policy implications for the 1990s. *Sex Roles*, **26**, 447–464.

Guerney, B. G. (1964). Filial therapy: Description and rationale. *Journal of Consulting Psychology*, **28**, 304–310.

Guerney, B. G. (1964). *Relationship Enhancement: Skill training programs for therapy, problem-prevention, and enrichment*. San Francisco: Jossey-Bass.

Gunther, B. (1968). *Sense relaxation below your mind*. New York: Collier Books.

Gurr, T. R. (1970). *Why men rebel*. Princeton: Princeton University Press.

Gurr, T. R. (1989). *Violence in America*. Newbury Park, CA: Sage.

Gutek, B. A. (1985). Sex and the workplace. *The impact of sexual behavior and harassment on women, men, and organizations*. San Francisco: Jossey-Bass.

Hagedorn, J. M. (1998). Gang violence in the postindustrial era. In M. Tonry & M. H. Moore (Eds.), *Youth violence*. Chicago: University of Chicago Press.

Hagedorn, J., & Macon, P. (1988). *People and folks*. Chicago: Lake View.

Halpin, A. W., & Winer, J. B. (1952). *The leadership behavior of the airplane commander*. Columbus: Ohio State University Research Foundation.

Hamilton, D. L, & Sherman, S. J. (1996). Perceiving persons and groups. *Psychological Review, 103*, 336–355.

Hamilton, D. L., & Trollier, T. K. (1986). Stereotypes and stereotyping: an overview of the cognitive approach. In J. F. Davidio & S. T. Gaertner (Eds.), *Prejudice, discrimination and racism*. New York: Academic Press.

Hamilton, D. L., Sherman, S. J., & Lickel, B. (1998). Perceiving social groups: The importance of the entativity continuum. In C. Sedikides, J. Schopler, & C. A. Insko (Eds.), *Intergroup cognition and intergroup behavior*. Mahwah, NJ: Erlbaum.

Hamilton, W. D. (1964). The genetical evolution of social behavior. *Journal of Theoretical Biology, 7*, 1–52.

Hammond, E. H. (1981). Fraternity hazing: Impact and implication. Unpublished manuscript, University of Louisville.

Hannerz, U. (1967). Gossip, networks, and culture in Black American ghetto. *Ethos, 32*, 35–60.

Harding, J., & Hogrefe, R. (1952). Attitudes of white department store employees towards negro co-workers. *Journal of Social Issues, 8*, 18–28.

Hardman, D. G. (1967). Historical perspectives on gang research. *Journal of Research in Crime and Delinquency, 4*, 5–27.

Hare, A. P. (1976). *Handbook of small group research*. New York: Free Press.

Harper, N. L., & Askling, L. R. (1980). Group communication and quality of task solution in a media production organization. *Communication Monographs, 47*, 77–100.

Hartford, R. J. (1972). A social penetration model for obscene language. Unpublished doctoral dissertation, University of Michigan.

Hatfield, E., Cacioppo, J. T., & Rapson, R. L. (1994). *Emotional contagion*. Paris: Cambridge University Press.

Hawkins, R., & Tiedemann, G. (1975). *The creation of deviance: interpersonal and organizational determinants*. Columbus, OH: Merrill.

Heller, K., Price, R. H., Reinharz, S., Riger, S., Wandersman, A., & D'Aunno, T. A. (1984). *Psychology and community change*. Homewood, IL: Dorsey Press.

Hemphill, J. K., & Coons, A. E. (1957). Development of the leader behavior description questionnaiare. In R. M. Stogdill & A. E. Coons (Eds.), *Leader behavior: Its description and measurement* (Research Monograph No. 88). Columbus, OH: Ohio State University, Bureau of Business Research.

Hensley, T. R., & Griffin, G. W. (1986). Victims of groupthink: The Kent State University Board of Trustees and the 1977 gymnasium controversy. *Journal of Conflict Resolution, 30*, 497–531.

Hersey, P., & Blanchard, K. H. (1977). *Management of organizational behavior: Utilizing human resources*. Englewood Cliffs, NJ: Prentice-Hall.

Hertz-Lazarowtiz, R., Sapir, C., & Sharan, S. (1981, April). *Academic and social effects of two cooperative learning methods in a desegregated classroom*. Paper presented at the meeting of the American Educational Research Association, New York.

Hertz-Lazarowitz, R., Sharan, S., & Steinberg, R. (1980). Classroom learning styles and co-operative behavior of elementary school children. *Journal of Educational Psychology, 72*, 99–106.

Hess, U., & Kirouac, G. (2000). Emotion expression in groups. In M. Lewis & J. M. Haviland-Jones (Eds.), *Handbook of Emotions*. New York: Guilford.

Hewitt, J. P. (1970). *Social stratification and deviant behavior*. New York: Random House.

Higgins, C. (1994). Improving the school ground environment as an antibullying intervention. In P. Smith & S. Sharp (Eds.), *School bullying: Insights and perspectives*. London: Routledge.

Higher Education Research Institute (1980). *Longitudinal follow-up of ACE 1971 college freshmen*. Los Angeles University of California at Los Angeles.

Hill, R. C. (1965). *Freedom's code: The historic American standards of character, conduct, and citizen responsibility*. San Antonio, TX: The Children's Fund.

Hirschi, T. (1969). *Causes of delinquency*. Berkeley: University of California Press.

Hodson, G., & Sorrentino, R. M. (1997). Groupthink and uncertainty orientation: Personality differences in reactivity to the group situation. *Group Dynamics: Theory, Research, and Practice*, **1**, 144–155.

Hoffman, M. L. (1977). Empathy, its development and prosocial implications. *Nebraska Symposium on Motivation*, **25**, 169–218.

Hogg, M. A. (1992). *The social psychology of group cohesiveness: From attraction to social identity*. New York: New York University Press.

Holmes, S. R., & Brandenburg-Ayers, S. J. (1998). Bullying behavior in school: A predictor of later gang involvement. *Journal of Gang Research*, **5**, 1–6.

Hoover, J. H.. & Juul, K. (1993). Bullying in Europe and the United States. *Journal of Emotional and Behavior Problems*, **2**, 25–29.

Hoover, J., & Hazler, R. J. (1991). Bullies and victims. *Elementary School Guidance & Counseling*, **25**, 212–219.

Horowitz, D. L. (2001). *The deadly ethnic riot*. Berkeley, CA: University of California Press.

Horowitz, R. (1987). Community tolerance of gang violence. *Social Problems*, **34**, 437–450.

Howard, J., & Rothbart, M. (1978). Social categorization and memory for ingroup and outgroup behaviour. *Journal of Personality and Social Psychology*, **38**, 301–310.

Howell, J. C. (1993). Gangs and youth violence: Recent research. In J. C. Howell, B. Krisberg, J. Hawkins & J. Wilson (Eds.). Thousand Oaks, CA: Sage.

Hudgins, W., & Prentice, N. (1973). Moral judgments in delinquent and non-delinquent adolescents and their mothers. *Journal of Abnormal Psychology*, **82**, 145–152.

Hughes, G. (1991). Swearing: A social history of foul language, oaths, and profanity in English. Oxford, UK: Blackwell.

Hunt, D. E. (1971). *Matching models in education: The coordination of teaching methods with student characteristics*. Toronto: Ontario Institute for Studies in Education.

Hyman, H. H., & Singer, E. (1981). *Readings in reference group theory and research*. New York: Free Press.

Illinois State Police (1989, January). *Criminal Intelligence Bulletin* (No. 42). Springfield, IL: Author.

Insko, C. A., & Schopler, J. (1998). Differential distrust of groups and individuals. In C. Sedikides, J. Schopler, & C. A. Insko (Eds.), *Intergroup cognition and intergroup behavior*. Mahwah, NJ: Erlbaum.

Ivey, A. E., & Authier, J. (1971). *Microcounseling*. Springfield, IL: Charles C. Thomas.

Jacovino, J. A. (1980). *The use of cooperatively structured games as a teaching strategy in a secondary school class to increase the group cooperation behaviors of its students*. Unpublished doctoral dissertation, University of Pennsylvania, Philadelphia.

Jaeger, M. E., Skleder, B. R., & Rosnow, R. L. (1994). Gossip, gossipers, gossipees. In R. F. Goodman & Ben-Ze'ev (Eds.), *Good gossip*. Lawrence: University Press of Kansas.

Jaffe, Y., & Yinon, Y. (1979). Retaliatory aggression in individuals and groups. *European Journal of Social Psychology*, **9**, 177–186.

Jaffe, Y., Shapiro, N., & Yinon, Y. (1981). Aggression and its escalation. *Journal of Cross-Cultural Psychology*, **12**, 21–36.

Jahoda, M., & West, P. (1951). Race relations in public housing. *Journal of Social Issues*, **7**, 132–139.

Janis, I. L. (1972). *Victims of groupthink*. Boston: Houghton Mifflin.

Janis, I. L. (1979). *Preventing groupthink in policy planning groups*. Paper presented at the meeting of the International Society of Political Psychology, Washington, DC.

Janis, I. L. (1982). Groupthink: *Psychological studies of policy decisions and fiascos.* Boston: Houghton Mifflin.

Janis, I. L., & Mann, L. (1977). *Decision making: A psychological analysis of conflict, choice, and commitment.* New York: Free Press.

Jankowski, M. S. (1991). *Islands in the streets.* Berkeley: University of California Press.

Jansyn, L. (1966). Solidarity and delinquency in a street corner group. *American Sociological Review,* **31,** 606–614.

Jay, T. B. (1992). Doing research with dirty words. *Maledicta,* **1,** 234–256.

Jervis, R. (1986). Deterrance, the spiral model and intentions of the adversary. In R. K. White (Ed.), *Psychology and the prevention of nuclear war.* New York: New York University Press.

Johnson, D. W., & Johnson, F. P. (1997). *Joining together: Group theory and group skills.* Needham Heights, MA: Allyn & Bacon.

Johnson, D. W., & Johnson, R. (1975). *Learning together and alone. Cooperation, competition and individualization.* Englewood Cliffs, NJ: Prentice-Hall.

Johnson, D.W., & Johnson, R. T., Johnson, J. H., & Anderson, D. (1976). Effects of cooperative versus individualized instruction on student prosocial behavior, attitudes toward learning, and achievement. *Journal of Educational Psychology,* **68,** 446–452.

Johnson, E. B., Gerard, H. G., & Miller, N. (1975). Teacher influence in the desegregated classroom. In H. B. Gerard & N. Miller (Eds.), *School desegregation: A long-term study.* New York: Plenum.

Johnson, R. E. (1979). *Juvenile delinquency and its origins.* Cambridge: Cambridge University Press.

Judd, C. H. (1902). Practice and its effects on the perception of illusions. *Psychological Review,* **9,** 27–39.

Kagan, S., Zahn, G. L., Widaman, K. F., Schwarzwald, J., & Tyrrell, G. (1985), Classroom structural bias. In R. Slavin, S. Sharan, S. Kagan, R. Hertz-Lazarowitz, C. Webb, & R. Schmuck (Eds.), *Learning to cooperate, cooperating to learn.* New York: Plenum.

Kahneman, D., & Tversky, A. (1979). On the psychology of prediction. *Psychological Review,* **80,** 237–251.

Katz, R. L. (1963). *Empathy: Its nature and uses.* New York: Free Press.

Keefe, T. (1976). Empathy: The critical skill. *Social Work,* **21,** 10–14.

Keen, S. (1970, October). Sing the body electric. *Psychology Today,* pp. 56–61.

Keen, S. (1986). *Faces of the enemy.* San Francisco: Harper & Row.

Kelley, H. H., & Thibaut, J. W. (1978). *Interpersonal relations: A theory of interdependence.* New York: Wiley.

Kelling, G. L., & Coles, C. M. (1996). *Fixing broken windows.* New York: Free Press.

Kelly, E., & Cohn, T. (1988). *Racism in schools—New research evidence.* Stoke-on-Trent, UK: Trentham Books.

Kelman, H. C. (1991). Interactive problem solving. In V. D. Volkan, J. V. Montville, & D. A. Julius (Eds.), *the psychodynamics of international relationships.* Lexington, MA: Lexington Books.

Kelman, H. C. (1998). Informal mediation by the scholar/practitioner. In E. Weiner (Ed.), *The handbook of interethnic coexistence.* New York: Continuum.

Keltner, D., Capps, L., Kring, A. M., Young, R. C., & Heerey, E. A. (2001). Just teasing: A conceptual analysis and empirical review. *Psychological Bulletin,* **127,** 229–248.

Keltner, D., Young, R. C., Heerey, E. A., Oemig, C., & Monarch, N. D. (1998). Teasing in hierarchical and intimate relations. *Journal of Personality and Social Psychology,* **75,** 1231–1247.

Kendon, A. (1970). Movement coordination in social interaction: Some examples described. *Arca Psychologica,* **32,** 1–25.

Kerner, O., Lindsay, J. V., Harris, F. R., Brooke, E. W., Corman, J. C., McCulloch, W. M., Abel, I. W., Thornton, C. B., Wilkins, R., Peden, K. G., & Jenkins, H. (1968). *Report of the National Advisory Commission on Civil Disorders.* New York: Bantam.

Kerr, J. H. (1994). *Understanding soccer hooliganism.* Buckingham, UK: Open University Press.

Kilpatrick, W. H. (1925). *Foundations of method.* New York: Columbia University Press.

Kinney, T. A. (1994). An inductively derived typology of verbal aggression and its association to distress. *Human Communication Research*, **21**, 183–222.

Kipnis, D. (1974). *The powerholders*. Chicago: University of Chicago Press.

Kipnis, D., & Consentino, J. (1969). Use of leadership powers in industry. *Journal of Applied Psychology*, **53**, 460–466.

Kipnis, D., Castell, P. J., Gergen, M., & Mauch, D. (1976). Metamorphic effects of power. *Journal of Applied Psychology*, **61**, 127–135.

Klandersman, B. (1984). Social-psychological expansions of resource mobilization theory. *American Sociological Review*, **49**, 1–17.

Klein, M. W. (1968a). Impressions of juvenile gang members. *Adolescence*, **3**, 53–78.

Klein, M. W. (1968b). *The Ladino Hills Project* (Final report). Washington, DC: Office of Juvenile Delinquency and Youth Development.

Klein, M. W. (1969). Violence in American juvenile gangs. In D. J. Mulvihill & M. M. Tumin (Eds.), *Crimes of violence*, Vol. 13. Washington, DC: National Commission on the Causes and Prevention of Violence.

Klein, M. W. (1971). *Street gangs and street workers*. Englewood Cliffs, NJ: Prentice-Hall.

Klein, M. W. (1995). *The American Street Gang*. New York: Oxford University Press.

Klein, M. W., & Crawford, L. Y. (1967). Groups, gangs and cohesiveness. In J. F. Short (Ed.), *Gang delinquency and delinquent subcultures*. New York: Harper & Row.

Klein, M. W., & Maxson, C. L. (1989). Street gang violence. In N. A. Weiner & N. W. Wolfgang (Eds.), *Violent crime, violent criminals*. Newbury Park, CA: Sage.

Knox, G. W. (1998). A survey of Chicago gangs. *Journal of Gang Research*, **5**, 1–16.

Kohlberg, L. (1969). Stage and sequence. The cognitive-developmental approach to socialization. In D. A. Goslin (Ed.), *Handbook of socialization theory and research* (pp. 347–480). Chicago: Rand McNally.

Kohlberg, L. (1971). Stages of moral development as a basis for moral education. In C. M. Beck, B. S. Crittenden, & E. V. Sullivan (Eds.), *Moral education: Interdisciplinary approaches* (1971). Toronto: University of Toronto Press.

Kohlberg, L. (1976). Moral stages and moralization: The cognitive-developmental approach. In T. Lickona (Ed.), *Moral development and behavior* (pp. 31–53). New York: Holt, Rinehart & Winston.

Kohn, A. (1992). Resistance to cooperative learning: Making sense of its deletion and dilution. *Journal of Education*, **174**, 38–55.

Kowalski, R. M. (2000). "I was only kidding!": Victims' and perpetrators' perceptions of teasing. *Personality and Social Psychology Bulletin*, **26**, 231–241.

Kowalski, R. M. (2001). Aversive interpersonal behavior: On being annoying, thoughtless, and mean. In R. M. Kowalski (Ed.), *Behaving badly*. Washington, DC: American Psychological Association.

Kowalski, R. M., Howerton, E., & McKenzie. (2001). Permitted disrespect: Teasing in interpersonal interactions. In R. M. Kowalski (Ed.), *Behaving badly*. Washington, DC: American Psychological Association.

Kramer, B. (1950). *Residential contact as a determinant of attitudes towards Negroes*. Unpublished PhD dissertation, Harvard University.

Kramer, R. M., & Messick, D. M. (1998). Getting by with a little help from our enemies: Collective paranoia and its role in intergroup relations. In C. Sedi kides, J. Schopler, & C. A. Insko (Eds.), *Intergroup cognition and intergroup behavior*. Mahwah, NJ: Erlbaum.

Krasner, L. (1980). *Environmental design and human behavior*. New York: Pergamon.

Krohn, M. D., Massey, J. L., & Skinner, W. F. (1987). A sociological theory of crime and delinquency: Social learning theory. In E. K. Morris & C. J. Braukmann (Eds.), *Behavioral approaches to crime and delinquency*. New York: Plenum.

Kruse, L. (1986). Conceptions of crowds and crowding. In C. F. Grauman & S. Moscovici (Eds.), *Changing conceptions of crowd mind and behavior*. New York: Springer-Verlag.

Labrell, F. (1994). A typical interaction behavior between fathers and toddlers: Teasing. *Early Development and Parenting*, **3**, 125–130.

Ladd, W. W. (1962). Effect of integration on property values. *American Economics Review*, **52**, 801–808.

Lagerspetz, K. M., Bjorkqvist, K., & Peltonen, T. (1988). Is indirect aggression typical of females? *Aggressive Behavior, 14*, 403–414.

Lagerspetz, K., Bjorkqvist, K., Berts, M., & King, E. (1982). Group aggression among school children in three schools in Finland. *Scandanavian Journal of Psychology, 23*, 45–52.

Laird, J. D., & Bresler, C. (1992). The process of emotional experience: A self-perception theory. In M. S. Clark (Ed.), *Review of personality and social psychology: Vol. 13. Emotion* (pp. 213–234). Newbury Park, CA: Sage.

Lamm, H., & Myers, D. G. (1978). Gang-induced polarization of attitudes and behavior. *Advances in Experimental Social Psychology, 11*, 145–195.

Landesco, J. (1932). Crime and failure of institutions in Chicago's immigrant areas. *Journal of Criminal Law and Criminology, 23*, 238–248.

Lane, D. A. (1989). Violent histories: Bullying and criminality. In D. P. Tattum & D. A. Lane (Eds.), *Bullying in schools*. Stoke-on-Trent, UK: Trentham Books.

Lang, K., & Lang, G. E. (1961). *Collective dynamics*. New York: Thomas Y. Crowell.

Latane, B., Williams, K., & Harkins, S. (1979). Many hands make light work: The causes and consequences of social loafing. *Journal of Personality and Social Psychology, 37*, 822–832.

Lawler, E. J., & Thompson, M. E. (1979). Subordinate response to a leader's cooptation strategy as a function of type of coalition power. *Representative Research in Social Psychology, 9*, 69–80.

Lax, D., & Sebenius, J. (1986). *The manager as negotiator*. New York: Free Press.

Le Blanc, M. (1996). Changing patterns in the perpetration of offences over time: Trajectories from early adolescence to the early 30s. *Studies on Crime & Crime Prevention, 5*, 151–165.

Le Bon, G. (1895). *The crowd*. London: Unwin (originally published in 1895).

Lee, V. E., Croninger, R. G., Linn, E., & Chen, X. (1996). The culture of sexual harassment in secondary schools. *American Educational Research Journal, 33*, 383–417.

Lemert, E. M. (1967). *Human deviance, social problems, and social control*. Englewood Cliffs, NJ: Prentice-Hall.

Lemon, H., & Myers, D. G. (1978). Group-induced polarization of attitudes and behavior. *Advances in Experimental Social Psychology, 11*, 145–195.

Lerner, M. J. (1980). *Belief in a just world: A fundamental delusion*. New York: Plenum.

Lesh, T. V. (1970). Zen meditation and the development of empathy in counselors. *Journal of Humanistic Psychology, 10*, 39–74.

Leventhal, H., & Mace, W. (1970). The effect of laughter on evaluation of a slapstick movie. *Journal of Personality, 38*, 16–30.

Levi, M., & Jones, S. (1985). Public and police perception of crime seriousness in England and Wales. *British Journal of Criminology, 25*, 234–250.

Levin, J., Arluke, A. (1987). *Gossip: The inside scoop*. New York: Plenum.

Levin, J., & Kimmel, A. J. (1977). Gossip columns: Media small talk. *Journal of Communicaiton, 27*, 169–175.

Levine, J. M., & Moreland, R. L. (1998). Small groups. In D. T. Gilbert, S.,T. Fiske, & G. Lindzey (Eds.), *The handbook of social psychology* (Fourth Ed.). New York: McGraw-Hill.

Levine, J. M., Moreland, R. L., & Ryan, C. S. (1998). Group socialization and intergroup relations. In C. Sedikides, J. Schopler, & C. A. Insko (Eds.), *Intergroup cognition and integroup behavior*. Mahwah, NJ: Erlbaum.

Lewin, K. (1943). Defining the field at a given time. *Psychological Review, 50*, 292–310.

Lewin, K. (1947). Frontiers in group dynamics. *Human Relations, 1*, 5–42.

Lewin, K., Lippitt, R., & White, R. K. (1939). Patterns of aggressive behavior in experimentally created "social climates." *Journal of Social Psychology, 10*, 271–299.

Lewin, M. (2000). "I'm not talking to you": Shunning as a form of violence. *Transactional Analysis Journal, 30*, 125–131.

Ley, D. (1976). The street gang in its milieu. In G. Gapport & H. M. Rose (Eds.). *Social economy of cities*. Newbury Park, CA: Sage.

Leyens, J. P., & Parke, R. D. (1975). Aggressive slides can induce a weapons effect. *European Journal of Social Psychology, 5*, 229–236.

Lieberman, S., & Silverman, A. R. (1970). The precipitants and underlying conditions of race riots. In E. I. Megarges & J. E. Hokanson (Eds.). *The dynamics of aggression*. New York: Harper & Row.

Limper, R. (2000). Cooperation between parents, teachers, and school boards to prevent bullying in education: An overview of work done in the Netherlands. *Aggressive Behavior*, **26**, 125–134.

Linden, R. (1978). Myths of middle-class delinquency. *Youth & Society*, **9**, 407–432.

Linville, P. W., & Jones, E. E. (1980). Polarized appraisals of out-group members. *Journal of Personality and Social Psychology*, **38**, 689–703.

Linville, P. W., Salovey, P., & Fischer, G. W. (1986). Stereotyping and perceived distributions of social characteristics: An application to ingroup–outgroup perception. In J. F. Dovidio & S. L. Gaertner (Eds.), *Prejudice, discrimination and racism*. New York: Academic.

Lipps, T. (1926). Das Wissen von Fremdden Ichen. *Psychologischen Untersuchungen*, **1**, 694–722 (original work published 1907).

Loeber, R., & Le Blanc, M. (1990). Towards developmental criminology. In M. Tonry & M. Morris (Eds.), *Crime and justice: An annual review of research*, Vol. 11. Chicago: University of Chicago Press.

Loeber, R., Wung, P., Keenan, K., Giroux, B., Stouthamer-Loeber, M., Van Kammen, W. B., & Maughan, B. (1993). Developmental pathways in disruptive child behavior. *Development and Psychopathology*, **5**, 103–133.

Lord, R. G. (1977). Functional leadership behavior: Measurement and relation to social power and leadership perceptions. *Administrative Science Quarterly*, **22**, 114–133.

Lott, A. J., & Lott, B. E. (1965). Group cohesiveness, as interpersonal attraction: A review of relationships with antecedent and consequent variables. *Psychological Bulletin*, **64**, 259–309.

Lowen, A. (1967). *The betrayal of the body*. New York: Macmillan.

Lowen, A., & Lowen, L. (1977). *The way to vibrant health: A manual of bioenergetic exercises*. New York: Harper & Row.

Lucker, G. W., Rosenfield, D., Sikes, J., & Aronson, E. (1976). Performance in the interdependent classroom: A field study. *American Educational Research Journal*, **13**, 115–123.

Lucore, P. (1975). Cohesiveness in the gang. In D. S. Cartwright, B. Tomson, & H. Schwartz (Eds.), *Gang delinquency*. Pacific Grove, CA: Brooks/Cole.

Lumley, F. E. (1925). *Means of social control*. New York: Century.

Lynch, A. (1996). *Thought contagion: How belief spreads through society*. New York: Basic Books.

Macrae, C. N., & Bodenhausen, G. V. (2000). Social cognition: Thinking categorically about others. *Annual Review of Psychology*, **51**, 93–120.

Magdid, K., & McKelvey, C. A. (1987). *High risk: Children without a conscience*. New York: Bantam.

Male, M. (1989). Cooperative learning and staff development. *Cooperation in Education*, **5**, 4–5.

Mandler, G. (1954). Transfer of training as function of degree of response overlearning. *Journal of Experimental Psychology*, **47**, 411–417.

Mann, L. (1981). The baiting crowd in episodes of threatened suicides. *Journal of Personality and Social Psychology*, **41**, 703–709.

Manning, M., Heron, J., & Marshall, T. (1978). Styles of hostility and of social interactions at nursery, at school and at home. An extended study of children. In L. A. Hersov & M. Berger (Eds.), *Aggression and anti-social behavior in childhood and adolescence*. Oxford: Pergamon.

Markus, H. R., & Kitayama, S. (1991). Culture and self: Implications for cognition, emotion, and motivation. *Psychological Review*, **98**, 224–253.

Marsh, P., Rosser, E., & Harre, R. (1978). *The rules of disorder*. London: Routledge.

Martino, L., & Johnson, D. W. (1979). The effects of cooperative versus individualistic instruction on interaction between normal-progress and learning-disabled students. *Journal of Social Psychology*, **107**, 177–183.

Marx, C., & Engels, F. (1947). *The German ideology*. New York: International Publishers.

Matarazzo, J. D., & Wiens, A. N. (1972). *The interview: Research on its anatomy and structure.* Chicago: Aldine-Atherton.

Matarazzo, J. D., Weitman, M., Saslow, G., & Wiens, A. N. (1963). Interviewer influence on durations of interviewee speech. *Journal of Verbal Learning and Verbal Behavior,* **1,** 451–458.

Matza, D. (1964). *Delinquency and drift.* New York: Wiley.

Maxson, C. L., Gordon, M. A., & Klein, M. W. (1985). Differences between gang and nongang homicides. *Criminology,* **23,** 209–221.

Mayer, H. C. (1964). *The good American program.* New York: American Viewpoint.

McClelland, D. C. (1975). *Power: The inner experience.* New York: Irvington.

McCord, W., & McCord, J. (1964). *Origins of crime: A new evaluation of the Cambridge–Somerville study.* New York: Columbia University Press.

McDougall, W. (1908). *An introduction to social psychology.* London: Methuen.

McGrath, J. E. (1984). *Groups: Interaction and performance.* New York: Holt.

McPhail, C. (1971). Civil disorder participation: A critical examination of recent research. *American Sociological Review,* **36,** 1058–1073.

McPhail, C. (1991). *The myth of the madding crowd.* New York: Aldine De Gruyter.

McPhail, P., Ungoed-Thomas, J. R., & Chapman, H. (1975). *Learning to care: Rationale and method of the lifeline program.* Niles, IL: Argus Communications.

Mead, G. H. (1934). *Mind, self and society.* Chicago: University of Chicago Press.

Meier, R. (1976). The new criminology: Continuity in criminological theory. *Journal of Criminal Law and Criminology,* **67,** 461–469.

Menesini, E., Esler, M., Smith, P. K., Genta, M. L., Giannetti, E., Fonzi A., & Constabile, A. (1997). Cross national comparison of children's attitudes toward bully/victim problems in school. *Aggressive Behavior,* **23,** 245–257.

Merton, R. K. (1938). Social structure and anomie. *American Sociological Review,* **3,** 672–682.

Miedzian, M. (1992). *Boys will be boys: Breaking the link between masculinity and violence.* New York: Doubleday.

Milgram, S., & Toch, H. (1969). Collective behavior: Crowds and social movements. In G. Lindzey & A. Aronson (Eds.), *The handbook of social psychology,* Vol, 4. Reading, MA: Addison-Wesley.

Miller, J. P. (1976). *Humanizing the classroom: Models of teaching in affective education.* New York: Praeger.

Miller, N., Brewer, M. B., & Edwards, K. (1985). Cooperative interaction in desegregated settings. A laboratory analogue. *Journal of Social Issues,* **41,** 63–79.

Miller, P. (1986). Teasing as a language socialization and verbal play in a White working class community. In B. B. Schieffelin & E. Ochs (Eds.), *Language socialization across cultures: Studies in the social and cultural foundations of language* (Vol. 3, pp. 199–212). New York Cambridge University Press.

Miller, W. B. (1958). Lower class culture as a generating milieu of gang delinquency. *Journal of Social Issues,* **14,** 5–19.

Miller, W. B. (1974). American youth gangs: Past and present. In A. Blumberg (Ed.), *Current perspectives on criminal behavior.* New York: Knopf.

Miller, W. B. (1974). American youth gangs: Past and present. In A. Blumberg (Ed.), *Current perspectives on criminal behavior.* Washington, DC: US Department of Justice.

Miller, W. B. (1975). *Violence by youth gangs and youth groups as a crime problem in major American cities.* Washington, DC: National Institute for Juvenile Justice and Delinquency Prevention.

Miller, W. B. (1982). *Crime by youth gangs and groups in the United States.* Washington, DC: National Institute for Juvenile Justice and Delinquency Prevention.

Miller, W. B., Geertz, H., & Cutter, H. S. G. (1968). Aggression in a boys' street-corner group. In J. F. Short (Ed.), *Gang delinquency and delinquent subcultures.* New York: Harper & Row.

Miller, W. I. (1993). *Humiliation.* Ithaca: Cornell University Press.

Mills, N. (1997). *The triumph of meanness.* Boston: Houghton Mifflin.

Moffitt, T. E. (1993). Adolescence-limited and life-course-persistent antisocial behavior: A developmental taxonomy. *Psychological Review,* **100,** 674–701.

Momboisse, R. M. (1970). *Riots, revolts and insurrections*. Springfield, IL: Charles C. Thomas.

Mooney, A., Creeser, R., & Blatchford, P. (1991). Children's views on teasing and fighting in junior schools. *Educational Research*, **33**, 103–112.

Moore, J., & Hagedorn, J. (2001). Female gangs: A focus on research. *Office of Juvenile Justice and Delinquency Prevention Juvenile Justice Bulletin*, March.

Moore, J. W. (1991). *Going down to the barrio: Home boys and home girls in change*. Philadelphia: Temple University Press.

Moore, J. W., Garcia, R., Garcia, C., Cerda, L., & Valencia, F. (1978). *Homeboys, gangs, drugs, and prison in the barrios of Los Angeles*. Philadelphia: Temple University Press.

Moore, J. W., Vigil, D., & Garcia, R. (1983). Residence and territoriality in Chicago gangs. *Social Problems*, **31**, 182–194.

Moos, R. H., & Insel, P. M. (1974). *Issues in social ecology*. Palo Alto, CA: National Press Books.

Moreno, J. L. (1960). *The sociometry reader*. Glencoe, IL: Free Press.

Morreall, J. (1994). Gossip and humor. In R. F. Goodman & A. Ben Ze'ev (Eds.), *Good gossip*. Lawrence, KS: University Press of Kansas.

Moscovici, S. (1985). *The age of the crowd: A historical treatise on mass psychology*. Cambridge: Cambridge University Press.

Mullen, B., Anthony, T., Salas, E., & Driskell, J. E. (1994). Group cohesiveness and quality of decision making: An integration of tests of the groupthink hypothesis. *Small Group Research*, **25**, 189–204.

Murphy, M. (1983). Emotional confrontations between Sevillano fathers and sons: Cultural foundations and social consequences. *American Ethnologist*, **17**, 650–664.

Murray, H. A. (1938). *Explorations in personality*. New York: Oxford.

Murray, J. A. (1986). Understanding competing theories of negotiation. *Negotiation Journal*, **2** (April), 179–186.

Myers, D. G. (1978). The polarizing effects of social comparison. *Journal of Experimental Social Psychology*, **14**, 554–563.

Nagin, D. S., Farrington, D. P., & Moffitt, T. E. (1995). Life-course trajectories of different types of offenders. *Criminology*, **33**, 111–139.

Natale, M. (1975). Convergence of mean vocal intensity in dyadic communication as a function of social desirability. *Journal of Personality and Social Psychology*, **32**, 790–804.

National Center for Educational Statistics (1981). *National longitudinal study of the high school class of 1972*. Washington, DC.

National Opinion Research Center (1973). *Southern schools: An evaluation of the effects of the Emergency School Assistance Program and school desegregation*. Chicago.

National Youth Gang Center (2000). *1998 National Youth Gang Survey*. Washington, DC: US Department of Justice.

Naylor, P., & Cowie, H. (1999). The effectiveness of peer support systems in challenging school bullying: The perspectives and experiences of teachers and pupils. *Journal of Adolescence*, **22**, 467–479.

Needle, J. A., & Stapleton, W. V. (1982). *Police handling of youth gangs*. Washington, DC: National Juvenile Justice Assessment Center.

Nettler, G. (1974). *Explaining crime*. New York: McGraw-Hill.

Nevo, O., Nevo, B., & Derech-Zehavi, A. (1994). The tendency to gossip as a psychological disposition: Constructing a measure and validating it. In R. F. Goodman & A. Ben Ze-ev (Eds.), *Good gossip*. Lawrence, KS: University Press of Kansas.

New York City Youth Board (1960). *Reaching the fighting gang*. New York.

Newman, D. A., Horne, A. M., & Bartolomucci, C. L. (2000). *Bully busters: A teacher's manual for helping bullies, victims, and bystanders*. Champaign, IL: Research Press.

Newman, F., & Oliver, D. (1970). *Clarifying public issues: An approach to teaching social studies*. Boston: Little, Brown.

Nietzel, M. T. (1979). *Crime and its modification*. Elmsford, NY: Pergamon.

Norwell, N., & Worchel, S. (1981). A re-examination of the relation between equal status contact and intergroup attraction. *Journal of Personality and Social Psychology*, **41**, 902–908.

Novelli, J. (1993). Better behavior for better learning. *Instructor*, July/August, 74–79.

Nye, F. I. (1958). *Family relationships and delinquent behavior*. New York: Wiley.

O'Connell, P., Pepler, D., & Craig, W. (1999). Peer involvement in bullying: Insights and challenges for intervention. *Journal of Adolescence, 22,* 437–452.

O'Donohue, W. (1997). Sample lesson plans. In W. O'Donohue (Ed.), *Sexual harassment: Theory, research, and treatment*. Boston, MA: Allyn & Bacon.

O'Moore, A. M. (1995). What do teachers need to know? In M. Elliott (Ed.), *Bullying: A practical guide to coping for schools*. London: Pitman Publishing.

O'Moore, A. M., Kirkham, C., & Smith, M. (1997). Bulllying behaviour in Irish schools: A nationwide study. *Irish Journal of Psychology, 18,* 141–169.

O'Moore, M., & Hillery (1991). What do teachers need to know. In M. Elliott (Ed.), *Bullying: A practical guide for coping for schools.* London: Longman.

Ohio State University Center for Human Resource Research (1981). *The national longitudinal surveys handbook*. Columbus, OH: College of Administrative Science, Ohio State University.

Olweus, D. (1978). *Aggression in the schools: Bullies and whipping boys*. New York: Wiley.

Olweus, D. (1987). Bully/victim problems among school children. In J. P. Mykelbust & R. Ommundsen (Eds.), *Psykologprofesjonen mot ar 2000*. Oslo: Universitetsforlget.

Olweus, D. (1989). Prevalence and incidence in the study of anti-social behavior: Definitions and measurements. In M. Klein (Ed.), *Cross-national research in self-reported crime and delinquency*. Dordrecht, The Netherlands: Kluwer.

Olweus, D. (1993). *Bullying at school: What we know and what we can do*. Oxford, UK: Blackwell.

Olweus, D. (1999). Sweden. In P. K. Smith, Y. Morita, J. Junger-Tas, D. Olweus, R. Catalano, & P. Slee (Eds.). *The nature of school bullying. A cross-national perspective*. London: Routledge.

Olweus, D. (2001). Peer harassment. A critical analysis and some important issues. In J. Juvonen & S. Graham (Eds.). *Peer harassment in school*. New York: Guilford Press.

Olzak, S. (1992). *The dynamics of ethnic competition and conflict*. Stanford: Stanford University Press.

Orlick, T. D. (1978). *The cooperative sports and games book*. New York: Pantheon.

Osborn, S. G., & West, D. J. (1979). Conviction records of fathers and sons compared. *British Journal of Criminology, 19,* 120–133.

Osgood, C. E. (1953). *Method and theory in experimental psychology*. New York: Oxford University Press.

Osgood, C. E. (1962). *An alternative to war or surrender*. Urbana, IL: University of Illinois Press.

Owens, S., Shute, R., & Slee, P. (2000). "Guess what I just heard!": Indirect aggression among teenage girls in Australia. *Aggressive Behavior, 26,* 67–83.

Padilla, F. M. (1992). *The gang as an American enterprise*. New Brunswick, NJ: Rutgers University Press.

Paludi, M. A. (1997). Sexual harassment in schools. In W. O'Donohue (Eds.), *Sexual harassment: Theory, research, and treatment*. Boston, MA: Allyn & Bacon.

Park, R. E. (1950). *Race and culture*. New York: Free Press.

Park, R. E., & Burgess, E. W. (1921). *The city*. Chicago: University of Chicago Press.

Park, W. (1990). A review of research on groupthink. *Journal of Behavioral Decision Making, 3,* 229–245.

Patterson, G. R. (1982). *Coercive family process*. Eugene, OR: Castalia.

Pearce, J. (1997). What can be done about the bully? In M. Elliott (Ed.), *Bullying: A practical guide to coping for schools*. London: Pitman Publishing.

Pepler, D. J., Craig, W. M., Ziegler, S., & Charach, A. (1994). An evaluation of an anti-bullying intervention in Toronto schools. *Canadian Journal of Community Mental Health, 13,* 95–110.

Pereira, G. J. (1978). *Teaching empathy through skill building versus interpersonal anxiety reduction methods*. Unpublished doctoral dissertation, Catholic University of America, Washington, DC.

Perry, D. G., Kusel, S. J., & Perry, L. C. (1988). Victims of peer aggression. *Developmental Psychology, 6,* 807–814.

Perry, D. G., Willard, J. C., & Perry, L. C. Peers' perceptions of the consequences that victimized children provide aggressors. *Child Development, 61,* 1310–1325.

Perry, J. B., & Pugh, M. D. (1978). *Collective behavior: Response to Social Stress.* New York: West Publishing.

Pesso, A. (1969). Movement in psychotherapy. New York: New York University Press.

Peterson, L., & Rigby, K. (1999). Countering bullying at an Australian secondary school with students as helpers. *Journal of Adolescence, 22,* 481–492.

Peterson, R. S. (1997). A directive leadership style in group decision making can be both virtue and vice. *Journal of Personality and Social Psychology, 72,* 1107–1121.

Pettigrew, T. F. (1971). *Racially separate or together?* New York: McGraw-Hill.

Pettigrew, T. F. (1986). The intergroup contact hypothesis reconsidered. In M. Hewstone & R. Brown (Eds.), *Contact and conflict in intergroup encounters.* Oxford: Basil Blackwell.

Plas, J. M. (1986). *Systems psychology in the schools.* New York: Pergamon.

Postmes, T., & Spears, R. (1998). Deindividuation and antinormative behavior. *Psychological Bulletin, 123,* 238–259.

Pruitt, D. G., & Rubin, J. Z. (1986). *Social conflict.* New York: Random House.

Puffer, J. A. (1912). *The boy and his gang.* Boston: Houghton Mifflin.

Quicker, J. C. (1983). *Homegirls: Characterizing Chicana gangs.* San Pedro, CA: International Universities Press.

Quinney, R. (1974). *Critique of legal order: Crime control in capitalist society.* Boston: Little, Brown.

Rabbie, J. M. (1982). *Are groups more aggressive than individuals?* Presented at British Psychological Society, Oxford.

Rabbie, J. M., & Huygen, K. (1974). Internal disagreements and their effects on attitudes toward in- and outgroups. *International Journal of Group Tensions, 4,* 222–246.

Rabbie, J. M., & Wilkins, G. (1971). Intergroup competition and its effects on intragroup and intergroup relations. *European Journal of Social Psychology, 1,* 215–234.

Ramey, D. T. (1981). Group climate, campus image and attitudes of fraternity men regarding pledge hazing. Unpublished doctoral dissertation, Indiana University.

Raphael, R. (1988). *The men from the boys: Rites of passage in male America.* Lincoln, NE: University of Nebraska Press.

Raths, L. E., Harmon, M., & Simon, S. B. (1966). *Values and teaching: Working with values in the classroom.* Columbus, OH: Charles Merrill.

Rausch, H. L. (1965). Interaction sequences. *Journal of Personality and Social Psychology, 2,* 487–499.

Rayner, C. & Hoel, H. (1997). A summary review of literature relating to workplace bullying. *Journal of Community & Applied Social Psychology, 7,* 181–191.

Reckless, W. C. (1961). *The crime problem.* New York: Appleton-Century-Crofts.

Reich, W. (1949). *Character analysis.* New York: Farrar, Straus & Giroux (original work published 1933).

Reicher, S. (1986). Contact, action and racialization: Some British evidence. In M. Hewstone & R. Brown (Eds.), *Contact and conflict in intergroup encounters.* Oxford: Blackwell.

Reiss, A. J., & Rhodes, A. L. (1964). Status deprivation and delinquent behavior. *The Sociological Quarterly, 4,* 135–149.

Renwick, P. (1977). The effects of sex differences on the perception and management of superior–subordinate conflict: An exploratory study. *Organizational Behavior and Human Performance, 19,* 403–415.

Reuterman, N. A. (1975). Formal theories of gangs. In D. Cartwright, B. Tomson, & H. Schwartz (Eds.), *Gang delinquency.* Pacific Grove, CA: Brooks/Cole.

Richmond, D. R. (1987). Putting an end to fraternity hazing. *NASPA Journal, 24,* 48–52.

Richter, P., & Kempster, N. (1997). 'Disgusted' by hazing, Cohen calls for 'Zero Tolerance'; Military: Marine Corps incident prompts criticism from defense chief. *Los Angeles Times.* Los Angeles, CA: The Times Mirror Company.

Rigby, K., & Cox, I. (1996). The contribution of bullying at school and low self-esteem to acts of delinquency among Australian teenagers. *Personality and Individual Differences, 2,* 609–612.

Rigby, K., & O'Brien, M. (1992). The influence of family factors on bully/victim behavior. Unpublished manuscript, Sydney, Australia.

Riordan, C. (1978). Equal status interracial contact: A review and revision of the concept. *International Journal of Intercultural Relations*, **2**, 161–185.

Rivers, I., & Smith, P. K. (1994). Types of bullying behaviors and their correlates. *Aggressive Behavior*, **20**, 359–368.

Robins, L. N., & Lewis, R. G. (1966). The role of the antisocial family in school completion and delinquency: A three-generation study. *Sociological Quarterly*, **7**, 500–514.

Robins, L. N., West, P. A., & Herjanic, B. L. (1975). Arrests and delinquency in two generations: A study of black urban families and their children. *Journal of Child Psychology and Psychiatry*, **16**, 125–140.

Rokeach, M. (1973). *The nature of human values*. New York: Free Press.

Roland, E. (1989). A system oriented strategy against bullying. In E. Roland & E. Munthe (Eds.), *Bullying: An international perspective*. London: Fulton.

Roland, E. (1993). Bullying: A developing tradition of research and management. In D. P. Tattum (Ed.), *Understanding and managing bullying*. Oxford: Heinemann.

Rolf, I. (1977) *Rolfing: The integration of human structures*. Boulder, CO: The Rolf Institute.

Roscoe, B., Strause, J. S., & Goodwin, M. P. (1992). Sexual harassment: Early adolescents' self-reports of experiences and acceptance. *Adolescence*, **29**, 515–522.

Rose, A. M., & Prell, A. E. (1955). Does the punishment fit the crime? A study in social valuation. *American Journal of Sociology*, **61**, 247–259.

Rose, S. D. (1977). *Grouptherapy: A behavioral approach*. Englewood Cliffs, NJ: Prentice-Hall.

Rose, T. L. (1981). Cognitive and dyadic process in intergroup contact. In D. L. Hamilton (Ed.), *Cognitive processes in stereotyping and intergroup behavior*. Hillsdale, NJ: Erlbaum.

Ross, D. M. (1996). *Childhood bullying and teasing: What school personnel, other professionals, and parents can do*. Alexandria, VA: American Counseling Association.

Rothbart, M. (1981). Memory processes and social beliefs. In D. L. Hamilton (Ed.), *Cognitive processes in stereotyping and intergroup behavior*. Hillsdale, NJ: Erlbaum.

Rothbart, M. (1993). Intergroup perception and social conflict. In S. Worchel & J. A. Simpson (Ed.), *Conflict between people and groups: Causes, processes, and resolutions*. Chicago: Nelson-Hall.

Rule, J. B. (1988). *Theories of civil violence*. Berkeley: University of California Press.

Runciman, W. G. (1966). *Relative deprivation and social justice*. Berkeley: University of California Press.

Rutter, M. (1980). *Changing youth in a changing society*. Cambridge, MA: Harvard University Press.

Rutter, M., & Giller, H. (1983). *Juvenile delinquency: Trends and perspectives*. New York: Guilford.

Rutter, M., Giller, H., & Hagell, A. (1998). *Antisocial behavior by young people*. Cambridge, UK: Cambridge University Press.

Ryen, A. H., & Kahn, A. (1975). The effects of intergroup orientation on group attitudes and proxemic behaviour: A test of two models. *Journal of Personality and Social Psychology*, **31**, 302–310.

Rynders, J., Johnson, R., Johnson, D. W., & Schmidt, B. (1980). Producing positive interaction among Down's syndrome and nonhandicapped teenagers through cooperative goal structuring. *American Journal of Mental Deficiency*, **85**, 268–273.

Sabella, R. A., & Myrick, R. D. (1995). Peer facilitators confront sexual harassment. *The Peer Facilitator Quarterly*, **13**, 17–23.

Saenger, G., & Gilbert, E. (1950). Customer reactions to the integration of Negro sales personnel. *International Journal of Opinion and Attitude Research*, **4**, 57–76.

Salmivalli, C. (2001). Group view on victimization. In J. Juvonen & S. Graham (Eds.), *Peer harassment in school*. New York: Guilford Press.

Salmivalli, C., Karhunen, J., & Lagerspetz, K. M. (1996). How do the victims respond to bullying? *Aggressive Behavior*, **22**, 99–109.

Salmivalli, C., Lagerspetz. K., Bjorkqvist, K., Osterman, K., & Kaukiainen, A. (1996). Bullying as a group process: Participant roles and their relations to social status within the group. *Aggressive Behavior*, **22**, 1–15.

Sampson, R. V. (1965). *Equality and power*. London: Heinemann.

San Diego Association of State Governments (1982). *Juvenile violence and gang-related crime*. San Diego.

Sanders, W. B. (1994). *Drive-bys: Grounded culture and juvenile gang violence*. New York: Aldine de Gruyter.

Sandler, B., & Paludi, M. (1993). *Educator's guide to controlling sexual harassment*. Washington, DC: Thompson.

Sandole, J. D., & Sandole-Staroste, I. (1987). *Conflict management and problem solving: Interpersonal to international applications*. New York: New York University Press.

Sapon-Shevin, M. (1986). Teaching cooperation. In G. Cartledge & J. F. Milburn (Eds.), *Teaching social skills to children*. New York: Pergamon.

Sappington, A. A. (1976). Effects of desensitization of white prejudice to blacks upon subjects' stereotypes of blacks. *Perceptual and Motor Skills*, **43**, 938.

Satino, J. (1990). The outlaw emotions: Narrative expressions on the rules and roles of occupational identity. *American Behavioral Scientist*, **33**, 318–329.

Savin-Williams, R. C. (1977). Dominance in a human adolescent group. *Animal Behavior*, **25**, 400–406.

Sawin, D. B., & Parke, R. D. (1979). The effects of interagent inconsistent discipline on children's aggressive behavior. *Journal of Experimental Child Psychology*, **28**, 528–535.

Schachter, S. (1959). *The psychology of affiliation*. Palo Alto, CA: Stanford University Press.

Schachter, S., Ellertson, N., McBride, D., & Gregory, D. (1951). An experimental study of cohesiveness and productivity. *Human Relations*, **4**, 229–238.

Schein, E. H. (1978). Career dynamics: Matching individual and organizational needs. Reading, MA: Addison-Wesley.

Schmuck, R. (1985). Learning to cooperate, cooperating to learn: Basic concepts. In R. Slavin, S. Sharan, S. Kagan, R. Hertz-Lazarowitz, C. Webb, & R. Schmuck (Eds.), *Learning to cooperate, cooperating to learn*. New York: Plenum.

Schofield, J. W. (1980). Cooperation as a social exchange: Resource gaps and reciprocity in academic work. In S. Sharan, P. Hare, C. D. Webb, & R. Hertz-Lazarowitz (Eds.), *Cooperation in education*. Provo, UT: Brigham Young University Press.

Schur, E. (1971). *Labeling deviant behavior: Its sociological implications*. New York: Random House.

Schuster, B. (1999). Outsiders at school: The prevalence of bullying and its relation with social status. *Group Processes and Intergroup Relations*, **2**, 175–190.

Schutz, W. C. (1967). *FIRO*. New York: Holt, Rinehart & Winston.

Scott, R., & McPartland, J. (1982). Desegregation as national policy. Correlates of racial attitudes. *American Educational Research Journal*, **19**, 397–414.

Selman, R. L. (1980). *The growth of interpersonal understanding: Developmental and clinical analyses*. New York: Academic.

Selman, R. L., & Demarest, A. P. (1984). Observing troubled children's interpersonal negotiation strategies: Implications of and for a developmental model. *Child Development*, **55**, 288–304.

Shantz, C. U. (1987). Conflicts between children. *Child Development*, **58**, 283–305.

Shapiro, J. P., Baumeister, R. F., & Kessler, J. W. (1991). A three-component model of children's teasing: Aggression, humor, and ambiguity. *Journal of Social and Clinical Psychology*, **10**, 459–472.

Sharan, S., Raviv, S., & Russell, P. L. (1982). *Cooperative and traditional classroom learning and the cooperative behavior of seventh-grade pupils in mixed-ethnic classrooms*. Unpublished manuscript, University of Tel Aviv, Israel.

Sharon, S., & Sharon, Y. (1976). *Small-group teaching*. Englewood Cliffs, NJ: Educational Technology.

Sharp, G. (1998). Nonviolent actions in acute interethnic conflicts. In E. Weiner (Ed.), *The handbook of interethnic coexistence*. New York: Continuum.

Sharp, S. (1995). How much does bullying hurt? *Educational & Child Psychology*, **12**, 81–88.

Sharp, S., & Thompson, D. (1994). How to establish a whole-school anti-bullying policy. In S. Sharp & P. K. Smith (Eds.), *Tackling bullying in your school*. London: Routledge.

Shaw, C. R., & McKay, H. D. (1942). *Juvenile delinquency and urban areas: A study of rates of delinquency in relation to differential characteristics of local communities in American cities*. Chicago: University of Chicago Press.

Shaw, M. E. (1964). Communication networks. In L. Berkowitz (Ed.), *Advances in experimental social psychology* (Vol. 1). New York: Academic.

Shaw, M. E. (1981). *Group dynamics: The psychology of small group behavior*. New York: McGraw-Hill.

Sherif, M., & Sherif, C. W. (1953). *Groups in harmony and tension*. New York: Harper & Row.

Sherif, M., Harvey, O. J., White, B. J., Hood, W. R., & Sherif, C. W. (1961). *Intergroup cooperation and competition*. Norman: University of Oklahoma.

Shore, E., & Sechrest, L. B. (1961). Concept attainment as a function of number of positive instances presented. *Journal of Educational Psychology, 52*, 303–307.

Short, J. F. (1974). Youth gangs and society: Micro- and macrosociological processes. *The Sociological Quarterly, 15*, 3–19.

Short, J. F., & Strodtbeck, F. L. (1965). *Group process and gang delinquency*. Chicago: University of Chicago Press.

Sidanius, J., & Pratto, F. (1999). *Social dominance: An intergroup theory of social hierarchy and oppression*. Cambridge, UK: Cambridge University Press.

Sighele, S. (1898). *Psychologie des sectes*. Paris: V. Giard & E. Briere.

Simmel, G. (1950). The sociology of Georg Simmel. New York: Free Press.

Simon, S. B., Howe, L. W., & Kirschenbaum, H. (1972). *Values clarification: A handbook of practical strategies for teachers and students*. New York: Hart.

Skogan, W. G. (1990). *Disorder and decline*. Berkeley: University of California Press.

Slavin, R. E. (1977). How student learning teams can integrate the desegregated classroom. *Integrated Education, 15*, 56–58.

Slavin, R. E. (1977). *Student learning team techniques: Narrowing the achievement gap between the races*. Baltimore: Johns Hopkins University, Center for Social Organization of Schools.

Slavin, R. E. (1978). Student teams and achievement divisions. *Journal of Research and Development in Education, 12*, 39–49.

Slavin, R. E. (1980). *Using student team learning* (revised edition). Baltimore: Johns Hopkins University, Center for Social Organization of Schools.

Slavin, R. E. (1983). *Cooperative learning*. New York: Longman.

Slavin, R. E. (1985). An introduction to cooperative learning research. In R. Slavin, S. Sharan, S. Kagan, R. Hertz-Lazarowitz, C. Webb, & R. Schmuck (Eds.), *Learning to cooperate, cooperating to learn*. New York: Plenum.

Slavin, R. E. (1985). Cooperative learning: Applying contact theory in desegregated schools. *Journal of Social Issues, 41*, 45–62.

Slavin, R. E., & Madden, N. A. (1979). School practices that improve race relations. *American Educational Research Journal, 16*, 169–180.

Slavin, R. E., & Oickle, E. (1981). Effects of cooperative learning teams on student achievement and race relations. *Sociology of Education, 54*, 174–180.

Slavin, R. E., Leavey, M., & Madden, N. A. (1982, April). *Effects of student teams and individualized instruction on student mathematics achievement, attitudes, and behavior*. Paper presented at the meeting of the American Educational Research Association, New York.

Smart, R. (1965). Social group membership, leadership, and birth order. *Journal of Abnormal Psychology, 86*, 528–535.

Smelser, N. J. (1962). *Theory of collective behavior*. New York: Free Press.

Smith, H. C. (1973). *Sensitivity training*. New York: McGraw-Hill.

Smith, P. K., & Brian, P. (2000). Bullying in schools: Lessons from two decades of research. *Aggressive Behavior, 26*, 1–9.

Smith, P. K., & Levan, S. (1995). Perceptions and experiences of bullying in younger pupils. *British Journal of Educational Psychology, 65*, 489–500.

Smith, P. K., & Sharp, S. (1994a). *School bullying: Insights and perspectives*. London: Routledge.

Smith, P. K., & Sharp, S. (1994b). The problem of school bullying. In P. Smith & S. Sharp (Eds.), *School bullying: Insights and perspectives*. London: Routledge.

Smorti, A., & Criraci, E. (2000). Narrative strategies in bullies and victims in Italian schools. *Aggressive Behavior, 26*, 33–48.

Snyder, J. J., & Patterson, G. R. (1987). Family interaction and delinquent behavior. In H. C. Quay (Ed.), *Handbook of juvenile delinquency*. New York: Wiley.

Snyder, M. (1981). On the self-perpetuating nature of social stereotypes. In D. L. Hamilton (Ed.), *Cognitive processes in stereotyping and intergroup behavior*. Hillsdale, NJ: Erlbaum.

Solomon, S., Greenberg, J., & Pyszczynski, T. (1991). A terror management theory of social behavior: The psychological functions of self-esteem and cultural worldviews. In M. P. Zanna (Ed.), *Advances in Experimental Social Psychology*, **24**, 93–159.

Sparks, R., Genn, H., & Dodd, D. (1977). *Surveying victims*. London: Wiley.

Spergel, I. A. (1964). *Racketville, Slumtown, and Haulberg*. Chicago: University of Chicago Press.

Spergel, I. A. (1965). *Street gang work: Theory and practice*. Reading, MA: Addison-Wesley.

Spergel, I. A. (1985). *The violent gang problem in Chicago*. Chicago: University of Chicago, School of Social Service Administration.

Spergel, I. A. (1990). Youth gangs: Continuity and change. In M. Tonry & N. Morris (Eds.), *Crime and justice: A review of research*. Chicago: University of Chicago Press.

Spergel, I. A., Ross, R. E., Curry, G. D., & Chance, R. (1989). *Youth gangs: Problem and response*. Washington, DC: Office of Juvenile Justice and Delinquency Prevention.

Staub, E. (1989). The roots of evil: The origins of genocide and other group violence. Cambridge, UK: Cambridge University Press.

Staub, E. (1993). The mob. In American Psychological Association, *Report of the American Psychological Association Commission on Youth Violence*, Washington, DC: Author.

Staub, E., & Rosenthal, L. H. (1999). Mob violence: Cultural-societal sources, instigators, group processes, and participants. In L. D. Eron, J. H. Gentry, & P. Schlegel (Eds.), *Reason to hope: A psychosocial perspective on violence and youth*. Washington, DC: American Psychological Association.

Stein, N. (1995). Sexual harassment in school: The public performances of gendered violence. *Harvard Educational Review*, **65**, 145–162.

Steiner, I. D. (1972). *Group process and productivity*. New York: Academic.

Steiner, I. D. (1976). Task-performing groups. In J. W. Thibaut, J. T. Spence, & R. C. Carson (Eds.), *Contemporary topics in social psychology*. Morristown, NJ: General Learning.

Stephan, W. G., & Brigham, J. C. (1985). Intergroup contact. *Journal of Social Issues*, **41**, 1–8.

Stephan, W. G., & Rosenfeld, D. (1978). Black self-rejection: Another look. *Journal of Educational Psychology*, **71**, 708–716.

Stephan, W. G., & Stephan, C. W. (1989). Antecedents of intergroup anxiety in Asian-Americans and Hispanic-Americans. *International Journal of Intercultural Relations*, **13**, 203–219.

Stephan, W. G., & Stephan, C. W. (1996). *Intergroup relations*. New York: Westview Press.

Stephenson, P., & Smith, D. (1997). Why some schools don't have bullies. In M. Elliott (Ed.), *Bullying: A practical guide to coping for schools*. London: Pitman Publishing.

Stokols, D. (1978). On the distinction between density and crowding: Some implications for future research. *Psychological Review*, **79**, 275–278.

Stouffer, S. A. (1949). *The American soldier*. Princeton: Princeton University Press.

Stouffer, S. A., Suchman, E. A., DeVinney, L. C., Star, S. A., & Williams, R. M., Jr. (1949). *The American soldier: Adjustment during army life* (Vol. 1). Hillsdale, NJ: Erlbaum.

Strauss, S. (1994, September). Sexual harassment at an early age. *Principal*, **74**, 26–30.

Street, R. L., Jr. (1984). Speech convergence and speech evaluation in fact-finding interviews. *Human Communication Research*, **11**, 139–169.

Streufert, S., & Streufert, S. C. (1986). The development of international conflict. In W. G. Austin & S. Worchel (Eds.), *The social psychology of intergroup conflict*. Monterey, CA: Brooks/Cole.

Strickland, L. H. (1958). Surveillance and trust. *Journal of Personality*, **26**, 206–215.

Sullins, E. S. (1991). Emotional contagion revisited: Effects of social comparison and expressive style on mood convergence. *Personality and Social Psychology Bulletin*, **17**, 166–174.

Suls, J. M. (1977). Gossip as social comparison, *Journal of Communicaton*, **27**, 164–168.

Sumner, W. G. (1906). *Folkways*. New York: Ginn.

Sutherland, E. H., & Cressey, D. R. (1974). *Criminology*. New York: Lippincott.

Sweet, S. (1999). Understanding fraternity hazing: Insights from symbolic interactionist theory. *Journal of College Student Development*, **40**, 355–363.

Sykes, G. M., & Matza, D. (1957). Techniques of neutralization: A theory of delinquency. *American Sociological Review*, **22**, 664–670.

Szwed, J. F. (1966). Gossip, drinking, and social control: Consensus and communication in a Newfoundland parish. *Ethnology*, **5**, 434–441.

Tajfel, H. (1970). Experiments in intergroup discrimination. *Scientific American*, **223**, 96–102.

Tajfel, H. (1978). The achievement of group differentiation. In H. Tajfel (Ed.), *Differentiation between social groups*. London: Academic Press.

Tajfel, H., Flament, C., Billig, M. G, & Bundy, R. F. (1971). Social categorization and intergroup behaviour. *European Journal of Social Psychology*, **1**, 149–177.

Tannen, D. (1998). *The argument culture*. New York: Random House.

Tannenbaum, F. (1938). *Crime and the community*. Boston: Ginn.

Tarde, G. (1898). *Etudes de psychologies sociale*. Paris: V. Giard & E. Briere.

Tattum, D. (1997). A whole-school response: From crisis management to suspension. *The Irish Journal of Psychology*, **18**, 221–232.

Taylor, G. (1994). Gossip as moral talk. In R. F. Goodman & A. Ben Ze'ev (Eds.), *Good gossip*. Lawrence, KS: University Press of Kansas.

Taylor, R. B., & Gottfredson, S. (1986). Environmental design, crime, and prevention: An examination of community dynamics. In A. J. Reiss & M. Tonry (Eds.), *Communities and crime*. Chicago: University of Chicago Press.

Taylor, S. E. (1981). The interface of cognitive and social psychology. In J. H. Harvey (Ed.), *Cognition, social behavior, and the environment*. Hillside, NJ: Erlbaum.

Taylor, S. E., & Fiske, S. T. (1981). Getting inside the head: Methodologies for process analysis in attribution and social cognition. In J. H. Harvey, W. Ickes, & R. F. Kidd (Eds.), *New directions in attribution research*. Hillsdale, NJ: Erlbaum.

Taylor, S. P., Shuntich, R. J., & Greenberg, A. (1979). The effects of repeated aggressive encounters on subsequent aggressive behavior. *The Journal of Social Psychology*, **107**, 199–208.

Tetlock, P. E. (1979). Identifying victims of groupthink from public statements of decision makers. *Journal of Personality and Social Psychology*, **35**, 1314–1324.

Thibaut, J. W., & Kelley, H. H. (1959). *The social psychology of groups*. New York: Wiley.

Thomas, C. W., & Bilchik, S. (1985). Prosecuting juveniles in criminal courts: A legal and empirical analysis. *Journal of Criminal Law and Criminology*, **76**, 439–479.

Thompson, D. W., & Jason, L. A. (1998). Street gangs and preventive interventions. *Criminal Justice and Behavior*, **15**, 323–333.

Thompson, K. M., Brownfield, D., & Sorenson, A. M. (1998). At-risk behavior and group fighting: A latent structure analysis. *Journal of Gang Research*, **5**, 1–14.

Thornberry, T. P., Krohn, M. D., Lizotte, A. J., & Chard-Wierschem, D. (1993). The role of juvenile gangs in facilitating delinquent behavior. *Journal of Research in Crime and Delinquency*, **30**, 55–87.

Thorndike, E. L., & Woodworth, R. S. (1901). The influence of improvement in one mental function upon the efficiency of other functions. *Psychological Review*, **8**, 247–261.

Thrasher, F. M. (1936). *The gang*. Chicago: University of Chicago Press (original work published 1927).

Tickle-Degnen, L., & Rosenthal, R. (1987). Group rapport and nonverbal behavior. *Review of Personality and Social Psychology*, **9**, 113–136.

Till, F. (1980). Sexual harassment: A report on the sexual harassment of students. Washington, DC: National Advisory Council on Women's Education.

Tilly, C. (1997). Collective violence in European perspective. In H. D. Graham & T. R. Gurr (Eds.), *Violence in America*. Beverly Hills, CA: Sage.

Tizard, B., Blatchford, P., Burke, J., Farquhar, C., & Plewis, I. (1988). *Young children at school in the inner city*. London: Erlbaum.

Tognacci, L. (1975). Pressures toward uniformity in delinquent gangs. In D. S. Cartwright, B. Tomson, & H. Schwartz (Eds.), *Gang delinquency*. Pacific Grove, CA: Brooks/Cole.

Tracy, P. E. (1979). *Subcultural delinquency: A comparison of the incidence and seriousness of gang and nongang member offensivity*. Philadelphia: University of Pennsylvania, Center for Studies in Criminology and Criminal Law.

Trevitt, V. (1964). *The American heritage: Design for national character*. Santa Barbara, CA: McNally & Loftin.

Truax, C. B., & Carkhuff, R. R. (1967). *Toward effective counseling and psychotherapy: Training and practice*. Chicago: Aldine.

Tuckman, B. W. (1965). Developmental sequences in small groups. *Psychological Bulletin*, **63**, 384–399.

Tuckman, B. W., & Jensen, M. A. C. (1977). Stages of small group development revisited. *Group and Organization*, **2**, 419–427.

Tuppern, C. J. S., & Gaitan, A. (1989). Constructing accounts of aggressive episodes. *Social Behavior*, **4**, 127–143.

Turner, C. W., Simons, L. S., Berkowitz, L., & Fordi, A. (1977). The stimulating and inhibiting effects of weapons on aggressive behavior. *Aggressive Behavior*, **3**, 355–378.

Turner, J. C. (1975). Social comparison and social identity. Some prospects for intergroup behaviour. *European Journal of Social Psychology*, **5**, 5–34.

Turner, J. C. (1978). Social comparison, similarity and ingroup favouritism. In H. Tajfel (Ed.), *Differentiation between social groups*. London: Academic Press.

Turner, J. C. (1980). Fairness or discrimination in intergroup behaviour? A reply to Branthwaite, Doyle and Lighbrown. *European Journal of Social Psychology*, **10**, 131–147.

Turner, J. C. (1981). The experimental social psychology of intergroup behavior. In J. C. Turner & H. Giles (Eds.), *Intergroup behavior*. Chicago: University of Chicago Press.

Turner, R. C., & Killian, L. M. (Eds). (1972). *Collective behavior* (2nd ed.). Englewood Cliffs, NJ: Prentice-Hall.

US Bureau of the Census (1993). *Population trends, 1990–2010*. Washington DC: US Government Printing Office.

US Merit Systems Protection Board. Sexual harassment in the federal workplace: Is it a problem? Washington, DC: US Government Printing Office.

US Riot Commission (1968). *Report*. New York: Bantam Books.

Underwood, B. J., & Schulz, R. W. (1960). *Meaningfulness and verbal behavior*. New York: Lippincott.

Van Gennep, A. (1908). *The rites of passage*. Chicago: University of Chicago Press.

Vaughan, G. (1978). Social categorization and intergroup behaviour in children. In H. Tajfel (Ed.), *Differentiation between social groups*. London: Academic Press.

Vermande, M. M., van den Oord, E. J., Goudena, P. P., & Rispens, J. (2000). Structural characteristics of aggressor-victim relationships in Dutch school classes of 4- to 5-year olds. *Aggressive Behavior*, **26**, 11–31.

Vermette, P. J. (1998). *Making cooperative learning work*. Upper Saddle River, NJ: Prentice Hall.

Vetter, H. J. (1969). *Language behavior and communication: An introduction*. Itasca, IL: Peacock.

Vigil, J. D. (1998). *Barrio gangs: Street life and identity in Southern California*. Austin: University of Texas Press.

Volkan, V. D. (1988). *The need to have enemies and allies*. Northvale, NJ: Jason Aronson.

Volpe, M. R. (1998). Using town meetings to foster peaceful coexistence. In E. Weiner (Ed.), *The handbook of intercultural coexistence*. New York: Continuum.

Voss, H. L. (1963). Ethnic differentials in delinquency in Honolulu. *Journal of Criminal Law, Criminology, and Police Science*, **54**, 322–327.

Vroom, V. H., & Yetton, P. W. (1973). *Leadership and decision making*. Pittsburgh: University of Pittsburgh Press.

Waddington, D., Jones, K., & Critcher, C. (1987). Flashpoints of public disorder. In G. Gaskell & R. Benewick (Eds.), *The crowd in contemporary Britain*. London: Sage.

Wagner, U., & Schonbach, P. (1984). Links between educational status and prejudice: Ethnic attitudes in West Germany. In N. Miller & M. B. Brewer (Eds.), *Groups in contact: The psychology of desegregation*. San Diego: Academic Press.

Walker, M. A. (1978). Measuring the seriousness of crimes. *British Journal of Criminology*, **18**, 348–364.

Wall, J. A., Jr. (1985). *Negotiation: Theory and practice*. Glenview, IL: Scott, Foresman & Company.

Warm, T. R. (1997). The role of teasing in development and vice versa. *Developmental and Behavioral Pediatrics*, **18**, 97–101.

Warr, M. (1989). What is the perceived seriousness of crimes? *Criminology*, **27**, 795–819.

Wattenberg, W. W., & Balistrieri, J. J. (1950). Gang membership and juvenile misconduct. *American Sociological Review*, **15**, 181–186.

Webb, W. M., & Worchel, P. (1986). Trust and distrust. In S. Worchel & W. G. Austin (Eds.), *Psychology of intergroup relations*. Chicago: Nelson-Hall.

Weiner, E., Ed. (1998). *The handbook of intercultural coexistence*. New York: Continuum.

Weinstein, G., & Fantini, M. (1970). *Toward humanistic education: A curriculum of affect*. New York: Praeger.

Weller, J., & Quarantelli, E. L. (1973). Neglected characteristics of collective behavior. *American Journal of Sociology*, **79**, 665–685.

West, D. J., & Farrington, D. P. (1977). The delinquent way of life. London: Heinemann.

Wetherell, M. (1982). Cross-cultural studies of minimal groups: Implications for the social identity theory of intergroup relations. In H. Tajfel (Ed.), *Social identity and intergroup relations*. Cambridge: Cambridge University Press.

Wetherell, M. (1987). Social identity and group polarization. In J. C. Turner (Ed.), *Rediscovering the social group: A self-categorization theory*. New York: Basil Blackwell.

Wetherell, M. S., & Vaughan, G. M. (1979). *Social class, sex, nationality and behaviour in minimal group situations*. Unpublished master's thesis, University of Auckland.

White, R. K. (1970). *Nobody wanted war: Misperception in Vietnam and other wars*. New York: Doubleday.

White, R. K. (1977). Misperception in the Arab–Israeli conflict. *Journal of Social Issues*, **33**, 190–221.

White, R. K. (1984). *Fearful warriors: A psychological profile of US–Soviet relations*. New York: Free Press.

White, R. K., & Lippitt, R. (1968). Leader behavior and member reaction in three "social climates." In D. Cartwright & A. Zander (Eds.), *Group dynamics: Research and theory*. New York: Harper & Row.

Whitney, I., & Smith, P. K. (1993). A survey of the nature and extent of bullying in junior/middle and secondary schools. *Educational Research*, **35**, 3–25.

Whyte, G. (1989). Groupthink reconsidered. *Academy of Management Review*, **14**, 40–56.

Wilder, D. A. (1984). Intergroup contact: The typical member and the exception to the rule. *Journal of Experimental Social Psychology*, **20**, 177–194.

Wilder, D. A. (1986). Cognitive factors affecting the success of intergroup contact. In S. Worchel & W. G. Austin (Eds.), *Psychology of intergroup relations* (pp. 49–66). Chicago: Nelson-Hall.

Wilder, D. A. (1986). Social categorization: Implications for creation and reduction of intergroup bias. *Advances in experimental social psychology*, **19**, 291–355.

Wilder, D. A., & Allen, V. L. (1978). Group membership and preference for information about other persons. *Personality and Social Psychology Bulletin*, **4**, 106–116.

Wilder, D., & Simon, A. (1998). Categorical and dynamic groups. In C. Sedikides, J. Schopler, & C. A. Insko (Eds.), *Intergroup cognition and intergroup behavior*. Mahwah, NJ: Erlbaum.

Wilder, D. A., & Thompson, J. E. (1980). Intergroup contact with independent manipulations of in-group and out-group interaction. *Journal of Personality and Social Psychology*, **38**, 589–603.

Williams, D. E., & Schaller, K. A. (1993). Peer persuasions: A study of children's dominance strategies. *Early Child Development and Care*, **88**, 31–41.

Williams, J., & Giles, H. (1978). The changing status of women in society: An intergroup perspective. In R. J. Brown (Ed.), *Differentiation between social groups*. London: Academic Press.

Williams, K. D. (1997). Social ostracisim. In R. M. Kowalski (Ed.), *Aversive interpersonal behaviors*. New York: Plenum.

Williams, K. D., & Sommer, K. L. (1997). Social ostracism by co-workers. Does rejection lead to loafing or competition? *Personality and Social Psychology Bulletin*, **23**, 693–706.

Williams, K. D., Cheung, C. K. T., & Choi, W. (2000). Cyberostracism: Effects of being ignored over the internet. *Journal of Personality and Social Psychology*, **79**, 748–762.

Williams, K. D., Sherman-Williams, B., Faulkner, S. [A survey of a representative US sample on the incidence of using the silent treatment.] Unpublished raw data.

Williams, K. D., Shore, W. J., & Grahe, J. E. (1998). The silent treatment: Perceptions of its behaviors and associated feelings. *Group Process and Intergroup Relations*, **1**, 117–141.

Williams, R. M. (1964). *Strangers next door: Ethnic relations in American communities.* Englewood Cliffs, NJ: Prentice-Hall.

Williams, R. M., Jr. (1977). *Mutual accommodation: Ethnic conflict and cooperation.* Minneapolis: University of Minnesota Press.

Wilmot, W. W., & Hocker, J. L. (2001). *Interpersonal conflict.* New York: McGraw-Hill.

Wilson, E. O. (1975). *Sociology: the new synthesis.* Cambridge, MA: Belknap.

Wilson, G. D. (1993). *The psychology of conservatism.* San Diego, CA: Academic.

Wilson, J. (1972). *Practical methods of moral education.* London: Heinemann Educational Books.

Wilson, J. Q., & Hernstein, R. J. (1985). *Crime and human nature.* New York: Simon & Schuster.

Wilson, J. Q., & Kelling, G. L. (1982). Broken windows: The police and neighborhood safety. *Atlantic*, **249**, 29–38.

Winters, A. M. (1993). You shouldn't talk like that: An analysis of factors that affect the perceived inappropriateness of swearing. Unpublished master's thesis, Illinois State University.

Winters, A. M., & Duck, S. (2001). You ****!: Swearing as an aversive and a relational activity. In R. M. Kowalski (Ed.), *Behaving badly.* Washington, DC: American Psychological Association.

Worchel, S. (1979). Co-operation and the reduction of intergroup conflict: Some determining factors. In W. G. Austin & S. Worchel (Eds.), *The social psychology of intergroup relations.* Monterey, CA: Brooks/Cole.

Worchel, S., Andreoli, V. A., & Folger, R. (1977). Intergroup co-operation and attraction: The effect of previous interaction and outcome of combined effort. *Journal of Experimental Social Psychology*, **13**, 131–140.

Yablonsky, L. (1967). *The violent gang.* New York: Penguin.

Zander, A., Cohen, A. R., & Stotland, E. (1959). Power and relations among the professions. In D. Cartwright (Ed.), *Studies in social power.* Ann Arbor, MI: University of Michigan, Institute for Social Research.

Zimbardo, P. G. (1960). Involvement and communication discrepancy as determinants of opinion change. *Journal of Abnormal and Social Psychology*, **60**, 86–94.

Zimbardo, P. G. (1969). The human choice: Individuation, reason and order versus deindividuation, impulse and chaos. In W. J. Arnold & D. Levine (Eds.), *Nebraska symposium on motivation.* Nebraska: University of Nebraska Press.

Zimring, F. (1981). Kids, groups and crime: Some implicatoins of a well-known secret. *Journal of Criminal Law and Criminology*, **72**, 867–885.

SUBJECT INDEX

Index compiled by Fiona Smith